BASEBALL

& Bubble Gum

THE 1952 TOPPS COLLECTION

BASEBALL
& Bubble Gum

THE 1952 TOPPS COLLECTION

Tom Zappala & Ellen Zappala

with John Molori

FOREWORD & CONTRIBUTIONS BY **JOE ORLANDO**

Peter E. Randall Publisher
Portsmouth, New Hampshire
2020

© 2020 by Tom Zappala and Ellen Zappala

ISBN: 978-1-942155-31-7

Library of Congress Control Number: 2020902011

Produced by Peter E. Randall Publisher
Box 4726, Portsmouth, New Hampshire 03802

www.perpublisher.com

Book design: Grace Peirce

Photography credit: Chrissie Good

Player card images provided by the John Branca Collection and
Professional Sports Authenticator (PSA).

Additional memorabilia and images provided by
Heritage Auctions, 707 Sportscards, Vintage Breaks, Pete Putman,
Staten Island Joe Marino, and collector Tom Killeen.

Additional copies available from: TomZappalaMedia.com and Amazon.com

Printed in China

To Lucy, Emmie, Anna, Johnny, Tommy, Sloane, and Enzo

Acknowledgments

This book was truly a collaborative effort, and it was rewarding to work with many of the same colleagues who have contributed greatly to our previous books.

Special thanks to our dear friend, Joe Orlando, president and CEO of Collectors Universe, Inc., the parent company of Professional Sports Authenticator (PSA). The in-depth information that Joe provided gives us a deeper understanding of the appeal, design, values, scarcity, and history of the iconic 1952 Topps Collection.

Thank you to John Molori, for his contributions to the player research and historical narratives. John's baseball knowledge and whimsical writing ability combine to make this book informative and fun to read.

A very special thank you to John Branca, the nephew of pitching great Ralph Branca, for allowing us to use the images of his complete 1952 Topps Collection throughout the pages of this book. His collection is one of the finest in existence, and it is a privilege to showcase it for the enjoyment of our readers.

We are pleased to include a tribute to Sy Berger, the father of the 1952 Topps Collection, written with eloquence and love by his son, Glenn Berger. Thank you, Glenn.

Special thanks to Jackie Curiel, PSA Chief of Staff, for her efforts to make this project successful. From image acquisition to photo-shoot coordination and set design, Jackie handled everything perfectly. We enjoyed the opportunity to work with her on yet another project and are very appreciative of all she does.

The beautiful photographic images within the book and on the cover are the work of the talented Chrissie Good, a senior photographer for Collectors Universe, Inc. This was our second project with Chrissie, and once again she captured our vision with creativity and flair. Thank you, Chrissie, for your amazing images.

We also want to extend our thanks to Chris Ivy of Heritage Auctions, Levi Bleam of 707 Sportscards, Leighton Sheldon of Vintage Breaks, Pete Putman, Staten Island Joe Marino, and collector Tom Killeen for contributing images and memorabilia to this project.

The two youngsters featured on the cover, brothers Roman and Luis Curiel, spent hours in the hot California sun posing in period costumes with various props until we got the shot that we envisioned. Thanks, boys, for putting up with the long day, but we think that we got it right!

This is the sixth book project we have worked on with Peter E. Randall Publisher. Because of their knowledge and expertise, the finished book is one we are all proud of. Special thanks to Deidre Randall for her unflagging pursuit of excellence, her patience, and her guidance. Thank you to designer Grace Peirce, for creating just the right look for the book, editor Zak Johnson for his careful attention to detail, and to Kate Crichton for her photo expertise. We have been fortunate to work with such a great team.

Thanks to all of the collectors and hobbyists who have supported every one of our projects over the last ten years. We greatly appreciate your kind words and support.

Finally, thanks to "The Mick," "Handy Andy," "Klu," and the rest of the 407 players that make up this outstanding collection.

Contents

The 1952 Topps Collection is not a stranger to baseball-card-collector adulation. At the very least, this iconic issue is considered one of the top trading card sets in the entire hobby, regardless of sport. Along with the "monstrous" 1909-11 T206 set and the colorful 1933 Goudey release, the 1952 Topps production has a secure place amongst "The Big Three" in the baseball card world. That's for sure.

To many, however, the 1952 Topps set is much more than just another great group of baseball cards.

The 1952 Topps set changed the game, maybe not the game of baseball itself, but it certainly ushered in a completely new era of collecting. It has also become a part of pop culture. Individual cards from the set have been used in various movies and television shows in different capacities. In some cases, the cards were mere props in the background, but other times the cards played significant roles in the story.

After watching from the sidelines as Bowman dominated the hobby landscape during the 1948–1951 period, Topps decided to make a significant move in 1952. While it's true that Topps dabbled in baseball card production before that time with mildly popular releases like the 1948 Magic Photos and the 1951 Connie Mack All-Stars sets, this was the company's first real attempt at challenging the reigning champion.

From 1952 to 1955, Bowman and Topps waged war against one another, but only one brand would be left standing at the end of the fight. After Bowman threw in the towel in 1955, Topps went on to dominate the hobby for decades, and today it stands as the only card manufacturer licensed by Major League Baseball to make trading cards. The company has faced many challenges and challengers along the way, but no brand can stake claim to the rich history that Topps possesses.

The clean and unmistakable design, the larger format, and the sheer size of the set enabled the 1952 Topps issue to make an undeniable impression on the youngsters opening packs in search of their favorite players and that prized stick of chewing gum. To place that initial impression in the proper context, just imagine holding a 1952 Topps Mickey Mantle and placing it right alongside a 1952 Bowman featuring the same New York Yankees idol.

You are left feeling that the 1952 Topps card is something more than what kids were used to seeing. Don't get me wrong, I still love the 1952 Bowman Mantle and believe it remains one of the most underrated cards in the market today. That said, when placed side-by-side with his Topps counterpart, there is no comparison from a visual appeal standpoint.

One card exhibits beautiful artwork and the other is, for some reason, unforgettable. It grabs your attention in a way that is hard to explain, yet easy to understand. For that reason and more, the Topps Mantle is worth substantially more than Mantle's true rookie card, issued a year prior by Bowman.

From its initial unveiling to the stories of unopened cases being dumped in the ocean around 1960 to the high-number find that stunned the hobby in 1986, the 1952 Topps set has captivated hobbyists young and old since it was born. It was a great time to be a baseball fan in the 1950s, and this set captures so many of the legendary players who remain household names today. Only their first names are necessary. Jackie, Yogi, Duke, Willie, Whitey, and of course, Mickey, all resonate with the collecting community.

". . . this iconic issue is considered one of the top trading card sets in the entire hobby, regardless of sport."

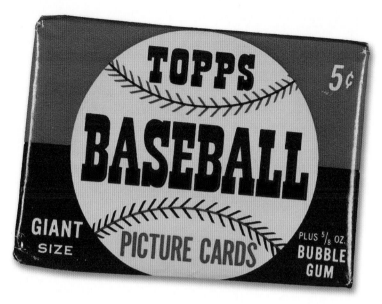

There are sets much older, many are tougher to assemble, and in some cases, there are those that are more valuable, but Topps changed the hobby forever in 1952. While the effort was well-received by kids at the time, the set gained greater momentum and respect as the years passed, perhaps in a more meaningful way than any other set that comes to mind.

Topps did a wonderful job of connecting with children in the beginning, but those children reconnected with the set as they became adults, which is part of the reason the hobby was taken to another level in the 1980s. Baby boomers now had the means to buy back all the cards their mom threw away years ago, and no set was more glorious than the 1952 Topps.

In this book, we tip our caps to the set that had more of an impact on the industry we know today than any other, and travel through time to meet the cardboard that acts more like a steel foundation to our hobby than a fragile collectible.

A Tribute to Sy Berger

by Glenn Berger

My first and most cogent memory of participating in my dad's extraordinary life with ballplayers, family, and bubble gum occurred when I was five years old. I was very excited when Dad said, "Son, we are going to spend the day at the Bubble Gum Factory." Dad often used the word "son" with me and with others when something extraordinary was about to happen.

First, we drove into Brooklyn, NY, to Dad's office. His domain was filled with papers, baseball stuff, boxes of cards, and a stenography machine into which he spoke for later transcription. At midday, we journeyed to the service elevator and followed the sweet smell of bubble gum into the factory where magical machines churned pink goo into small rectangles. Dad was greeted by everyone from the foreman to the workers who were loading sugar into the vats. It was as if they were his best friends. They certainly became my buddies, especially when they handed me boxes of bubble gum.

Once back in his office, Dad had happy and smiling visitors filing in and out. Sometimes, Dad reached into his desk and handed them a Mickey Mantle card. How was I to know that Dad had loaded much of the 1952 card production onto a barge and dumped the cards into the bay because they were not selling and the storage capacity at Topps was limited? If he had only saved 1,000 Mantles for the family!

Most nights after supper, Dad worked late into the evening, writing on long yellow sheets of paper with an ink pen. As I discovered later, he was figuring out batting averages and creating templates for the next year's cards.

HISTORY of TOPPS

1952 — Sy Berger creates the first complete set

For me, the most exciting part of hanging out with Dad was when he took me to the team clubhouses, especially when we visited the old Yankee Stadium. On one occasion Dad was chatting with his dear friends Bob Keegan, a pal from Bucknell University, and Billy Pierce, the great left-handed pitcher of the Chicago White Sox. Minnie Minoso got ahold of me and shared just how to use chewing tobacco. I was ten years old at the time.

When we entered the clubhouses, everyone greeted Dad as if their personal mentor and special friend had just arrived. Once, when Dad was having a serious discussion with Mickey Mantle, I stood next to the great slugger and watched in total awe as he wrapped his aching leg in gauze and tape. He then sat me on his knee and talked to me with kindness.

There was always a great deal of hugging and genuine love between Dad, the ballplayers, the managers, and the coaches. It was as if they were long-lost brothers reconnecting for the first time. Dad was a very affectionate man and to this day I miss the meaningful kiss on my cheek that became the kernel for a father's love for his child. Thank you, Dad, for enriching my life with so much love and many wonderful memories.

Introduction

As a kid who grew up in an industrial city north of Boston in the 1950s and '60s, baseball was a passion for me and my core group of friends. Every summer, if we were not playing ball or having a catch, we were kneeling in front of a brick wall playing "scalers." Most kids across the country were either flipping baseball cards or scaling them.

We loved to play "scalers" because it required great hand-eye coordination and a precise flick of the wrist. We took turns tossing our cards at a wall about 15 feet away. The first one to land a card on another card, or "kiss" it (as we called it), won all the cards that had accumulated on the ground. If a card landed up against the wall, we would take turns trying to knock down the "leaner" with another card. Whoever knocked it down won the whole pile. My friend Wayne was a great card scaler and pretty much wiped me out every time we played.

I started collecting cards in the late 1950s. I loved walking down to the store to get a new pack of cards and chew the bubble gum while checking to see if I got one of my favorite players. The 1952 Topps set was introduced the same year that I was born, and, as a kid, I never owned cards from this particular set, but I had a great collection of cards from 1959 through 1966. Somehow, Wayne wound up with most of them. Like everyone else, at some point my cards were thrown in the trash by, yes, my mother. I think mothers across the country must have attended a card trashing convention and voted unanimously to throw out the baseball cards in every home in America.

This book is about the players and the set that really laid the groundwork for card collecting. The 1952 Topps set was introduced at a time when baseball was in transition. Many players had returned from World War II or were serving in the Korean War, and baseball's color barrier had recently been broken. Baseball reached new heights of popularity as fans across the country could now watch their favorite players and teams right in their living rooms on television. Just like me, kids from all over the country were collecting cards, hoping to find their favorite players in that pack along with the flat, powdery piece of bubble gum. It was gold!

This book tells the story of all the players who made this iconic set so popular. From "Commons" to "Uncommons" to "Hall of Famers," we discuss every one of them. Some came up for the proverbial "cup of coffee," some lost key years to serving our country, some had stellar careers, and some were the hard-working "dirt dogs" of the game.

As an added feature, our colleague and friend, Joe Orlando, president and CEO of Collectors Universe, Inc., parent company of Professional Sports Authenticator (PSA), takes it full circle by discussing every aspect of the 1952 Topps Collection, including the history, design, rarities, variations, and major finds.

We hope that you enjoy the book. Take your bike out, stick that Mantle card in your spokes, and enjoy the ride. By the way, I forgave my mom many years ago for tossing my cards. She looked at me like I had two heads and said, "Forgive me for throwing out those worthless pieces of cardboard?" I just looked at her and smiled.

Tom Zappala

The Hall of Famers

The Hall of Famers in the 1952 Topps Collection

represent what has become known as the Golden Age of Baseball. Dating back to the turn of the twentieth century, fans idolized players like Cobb, Johnson, Mathewson, and Speaker. The next wave of greats like Ruth, Gehrig, Foxx, and Hornsby then arrived on the scene. They were followed by Williams, DiMaggio, Mantle, Robinson, Musial, Mays, Ford, and Spahn. Of course Ted Williams, Stan Musial, Joe DiMaggio, and Whitey Ford are not in the 1952 Topps

set because Williams and Musial had contractual obligations with another company, Ford was serving in the Korean War, and Joltin' Joe had recently retired. The others certainly picked up the gauntlet. This group of Hall of Famers was as good as any before them. Meet the Hall of Famers of the 1952 Topps Collection.

Richie Ashburn

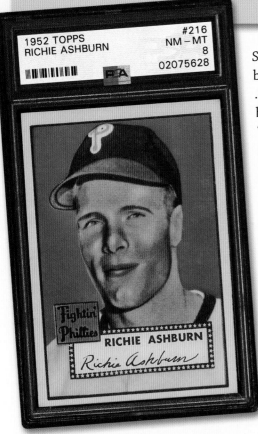

Simply put, Richie Ashburn was a great ballplayer. As a rookie in 1948, he batted .333 and led the league with 32 stolen bases. A member of the 1950 Phillies "Whiz Kids," Ashburn appeared in six All-Star games, was the NL Batting Champ twice, and led the league in walks four times. Ashburn batted over .300 in nine of his 15 seasons, with high points in 1951, when he batted .344 with 221 hits, and 1958, when he batted .350 with 215 hits. Outstanding defensively, the center fielder led the NL in putouts nine times. With his dry sense of humor, Ashburn was a natural in the broadcast booth after his playing days. Extremely popular, he was the Phillies broadcaster for 35 years until 1997, when he died from a heart attack at age 70. He was elected to the Hall of Fame two years prior in 1995.

Career Stats

AB:	8,365	HR:	29
R:	1,322	RBI:	586
H:	2,574	OPS:	.778
BA:	.308		

Teams

Philadelphia Phillies NL (1948-1959)
Chicago Cubs NL (1960-1961)
New York Mets NL (1962)

Yogi Berra

Berra or Bench? Bench or Berra? Either Yogi Berra or Johnny Bench could be considered the greatest catcher of all-time. In the case of Yogi Berra, what can you say? He was an 18-time All-Star, played in 14 World Series, was a three-time American League MVP, and was named to the All-Century Team. A .285 lifetime hitter who banged out 358 home runs, Berra was outstanding defensively and a genius at calling games and handling pitchers. Yogi also managed the Yankees to the 1964 AL pennant, coached the 1969 "Miracle Mets," and won the NL pennant as manager of the Mets in 1973. He managed seven years and coached for 18 years, finishing in 1989 with the Astros. And let's not forget his "Yogisms." What more needs to be said? Yogi was simply a great player. He died in 2015 at the age of 90.

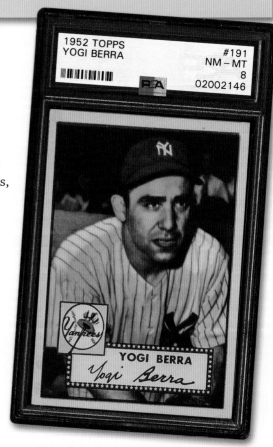

Career Stats

AB:	7,555	HR:	358
R:	1,175	RBI:	1,430
H:	2,150	OPS:	.830
BA:	.285		

Teams

New York Yankees AL (1946-1963)
New York Mets NL (1965)

Roy Campanella

Sadly, the lasting image of Roy Campanella for many is that of the stately Hall of Fame catcher confined to a wheelchair after a 1958 motor-vehicle accident. Campanella was one of the finest backstops the game has ever known, a rock of stability from 1948 through 1957 for the Brooklyn Dodgers. An eight-time All-Star, Campanella won three MVP Awards and drove in a gaudy 142 runs in 1953. Moreover, he deftly handled a pitching staff that included some of the true greats of the game. The Philly native led the Dodgers to five NL pennants and a world championship in 1955. In his post-accident life, "Campy" stayed positive. He owned a liquor store, worked in radio, and worked for the Dodgers organization. A team award for spirit and leadership bears his name. The 1969 Hall of Fame inductee died of a heart attack in 1993 at age 71.

Career Stats

AB:	4,205	HR:	242
R:	627	RBI:	856
H:	1,161	OPS:	.860
BA:	.276		

Teams
Brooklyn Dodgers NL (1948-1957)

Bill Dickey

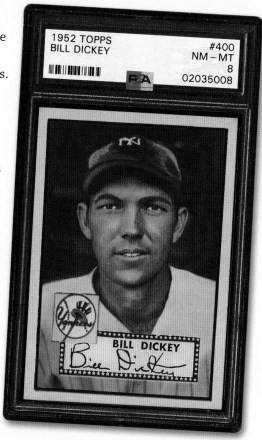

A career Yankee, Bill Dickey was an 11-time All-Star and batted over .300 eleven times. He backstopped the Yankees to seven World Series titles. At his best in the postseason, he batted .438 in the 1932 World Series and .400 in the 1938 fall classic. Dickey smashed 202 career home runs with 1,209 RBI and a .313 batting average. After serving in WWII, he managed the Yankees in 1946, and as coach for the Yanks, he groomed both Yogi Berra and Elston Howard. He later coached for Casey Stengel's Mets. The 1954 Hall of Fame inductee's jersey was retired in 1972, and he joined the pantheon of legends in Yankee Stadium's Monument Park in 1988. Dickey died at age 86 in 1993. He may have played third fiddle to Babe Ruth and Lou Gehrig in popularity, but he was a true maestro behind and at the plate.

Career Stats

AB:	6,300	HR:	202
R:	930	RBI:	1,209
H:	1,969	OPS:	.868
BA:	.313		

Teams
New York Yankees AL (1928-1943, 1946)

Larry Doby

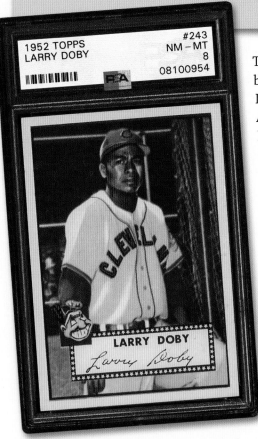

Three months after Jackie Robinson broke baseball's color barrier in April of 1947, Larry Doby became the first African American player in American League history. The seven-time All-Star hit 253 home runs with 970 RBI and batted .283 in his 13-year Hall of Fame career. In 1952, Doby led the league with 104 runs scored, 32 home runs, and his .541 slugging percentage. Two years later, he smashed a league-leading 32 homers and 126 RBI. The US Navy veteran became the first African American player to hit a World Series home run, helping Cleveland to the 1948 title. Thirty years later, as skipper of the 1978 White Sox, Doby became the second African American manger in MLB history. In 1997, the Indians retired Doby's number "14," and he was inducted into the Hall of Fame in 1998. The iconic trailblazer passed away in 2003 at age 79.

Career Stats

AB:	5,348	HR:	253
R:	960	RBI:	970
H:	1,515	OPS:	.876
BA:	.283		

Teams

Cleveland Indians AL (1947–1955, 1958)
Chicago White Sox AL (1956–1957, 1959)
Detroit Tigers AL (1959)

Leo Durocher

Abrasive, explosive, aggressive—"Leo the Lip" Durocher was one of the most colorful, hard-edged men to ever lace up the spikes. A feisty shortstop and second sacker, he was a three-time All-Star who played 17 years for the Yanks, Reds, Cards, and Dodgers. It was as manager, however, that the fiery, competitive Durocher achieved lasting notoriety. As player-manager of the Dodgers, Durocher led "Dem Bums" to the NL pennant in 1941. Although instrumental in bringing Jackie Robinson to the Dodgers, Durocher missed managing their historic 1947 season while suspended for a smorgasbord of transgressions. In 1948, he moved on to manage crosstown rivals, the New York Giants, winning two pennants and a World Series championship in 1954. He later managed the Cubs and Astros and compiled a 2008–1709 record in 24 years. Durocher died in 1991 at age 86, three years before his Hall of Fame induction.

Career Stats

AB:	5,350	HR:	24
R:	575	RBI:	567
H:	1,320	OPS:	.619
BA:	.247		

Teams

New York Yankees AL (1925, 1928–1929)
Cincinnati Reds NL (1930–1933)
St. Louis Cardinals NL (1933–1937)
Brooklyn Dodgers NL (1938–1941, 1943, 1945)

Bob Feller

One of the most dominant pitchers of the era, Bob "Rapid Robert" Feller led the American League in wins six times, strikeouts seven times, and threw three no-hitters. While still in high school, Feller jumped right into the fire with the Indians in 1936, at the age of 17. One of the best from 1938 through 1941, he led the league with 24 wins in 1939, 27 wins and 2.61 ERA in 1940, and 25 wins in 1941. Feller served in the US Navy from December 1941 through August 1945 and returned to lead the league with 26 wins in 1946, 20 in 1947, and 22 in 1951. If he hadn't lost nearly four seasons to military service, Feller would likely have compiled more than 300 career wins. The eight-time All-Star and 1962 Hall of Fame inductee passed away in 2010 at the age of 92.

Career Stats

Record:	266–162
ERA:	3.25
IP:	3,827.0
Ks:	2,581
Threw:	RH

Teams
Cleveland Indians AL (1936–1941, 1945–1956)

Billy Herman

Hall of Famer Billy Herman played in ten straight All-Star games from 1934 to 1943. A Cubby for 11 seasons, he led the league with 227 hits in 1935. Over his 15 MLB seasons, Herman hit just 47 home runs but he doubled and tripled pitchers to death. Although he served in the US Navy from 1944 to 1945, Herman amassed 2,345 career hits. He had three 200-hit seasons and batted .304 for his career. The second sacker played in three World Series with the Cubs and one with Brooklyn, but never won a title. Lending credence to the theory that great players do not make great managers, Herman never finished higher than seventh place while managing the Pirates in 1947 and the Red Sox from 1964 to 1966. He also coached for several teams. This grand old man of baseball passed away at age 83 in 1992.

Career Stats

AB:	7,707	HR:	47
R:	1,163	RBI:	839
H:	2,345	OPS:	.774
BA:	.304		

Teams
Chicago Cubs NL (1931–1941)
Brooklyn Dodgers NL (1941–1943, 1946)
Boston Braves NL (1946)
Pittsburgh Pirates NL (1947)

Monte Irvin

1952 TOPPS #26
MONTY IRVIN
MINT 9
01145456

A star for the Newark Eagles in the Negro Leagues, Monte Irvin was signed by the New York Giants two years after Jackie Robinson broke the color barrier. The 30-year-old rookie outfielder quickly established himself in the majors, and was instrumental in the Giants' drive to the pennant in 1951 and their World Series win in 1954. Irvin, along with fellow Giants integration trailblazers Hank Thompson and Willie Mays, comprised the first all-black outfield in MLB history. The 1952 All-Star played only eight years in the majors, but he left his mark on baseball history. After his retirement, Irvin scouted for the Mets before working for many years as public relations specialist and assistant to the commissioner of baseball. The 1973 Hall of Fame inductee kept close ties with the Giants, who retired his number "20" in 2010. Monford Merrill Irvin was 96 when he died in 2016.

Career Stats

AB:	2,499	HR:	99
R:	366	RBI:	433
H:	731	OPS:	.858
BA:	.293		

Teams
New York Giants NL (1949–1955)
Chicago Cubs NL (1956)

George Kell

One of the best hitters of his generation, ten-time All-Star George Kell, batted over .300 nine times and finished his career with a .306 batting average and 2,054 hits. Overshadowed in the American League by Ted Williams, Kell batted .343 in 1949 to best Williams and win the batting crown. In an incredible 1950 season, the Arkansas native batted .340 and led the league with 218 hits and 56 doubles. Kell began his career with the 1943 Athletics and tripled in his first at-bat. With Detroit from 1946 to 1952, the third sacker batted over .300 every season and made six straight All-Star teams. He also played for the Red Sox, White Sox, and Orioles before his second career in the Tigers broadcasting booth where he charmed fans with his folksy manner for 37 years. The 1983 Hall of Fame inductee passed away in 2009 at age 86.

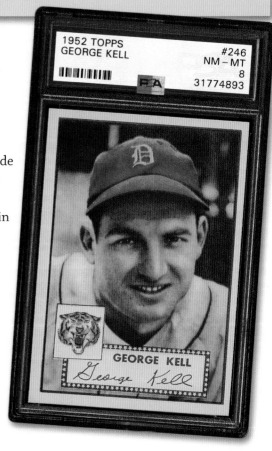

1952 TOPPS #246
GEORGE KELL
NM – MT 8
31774893

Career Stats

AB:	6,702	HR:	78
R:	880	RBI:	870
H:	2,054	OPS:	.781
BA:	.306		

Teams
Philadelphia Athletics AL (1943–1946)
Detroit Tigers AL (1946–1952)
Boston Red Sox AL (1952–1954)
Chicago White Sox AL (1954–1956)
Baltimore Orioles AL (1956–1957)

Bob Lemon

After serving in the US Navy from 1943 through 1945, Bob Lemon served up a Hall of Fame pitching career beginning in 1946. With Cleveland for his entire career, Lemon won 207 games, reached the 20-win plateau seven times, and was an All-Star every year from 1948 to 1954. He led the American League in games started three times, complete games five times, and innings pitched four times. In Cleveland's 1948 World Series win vs. Boston, Lemon went 2–0 with a 1.65 ERA. A solid hitter, Lemon actually began his career as an outfielder. After retiring in 1958, Lemon managed for eight MLB seasons, compiling a 430–403 record. His greatest success came in 1978 when Lemon replaced Billy Martin midseason and the Yankees surged from fourth place to a World Series championship vs. the Dodgers. A true baseball man, Bob Lemon died in 2000 at age 79.

Career Stats

Record:	207–128
ERA:	3.23
IP:	2,850.0
Ks:	1,277
Threw:	RH

Teams

Cleveland Indians AL (1946–1958)

Mickey Mantle

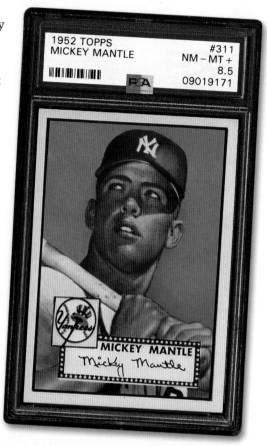

One of the greatest players in the history of the game, Mickey Mantle remains one of baseball's greatest "What If's." What if he had not battled knee injuries and other ailments throughout his career? What if he had not caroused at such a high level while he played baseball? What if the pressure of replacing Yankees legend Joe DiMaggio and the death of his father at age 40 had not haunted him? In his 18-year career, Mantle smashed 536 home runs, he won three MVP Awards, and was an All-Star 16 times. Despite his bad wheels, Mantle motored around the bases to the tune of 1,676 career runs scored. He died in 1995 at age 63, but the blonde bomber remains one of baseball's great enigmas, with a legacy of melancholy as well as mastery. His card featured in this collection is the most sought-after of the set.

Career Stats

AB:	8,102	HR:	536
R:	1,676	RBI:	1,509
H:	2,415	OPS:	.977
BA:	.298		

Teams

New York Yankees AL (1951–1968)

Eddie Mathews

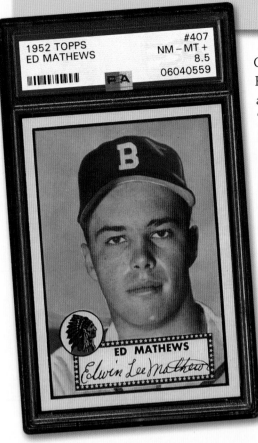

One of baseball's all-time greats, Hall of Famer Eddie Mathews hit 25 homers as a rookie with the Boston Braves in 1952. The next season, the team moved to Milwaukee and Mathews led the National League with 47 home runs. He would smash 512 homers and knock in 1,453 runs in his 17-year career. Mathews combined power with patience, leading the NL in walks on four occasions. The third baseman made nine All-Star teams and was part of Milwaukee's 1957 world champion team. When the Braves moved to Atlanta in 1966, Mathews became the only man to play for the club in all three cities. He wrapped up his career with the 1968 world champion Detroit Tigers. Mathews was Braves manager in 1974 when former teammate Hank Aaron surpassed Babe Ruth's home run record. One of baseball's iconic sluggers, Mathews died in 2001 at age 69.

Career Stats

AB:	8,537	HR:	512
R:	1,509	RBI:	1,453
H:	2,315	OPS:	.885
BA:	.271		

Teams

Boston/Milwaukee/Atlanta Braves NL (1952–1966)
Houston Astros NL (1967)
Detroit Tigers AL (1967–1968)

Willie Mays

The "Say Hey Kid" broke in with the Giants in 1951 and set new standards for excellence. Mays's stats are incredible: 660 homers, 1,903 RBI, and 2,062 runs. Beyond the numbers, his style, enthusiasm, and knowledge of the game were singular. The Alabama native played in 20 All-Star games, 19 consecutively between 1954 and 1972. The epitome of power and speed, he led the league in home runs four times, stolen bases four times, slugging five times, and triples three times. Mays eclipsed the 50-homer plateau twice and won 12 consecutive Gold Gloves from 1957 to 1968. He was the catalyst for the Giants' 1954 world championship, batting a career-high .345 with 41 homers. After 21 seasons with the Giants, Mays joined the Mets for his final two seasons. The Hall of Famer will forever be revered as one of baseball's icons, perhaps the greatest of all-time.

Career Stats

AB:	10,881	HR:	660
R:	2,062	RBI:	1,903
H:	3,283	OPS:	.941
BA:	.302		

Teams

New York/San Francisco Giants NL (1951–1952, 1954–1972)
New York Mets NL (1972–1973)

Johnny Mize

A true star, Johnny "Big Cat" Mize was a heck of a first baseman. The ten-time All-Star played on five consecutive Yankees World Series championship teams. However, his best offensive years took place with the St. Louis Cardinals and the New York Giants before and after his three years of military service. When he played for the Giants in 1947, he had a monster year, batting .302, and his 51 home runs tied with Ralph Kiner to lead the majors. He also led MLB with 137 runs and 138 RBI that year. One of the top-ten first basemen of all time, Mize retired in 1953 with a .312 lifetime batting average, 359 home runs, and a .992 fielding average. Mize then became a color commentator and did some coaching and scouting. The 1981 Hall of Fame inductee passed away in 1993 at the age of 80.

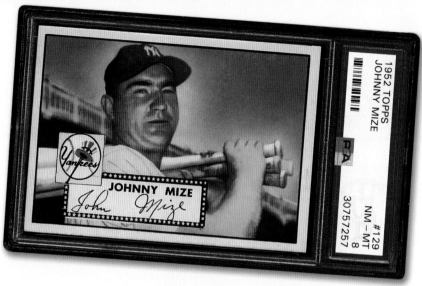

Teams
St. Louis Cardinals NL (1936–1941)
New Your Giants NL (1942, 1946–1949)
New York Yankees AL (1949–1953)

Career Stats
AB:	6,443	HR:	359
R:	1,118	RBI:	1,337
H:	2,011	OPS:	.959
BA:	.312		

Pee Wee Reese

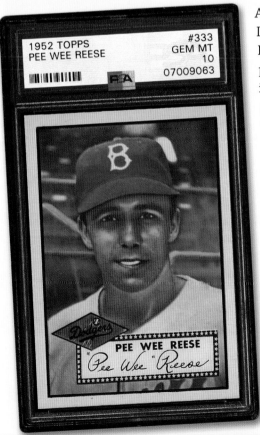

A ten-time All-Star, Harold "Pee Wee" Reese played 16 seasons for the Dodgers. The 5-foot-10, 160-pound shortstop epitomized the grit of Brooklyn's fabled baseball team. A standout player and standup guy, Reese publicly befriended Jackie Robinson when #42 broke baseball's color barrier in 1947. Beloved by fans, Reese was a pest to pitchers, working counts, getting on base, and using his speed to score runs. In 1949, he led the NL in plate appearances and runs scored. Reese was the engine that fueled the Dodgers to seven pennants and the 1955 world championship. He served in World War II from 1943 to 1945 and was a field general for his clubs throughout his career. In 1984, Reese was inducted into the Baseball Hall of Fame and his number "1" was retired by the Dodgers. He died in 1999 at the age of 81.

Career Stats
AB:	8,058	HR:	126
R:	1,338	RBI:	885
H:	2,170	OPS:	.743
BA:	.269		

Teams
Brooklyn/Los Angeles Dodgers NL (1940–1942, 1946–1958)

Phil Rizzuto

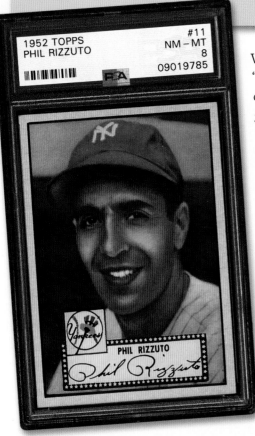

1952 TOPPS #11
PHIL RIZZUTO
NM – MT 8
09019785

Volumes could be written about Phil "The Scooter" Rizzuto. One of the best defensive shortstops to ever play the game, the diminutive Rizzuto was a five-time All-Star who played on seven Yankees World Series championship teams and was the American League MVP in 1950. He also took home the Babe Ruth Award in 1951. A student of "small ball," Rizzuto is considered one of the best bunters in baseball history. With a repertoire of bunts in his arsenal for any situation, Rizzuto consistently led the league in sacrifice hits. After his playing days were over, Rizzuto became a beloved broadcaster for the Yankees on both radio and TV for over 40 years. His signature expression, "Holy Cow!" still resonates to this day. Inducted into the Hall of Fame in 1994, Rizzuto passed away in 2007 at the age of 89.

Career Stats

AB:	5,816	HR:	38
R:	877	RBI:	563
H:	1,588	OPS:	.706
BA:	.273		

Teams

New York Yankees AL (1941–1942, 1946–1956)

Robin Roberts

One of the most dominant pitchers in the National League between 1950 and 1955, Robin Roberts was durable with a quick, moving fastball and pinpoint control. With the Philadelphia Phillies, Roberts had a stretch of six 20-game seasons. Part of the 1950 "Whiz Kids" team, his 20 wins helped the Phillies secure the pennant for the first time in 35 years. In 1952, Roberts compiled a sparkling 28–7 record with a 2.59 ERA. He was so durable that between July 1952 and June 1953, he pitched 28 complete games in a row. A seven-time All-Star, Roberts led the NL in complete games five times, innings pitched five times, wins four times, and strikeouts twice. After his MLB career, Roberts coached and managed at the collegiate level and spent time as a broadcaster. The 1976 Hall of Fame inductee passed away at the age of 83 in 2010.

1952 TOPPS
ROBIN ROBERTS #59
NM – MT 8
07049300

Career Stats

Record:	286–245
ERA:	3.41
IP:	4,688.2
Ks:	2,357
Threw:	RH

Teams

Philadelphia Phillies NL (1948–1961)
Baltimore Orioles AL (1962–1965)
Houston Astros NL (1965–1966)
Chicago Cubs NL (1966)

Jackie Robinson

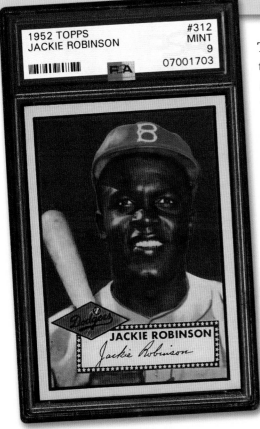

The man who broke baseball's color barrier in 1947 when he proudly strode onto the field for the Brooklyn Dodgers, Jack Roosevelt Robinson, did more than make six All-Star teams in his 10-year MLB career. He posted 203 hits and won a batting title in 1949, and propelled the Dodgers to their first world championship in 1955. Over his MLB career, Robinson batted .311 and had an astounding 19 steals of home. But there is more. He was a star at UCLA, a Negro Leagues standout, and a second lieutenant in the US Army. Robinson even played himself in the film, *The Jackie Robinson Story*. His stellar career paved the way for Robinson to become the first African American inductee to the Baseball Hall of Fame in 1962. Simply said, he changed America. Sadly, soon after the Dodgers retired his number "42," Robinson, a diabetic, died at 53 years old in 1972.

Career Stats

AB:	4,877	HR:	137
R:	947	RBI:	734
H:	1.518	OPS:	.883
BA:	.311		

Teams

Brooklyn Dodgers NL (1947–1956)

Red Schoendienst

Hall of Famer and ten-time All-Star Albert "Red" Schoendienst was a great ballplayer, manager, and coach. A hitting machine and standout second baseman, Schoendienst banged out 2,449 hits to go along with his .289 lifetime batting average. Also a defensive standout, his .9934 fielding percentage in 1956 stood as a National League record for second basemen for 40 years. As a player, Schoendienst won the 1946 World Series with the St. Louis Cardinals, the 1957 Series with the Milwaukee Braves, and he led the NL with 200 hits in 1957. He coached the 1964 world champion Cardinals and as the Cards manager, he won the 1967 World Series, the 1968 NL pennant, and posted a 1041–955 record in 14 years. He coached the Cardinals until 2011, winning three more Series. The 1989 Hall of Fame inductee and baseball lifer passed away in 2018 at the age of 95.

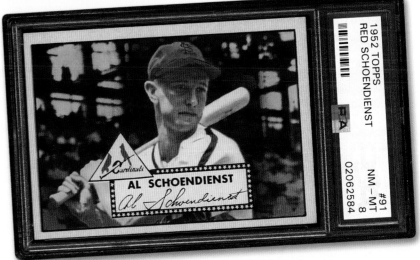

Teams

St. Louis Cardinals NL (1945–1956, 1961–1963)

New York Giants NL (1956–1957)

Milwaukee Braves NL (1957–1960)

Career Stats

AB:	8,479	HR:	84
R:	1,223	RBI:	773
H:	2,449	OPS:	.724
BA:	.289		

Enos Slaughter

1952 TOPPS #65
ENOS SLAUGHTER NM – MT 8
11608654

Nicknamed "Country" because of his North Carolina roots, Enos Slaughter was your prototypical contact hitter who had an outstanding 19-year career. The sweet-swinging lefty compiled 2,383 hits, batted a career .300, and played on four World Series championship teams. Imagine what he would have accomplished had he not lost three seasons to military service. A ten-time All-Star with the Cardinals, Slaughter will always be remembered by Boston fans for scoring the winning run against their beloved Red Sox in Game Seven of the 1946 World Series. Known for his hustle, Slaughter would run full-speed up the first-base line even if he drew a walk. After baseball, Slaughter retired to his North Carolina farm, coached baseball at Duke University, and wrote *Country Hardball*, his autobiography. In 1996, the Cardinals retired his number "9." The 1985 Hall of Fame inductee passed away in 2002 at the age of 86.

Career Stats

AB:	7,946	HR:	169
R:	1,247	RBI:	1,304
H:	2,383	OPS:	.834
BA:	.300		

Teams

St. Louis Cardinals NL (1938–1942, 1946–1953)
New York Yankees AL (1954–1955, 1956–1959)
Kansas City Athletics AL (1955–1956)
Milwaukee Braves NL (1959)

Duke Snider

The batting epicenter for the great Brooklyn Dodgers teams of the 1950s, Duke Snider, power-pal, Gil Hodges, and teammates Jackie Robinson, Pee Wee Reese, and Roy Campanella, were the fabled "Boys of Summer" 1955 World Series champions. For five straight seasons, "The Duke of Flatbush" hit at least 40 home runs, and was an RBI machine. Snider was a cog on the 1959 LA Dodgers World Series champion team. Over his great career, the eight-time All-Star, hit 407 home runs with a .295 lifetime batting average. As his career wound down, Snider wound up with the hapless 1963 New York Mets and ended up with the 1964 San Francisco Giants. Following his retirement, Snider was a respected television broadcaster and analyst for the Padres and Expos. He was elected to the Hall of Fame in 1980 and passed away in 2011 at the age of 84.

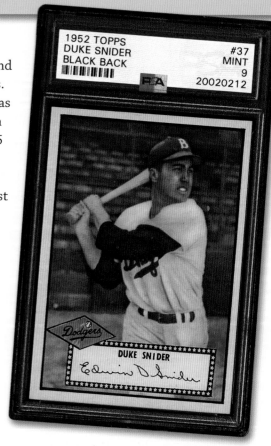

1952 TOPPS #37
DUKE SNIDER
BLACK BACK MINT 9
20020212

Career Stats

AB:	7,161	HR:	407
R:	1,259	RBI:	1,333
H:	2,116	OPS:	.919
BA:	.295		

Teams

Brooklyn/Los Angeles Dodgers NL (1947–1962)
New York Mets NL (1963)
San Francisco Giants NL (1964)

Warren Spahn

1952 TOPPS #33
WARREN SPAHN MINT
BLACK BACK 9
17693769
PSA

Arguably the greatest left-handed pitcher in baseball history, Warren Spahn won an amazing 363 games over his brilliant career, pitching primarily for the Boston Braves/ Milwaukee Braves. The 1957 Cy Young Award winner and 17-time All-Star led the National League in wins eight times. Spahn was the league ERA leader three times, strikeout leader four times, and he pitched two no-hitters to go along with his thirteen 20-win seasons. Spahn's pitching philosophy was simple: "Hitting is timing. Pitching is upsetting timing." During the 1948 pennant drive, Spahn and teammate Jonny Sain were so dominant that a popular verse was written about them, "Spahn and Sain; then pray for rain." Warren Spahn was voted to the All-Century Team in 1999 and was elected to the Hall of Fame in 1973. A decorated World War II veteran, Spahn passed away in 2003 at the age of 82.

Career Stats

Record: 363–245
ERA: 3.09
IP: 5,243.2
Ks: 2,583
Threw: LH

Teams

Boston Braves/Milwaukee Braves NL (1942, 1946–1964)
New York Mets NL (1965)
San Francisco Giants NL (1965)

Hoyt Wilhelm

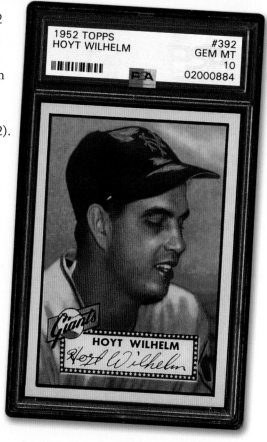

1952 TOPPS #392
HOYT WILHELM
GEM MT
10
02000884
PSA

When he died in 2002 at the age of 80, Hoyt Wilhelm left a unique pitching legacy—from the knuckleball, to the tilted cap, to the longevity (1952–1972). He broke in with the Giants, posting 15 wins with a league-leading 2.43 ERA. A five-time All-Star, "Old Sarge" played for nine teams and posted an ERA under 2.00 seven times. During his career, Wilhelm struck out more than twice as many hitters as he walked. He amassed 143 wins and 228 saves, with a career 2.52 ERA. Wilhelm played in just one World Series, winning with the Giants in 1954. In September of 1958, playing for the Orioles, he tossed a no-hitter vs. the Yankees. A decade later, he passed Cy Young for most games pitched and remains sixth on the all-time list. Wilhelm pitched to age 49 and was inducted into the Hall of Fame in 1985.

Career Stats

Record: 143–122
ERA: 2.52
IP: 2,254.1
Ks: 1,610
Threw: RH

Teams

New York Giants NL (1952–1956)
St. Louis Cardinals NL (1957)
Cleveland Indians AL (1957–1958)
Baltimore Orioles AL (1958–1962)
Chicago White Sox AL (1963–1968)
California Angels AL (1969)
Atlanta Braves NL (1969–1970, 1971)
Chicago Cubs NL (1970)
Los Angeles Dodgers NL (1971–1972)

Dick Williams

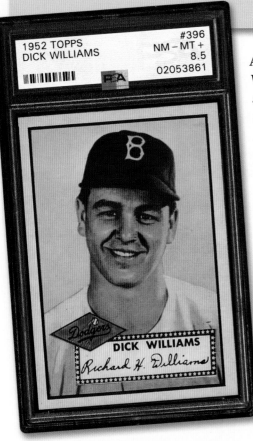

1952 TOPPS
DICK WILLIAMS
#396
NM – MT +
8.5
02053861

A feisty outfielder and infielder, Dick Williams played for 13 seasons. He was an extra in the film *The Jackie Robinson Story* and debuted with Brooklyn in 1951. A shoulder injury in 1952 hindered his career, inspiring him to learn baseball strategy from the likes of Bobby Bragan, Paul Richards, and Chuck Dressen. Williams' last stop as a player was with the Red Sox in 1964. He was named Boston's manager in 1967 and fueled the "Impossible Dream" turnaround from ninth place to the pennant. Williams eventually moved to Oakland where he battled meddling owner Charlie Finley and won the 1972 and 1973 World Series with a roster of free-spirited and talented players. He also turned losers into winners in Montreal and San Diego. In 21 seasons as a manager, Williams won 1,571 games. The 2008 Hall of Fame inductee died in 2011 at age 82.

Career Stats

AB:	2,959	HR:	70
R;	358	RBI:	331
H:	768	OPS:	.704
BA:	.260		

Teams

Brooklyn Dodgers NL (1951–1954, 1956)
Baltimore Orioles AL (1956–1957, 1958, 1961–1962)
Cleveland Indians AL (1957)
Kansas City Athletics AL (1959–1960)
Boston Red Sox AL (1963–1964)

Early Wynn

The length of Early Wynn's career was matched only by the shortness of his temper. An intimidating figure on the hill during his 23 seasons, Wynn won 20 games or more five times and hit the coveted 300-wins milestone. A 19-year-old rookie with the 1939 Senators, Wynn served in the military in 1945 and returned to become a seven-time All-Star. From 1949 through 1956, Wynn teamed with Bob Lemon and Bob Feller, giving the Indians a rotation of three future Hall of Famers and a 1954 pennant win. In 1959, at age 39, Wynn posted a 22–10 record, won the Cy Young Award, and helped the White Sox to the pennant. After retiring in 1963 at age 43, Wynn coached, managed in the minors, and was a broadcaster for the Blue Jays and White Sox. The 1972 Hall of Fame inductee passed away in 1999 at age 79.

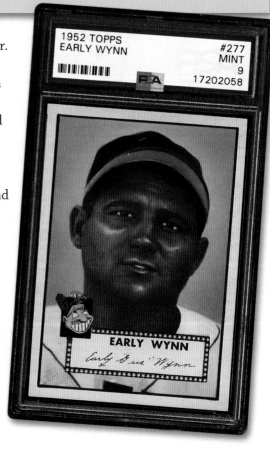

1952 TOPPS
EARLY WYNN
#277
MINT
9
17202058

Career Stats

Record:	300–244
ERA:	3.54
IP:	4,564.0
Ks:	2,334
Threw:	RH

Teams

Washington Senators AL (1939, 1941–1944, 1946–1948)
Cleveland Indians AL (1949–1957, 1963)
Chicago White Sox AL (1958–1962)

2

The Uncommons

The word "uncommon" refers to someone or something "out of the ordinary," or "unusual."

In this chapter, we discuss the players who were not Hall of Famers, yet were not your everyday common players. Although not worthy of Cooperstown, some of these men had excellent careers. Others had experiences outside of the diamond that warrant additional attention. Whether they had very successful Major League Baseball careers, were war heroes, or became famous or infamous after their careers ended, they were all certainly a bit unique. Meet the "Uncommons" of the 1952 Topps Collection.

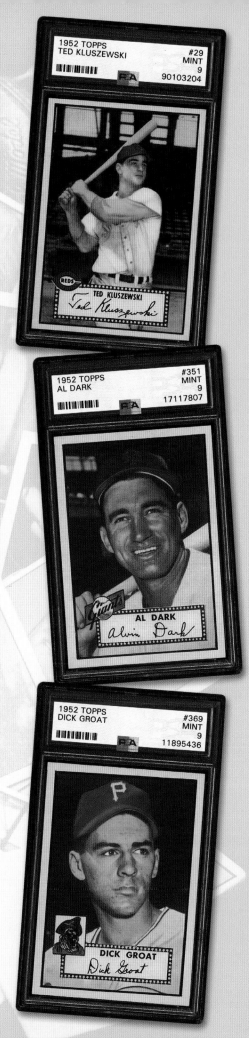

Joe Adcock

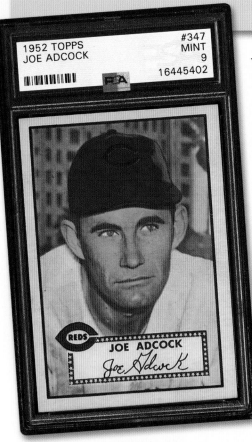

With his 336 career home runs and 1,122 RBI, power-hitting first baseman and outfielder Joe Adcock was overshadowed by the likes of Gil Hodges, Ted Kluszewski, Willie Mays, and longtime Braves teammate, Hank Aaron. He was an All-Star twice in 1960, but he was more than deserving in 1956 when he slammed 38 homers and 103 RBI, and in 1961 with his 35 dingers and 108 RBI. After starting in Cincinnati, Adcock starred with Milwaukee from 1953 through 1962. He won a World Series with the Braves in 1957 and batted .308 in the 1958 fall classic, which the Braves lost to the Yankees. He ended his career in style, smashing 18 home runs in just 83 games for the Angels in 1966. Adcock managed the 1967 Indians and later owned racehorses. He died in 1999 at age 71 from Alzheimer's disease.

Career Stats

AB:	6,606	HR:	336
R:	823	RBI:	1,122
H:	1,832	OPS:	.822
BA:	.277		

Teams
Cincinnati Reds NL (1950–1952)
Milwaukee Braves NL (1953–1962)
Cleveland Indians AL (1963)
Los Angeles/California Angels AL (1964–1966)

Johnny Antonelli

The biggest bonus baby in baseball history at the time, 18-year-old Johnny Antonelli reportedly received more than $50,000 to sign with the Braves in 1948. The southpaw had a slow start but honed his skills while pitching for the US Army in 1951 and 1952. He flourished after joining the New York Giants in 1954. That year, Antonelli went 21–7 and led the majors with his 2.30 ERA and six shutouts. He pitched a complete game win in Game Two of the 1954 Series and got the save in Game Four as the Giants swept the Indians for the Title. The six-time All-Star and two-time 20-game winner had a great seven-year run with the Giants. After stints with Cleveland and Milwaukee, Antonelli returned to Rochester, New York, to run his Firestone/Michelin tire distribution business until 1994. Antonelli passed away in 2020 at 89 years old.

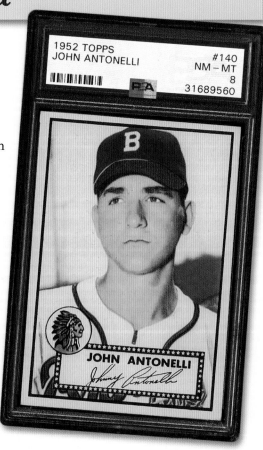

Career Stats

Record:	126–110
ERA:	3.34
IP:	1,992.1
Ks:	1,162
Threw:	LH

Teams
Boston/Milwaukee Braves NL (1948–1950, 1953)
New York/San Francisco Giants NL (1954–1960)
Cleveland Indians AL (1961)
Milwaukee Braves NL (1961)

Bobby Avila

Born in Veracruz, Mexico, Bobby Avila became an iconic figure for future Mexican ballplayers with his drive and excellence. He won the American League batting title while playing for the 1954 AL champion Indians. That season, Avila hit .341 with 15 home runs, 112 runs scored, and 67 RBI. He batted a disappointing .133 in the team's fall classic loss to the Giants, but for his entire career, Avila was non-stop at second base, playing with an unmatched competitive fire. He spent ten seasons and made three All-Star teams with Cleveland. In 1959, his final season, he played for the Orioles, Red Sox, and Braves. Avila was part-owner of the Mexico City Reds and president of the Veracruz League, which was subsequently named after him. He eventually became mayor of Veracruz and a congressman in Mexico. Avila died in 2004 at age 80.

Career Stats

AB:	4,620	HR:	80
R:	725	RBI:	467
H:	1,296	OPS:	.747
BA:	.281		

Teams
Cleveland Indians AL (1949–1958)
Baltimore Orioles AL (1959)
Boston Red Sox AL (1959)
Milwaukee Braves NL (1959)

Hank Bauer

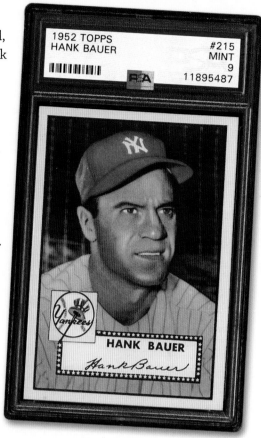

A right fielder with a great arm, good speed, and some power, Hank Bauer was known for his hard-nosed style of play. As a member of the juggernaut Yankees of the 1950s, the three-time All-Star played in nine World Series and helped the team to seven championships. Bauer; along with friends Mickey Mantle, Whitey Ford, and Billy Martin; made the Yankees a very colorful team both on and off the field. After 12 seasons in pinstripes, Bauer played briefly for Kansas City before he coached and managed the Athletics. Bauer managed the Orioles to the 1966 world championship, and later managed Oakland A's. He posted a 594–544 record in eight years as a Major League manager. Bauer also managed in the minors, ran his liquor store, and scouted for the Yankees. The US Marine Corps veteran who was injured on Guam and Okinawa died in 2007 at age 84.

Career Stats

AB:	5,145	HR:	164
R:	833	RBI:	703
H:	1,424	OPS:	.785
BA:	.277		

Teams
New York Yankees AL (1948–1959)
Kansas City Athletics AL (1960–1961)

Frank Baumholtz

Where do we start when it comes to Frank Baumholtz? Yes, he had a .290 lifetime batting average in the majors and was quite an outfielder. Good with the bat, Baumholtz batted .325 in 1952 and .306 in 1953 for the Cubs. We are not even sure that baseball was his best sport. Baumholtz was also a first-team All-American basketball player who led the Ohio University Bobcats to the National Invitation Tournament final in 1941, and he played professional basketball averaging 14 points per game. Above and beyond his athletic endeavors, he served four years in the US Navy. Lieutenant Baumholtz saw extensive action in World War II as his ship was involved in the final battles in the Pacific, off Iwo Jima and Okinawa. A star on the baseball diamond, basketball court, and the battlefield, Baumholtz passed away in 1997 at the age of 79.

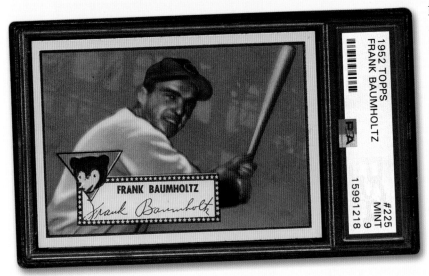

Career Stats

AB:	3,477	HR:	25
R:	450	RBI:	272
H:	1,010	OPS:	.730
BA:	.290		

Teams

Cincinnati Reds NL (1947–1949)

Chicago Cubs NL (1949–1955)

Philadelphia Phillies NL (1956–1957)

Gene Bearden

While in the minors, Gene Bearden served on the USS *Helena*. His battle injuries in 1943 left him with a metal plate in his skull, a metal hinge in his knee, and a lifetime of pain. It's amazing he could pitch again, but in 1948, his first full season in the majors, he posted a 20–7 record and a league-leading 2.43 ERA, helping the Cleveland Indians to a World Series title. In Game Three of the fall classic vs. the Braves, Bearden pitched a complete game shutout, and he got the save in Game Six. Sadly, he never reached his 1948 heights again. Bearden won just 25 more games in his career, playing with the Senators, Tigers, Browns, and White Sox. After baseball, he became a fast food entrepreneur, American Legion baseball supporter, and Cleveland Baseball Hall of Famer. Bearden passed away at age 83 in 2004.

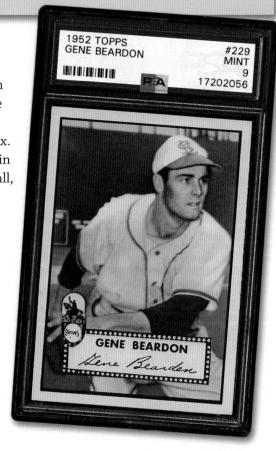

Career Stats

Record:	45–38
ERA:	3.96
IP:	788.1
Ks:	259
Threw:	LH

Teams

Cleveland Indians AL (1947–1950)

Washington Senators AL (1950–1951)

Detroit Tigers AL (1951)

St. Louis Browns AL (1952)

Chicago White Sox AL (1953)

Gus Bell

The patriarch of the four-generation Bell baseball family, Gus Bell had a solid 15-year MLB career. With Pittsburgh in 1951, the 22-year-old right fielder led the league with 12 triples. The four-time All-Star's best seasons were with Cincy in 1953, when he batted .300 with 30 home runs, and 1955, when he batted .308 with 27 homers. Very good defensively, Bell led the league in fielding percentage in 1958 and 1959. He wrapped up with Cincinnati after playing in three games of the Reds' 1961 World Series loss to the Yankees. After stints with the Mets and the Braves, Bell retired in 1964 with a lifetime .281 BA and 206 career home runs. His son Buddy was a five-time All-Star third baseman and MLB manager. Grandsons David and Mike were MLB infielders, and great-grandson Luke was drafted in 2019. Gus Bell passed away in 1995 at age 66.

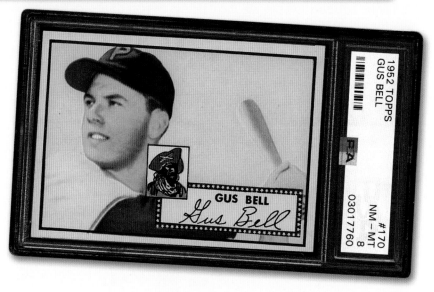

Teams

Pittsburgh Pirates NL (1950–1952)
Cincinnati Reds/Redlegs NL (1953–1961)
New York Mets NL (1962)
Milwaukee Braves NL (1962–1964)

Career Stats

AB:	6,478	HR:	206
R:	865	RBI:	942
H:	1,823	OPS:	.775
BA:	.281		

Al Benton

A serviceable starter and reliever, Al Benton started with the Athletics in 1934. With Detroit for most of his career, the two-time All-Star led the American League with 17 saves in 1940 and won 15 games in 1941. He missed two seasons serving in the US Navy and returned in 1945 to post 13 wins and a miniscule ERA of 2.02 for Detroit. That season, he helped the Tigers to a World Series win vs. the Cubs, appearing in three fall classic games with a 1.93 ERA. Over his 14-year career, Benton faced many exceptional hitters, and he was the only hurler to face both Babe Ruth and Mickey Mantle. Benton's fortunes dropped after baseball, but he turned things around after arrests for auto theft and forgery. A motel manager in 1968, Benton died at age 57 after he was severely burned by an explosion at the motel.

Teams

Philadelphia Athletics AL (1934–1935)
Detroit Tigers AL (1938–1942, 1945–1948)
Cleveland Indians AL (1949–1950)
Boston Red Sox AL (1952)

Career Stats

Record:	98–88
ERA:	3.66
IP:	1,688.1
Ks:	697
Threw:	RH

Johnny Berardino

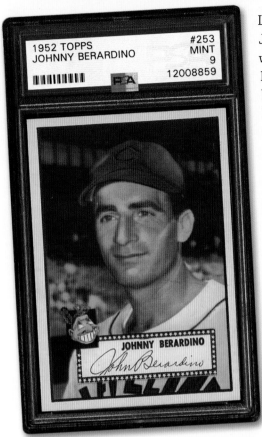

1952 TOPPS
JOHNNY BERARDINO
#253
MINT
9
12008859

Los Angeles native Johnny Berardino would return to Hollywood after baseball and achieve lasting fame. A versatile infielder, he broke in with the St. Louis Browns in 1939 and batted .271 in 128 games in 1941. Berardino served in both the US Army Air Force and the US Navy during WWII and missed the Browns' AL pennant run in 1944. The USC product moved on to Cleveland and was a member of the 1948 world champion Indians squad. Berardino acted in a few films before and during his MLB days, and, after leaving baseball in 1952, he focused on acting. In 1963, he landed the role of a lifetime on television. As Dr. Steve Hardy on *General Hospital*, he gained worldwide notoriety and in 1993 was honored with a star on Hollywood's Walk of Fame. Berardino would play Dr. Hardy until succumbing to cancer in 1996 at age 79.

Career Stats

AB:	3,028	HR:	36
R:	334	RBI:	387
H:	755	OPS:	.672
BA:	.249		

Teams

St. Louis Browns AL (1939–1942, 1946–1947, 1951)
Cleveland Indians AL (1948–1950, 1952)
Pittsburgh Pirates NL (1950, 1952)

Joe Black

New Jersey-born Joe Black had one of the best all-around pitching seasons of the decade in 1952. He won the Rookie of the Year Award and finished third in MVP voting with a 15–4 record for the Dodgers. A stellar reliever, the 28-year-old Black posted a miniscule 2.15 ERA and had 15 saves, finishing a league-high 41 games for "Dem Bums." The 1952 Series Game One starter pitched a six-hit complete game win, becoming the first black pitcher to win a World Series game. A former star in the Negro Leagues, Black's MLB fall was as sharp as his rise. He won just 15 more games and recorded only ten saves during his remaining five MLB seasons, with stops in Cincy and Washington. Black was later an executive for Greyhound and worked in community relations for the Arizona Diamondbacks. He died in 2002 at age 78.

1952 TOPPS
JOE BLACK
#321
NM – MT
8
40525237

Career Stats

Record:	30–12
ERA:	3.91
IP:	414.0
Ks:	222
Threw:	RH

Teams

Brooklyn Dodgers NL (1952–1955)
Cincinnati Redlegs NL (1955–1956)
Washington Senators AL (1957)

Ewell Blackwell

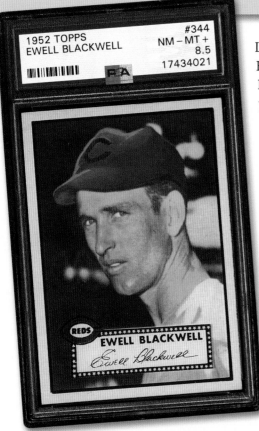

1952 TOPPS
EWELL BLACKWELL
#344
NM – MT +
8.5
17434021

Lanky fireballer Ewell "The Whip" Blackwell made his debut with the Reds in 1942 and spent the next three years in the US Army. Upon his return, he made six straight All-Star teams. In 1947, Blackwell may have been baseball's best pitcher, with his 22–8 record and 2.47 ERA. Second in 1947 MVP voting, he led the league with 23 complete games, 193 strikeouts, and led MLB with those 22 wins. Blackwell's talent made him nearly unhittable. He won 17 games in 1950 and 16 in 1951, while his penchant for hitting batters grew in legend and fact. Blackwell led the NL in both hit batsmen and wild pitches in 1950. He was a nasty hurler who intimidated even the likes of Ted Williams and Stan Musial. Injuries curtailed his career in 1955. The 1960 Reds Hall of Fame inductee died of cancer in 1996 at age 74.

Career Stats

Record:	82–78
ERA:	3.30
IP:	1,321.0
Ks:	839
Threw:	RH

Teams
Cincinnati Reds NL (1942, 1946–1952)
New York Yankees AL (1952–1953)
Kansas City Athletics AL (1955)

Ray Boone

1952 TOPPS
RAY BOONE
#55
NM – MT +
8.5
15189012

The patriarch of baseball's Boone family, Ray Boone was a solid infielder. The two-time All-Star played for the 1948 world champion Indians as a rookie. Over his 13-year career, Boone played for six teams, but he was most productive in the mid-1950s as Detroit's third sacker. Boone had four consecutive 20-home run seasons, led the AL with 116 RBI in 1955, and batted .308 while slamming 25 home runs in 1956. He wrapped up his career with the Red Sox in 1960 and went on to scout for Boston for 30 years. The first Boone family member to play Major League Baseball, Ray is the father of All-Star Bob Boone and grandfather of All-Stars Aaron Boone and Bret Boone. Potentially, Ray's great-grandson Jake Boone could be a fourth generation MLB player. A descendant of frontiersman Daniel Boone, Ray Boone passed away in 2004 at the age of 81.

Career Stats

AB:	4,589	HR:	151
R:	644	RBI:	737
H:	1,260	OPS:	.789
BA:	.275		

Teams
Cleveland Indians AL (1948–1953)
Detroit Tigers AL (1953–1958)
Chicago White Sox AL (1958–1959)
Kansas City Athletics AL (1959)
Milwaukee Braves NL (1959–1960)
Boston Red Sox AL (1960)

Ralph Branca

1952 TOPPS   #274
RALPH BRANCA   MINT   9
12281791

Ralph Branca of the Brooklyn Dodgers surrendered Bobby Thomson's "Shot Heard 'Round the World" pennant-winning home run, giving new meaning to the phrase "Dodger Blue." The Giants went to the 1951 World Series and Branca went into baseball infamy. Also known for his close friendship with teammate Jackie Robinson, Branca was a three-time All-Star and winner of 21 games in 1947. He led the NL with a .722 winning percentage in 1949, played in both the 1947 and 1949 fall classics vs. the Yankees, and won 13 games for Brooklyn in 1951. Branca played briefly for the Tigers and Yankees but retired as a Dodger in 1956. A successful businessman, Branca was chairman of the Baseball Assistance Team, which helps retired ballplayers financially. He passed away in 2016 at age 90.

Career Stats

Record:	88–68
ERA:	3.79
IP:	1,484.0
Ks:	829
Threw:	RH

Teams
Brooklyn Dodgers NL (1944–1953, 1956)
Detroit Tigers AL (1953–1954)
New York Yankees AL (1954)

Al Brazle

At age 29, in his debut season, Al Brazle was a key factor in the Redbirds' surge to the 1943 NL pennant. St. Louis lost to the Yankees in the World Series, but went on to beat the Red Sox in the 1946 fall classic—a satisfying win for Brazle, a former Red Sox farmhand who once roomed with Ted Williams. Chronic arm woes forced the hard-throwing lefty to change his pitching motion to a sidearm delivery, a move that saved his career. In 1952 and 1953, Brazle led the National League in saves with 16 and 18 respectively—both single-season records at that time. After ten years with St. Louis, where he fashioned a nifty 97–64 career record with 59 saves, Brazle retired at age 40. He later became the head baseball coach at Florida Presbyterian College. The WWII US Army veteran died at age 60 in 1973.

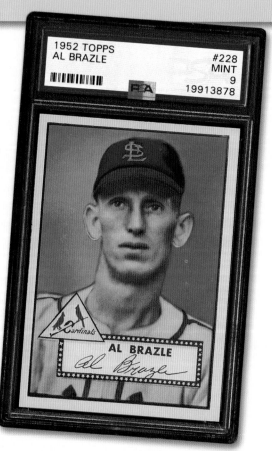

1952 TOPPS   #228
AL BRAZLE   MINT   9
19913878

Career Stats

Record:	97–64
ERA:	3.31
IP:	1,377.0
Ks:	554
Threw:	LH

Teams
St. Louis Cardinals NL (1943, 1946–1954)

Harry Brecheen

A very effective pitcher, Oklahoma-born Harry "The Cat" Brecheen racked up 105 wins for the Cardinals from 1943 through 1949 and led the National League in winning percentage in 1945 and ERA in 1948. A tough competitor with excellent command, Brecheen was an All-Star in 1947 and 1948, and he helped the Cards to three World Series, winning titles in 1944 and 1946. In the 1946 fall classic vs. Boston, Brecheen became the first left-hander to win three World Series games. Overall, he posted a 4–1 record and a spectacular 0.83 ERA in the postseason. After 11 years with the Cardinals, Brecheen joined the neighboring Browns for his final MLB season in 1953 and continued to work in the Browns/Orioles organization for many years. The Oklahoma Sports Hall of Fame and St. Louis Cardinals Hall of Fame inductee died at the age of 89 in 2004.

Career Stats

Record: 133–92
ERA: 2.92
IP: 1,907.2
Ks: 901
Threw: LH

Teams

St. Louis Cardinals NL (1940, 1943–1952)
St. Louis Browns AL (1953)

Lou Brissie

Not many in baseball history had the determination and courage of Lou Brissie. On December 7, 1944, Brissie was felled by a German artillery shell. The damage included shrapnel in his shoulder, hands, and thighs, and a shattered left tibia and shinbone. Amazingly, Brissie joined the pitching staff of the Philadelphia Athletics three years and numerous operations later. After his US Army experience, Brissie's baseball stats seem meaningless. Still, he had 14 wins in 1948 and was an All-Star in 1949 with a 16–11 record. Traded to Cleveland in 1951, Brissie finished in 1953 with a 44–48 record. After baseball, he was commissioner of American Legion Junior Baseball and worked for the South Carolina Board of Technical Education. The South Atlantic League Hall of Fame member and subject of the Ira Berkow book entitled *The Corporal was a Pitcher*, Brissie died in 2013 at age 89.

Career Stats

Record: 44–48
ERA: 4.07
IP: 897.2
Ks: 436
Threw: LH

Teams

Philadelphia Athletics AL (1947–1951)
Cleveland Indians AL (1951–1953)

Smoky Burgess

1952 TOPPS #357
SMOKY BURGESS NM – MT +
8.5
11895429
PSA

The starting catcher for the 1960 world champion Pittsburgh Pirates, Forrest "Smoky" Burgess batted .294 for the Bucs that season and was a six-time All-Star over an 18-year career. He batted over .300 five times, including a career-high .368 for the Phillies in 1954. A terrific defensive catcher, at 5-foot-8 and 185 pounds, Burgess was known as much for his girth as his worth. In Pittsburgh, Burgess was behind the plate for Harvey Haddix's 12-inning perfect game loss in 1959. The wide-bodied backstop batted .333 in that fabled 1960 Series vs. the Yankees, won by Bill Mazeroski's Game Seven walk-off home run. He also posted 16 career pinch-hit home runs, second on the all-time list when he retired in 1967. In retirement, he scouted for the Atlanta Braves and instructed future big leaguers including two-time NL MVP Dale Murphy. Burgess died in 1991 at age 64.

Career Stats

AB:	4,471	HR:	126
R:	485	RBI:	673
H:	1,318	OPS:	.807
BA:	.295		

Teams
Chicago Cubs NL (1949, 1951)
Philadelphia Phillies NL (1952–1955)
Cincinnati Redlegs NL (1955–1958)
Pittsburgh Pirates NL (1959–1964)
Chicago White Sox AL (1964–1967)

Tommy Byrne

US Navy veteran Tommy Byrne won 85 games in his 13-year career and was a key contributor to four Yankees pennants and two World Series crowns. The 1950 All-Star won 15 games in both 1949 and 1950. Traded to the Browns in 1951, Byrne also pitched for the White Sox and Senators before returning to the Yanks in 1954. He posted a career-best 16–5 record and 3.15 ERA in 1955. Byrne could hit, too. He batted over .300 twice and had 14 career home runs. The Baltimore native earned a mathematics degree from Wake Forest College in North Carolina. In retirement, Byrne worked for the Mets organization, was a successful businessman, and served as mayor of Wake Forest from 1973 to 1987. A member of the North Carolina, Maryland, Wake Forest College, and Baltimore City College High School halls of fame, Byrne died in 2007 at age 87.

1952 TOPPS #241
TOMMY BYRNE NM – MT
8
06393835
PSA

Career Stats

Record:	85–69
ERA:	4.11
IP:	1,362.0
Ks:	766
Threw:	LH

Teams
New York Yankees AL (1943, 1946–1951, 1954–1957)
St. Louis Browns AL (1951–1952)
Chicago White Sox AL (1953)
Washington Senators AL (1953)

Chico Carrasquel

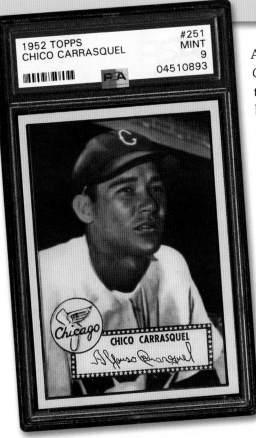

1952 TOPPS
CHICO CARRASQUEL
#251
MINT
9
04510893
PSA

A trailblazer for Latino players, Chico Carrasquel was a gem at shortstop for ten seasons. The four-time All-Star batted .282 in 1950 as the top rookie for the White Sox. Carrasquel used his quickness both at the plate and in the field, extending singles to doubles and covering ample infield ground. The Venezuelan was traded to the Indians for future Hall of Famer Larry Doby in 1955. He finished his career in 1959 with the Orioles after he was traded for future Hall of Famer Dick Williams. One of the first international players to be embraced by fans, Carrasquel was known for his enthusiasm on the diamond. He eventually became a MLB scout and a broadcaster on Spanish radio.

He was also active in youth baseball in Venezuela where the Puerto La Cruz stadium bears his name. Carrasquel passed away in 2005 at age 79.

Career Stats

AB:	4,644	HR:	55
R:	568	RBI:	474
H:	1,199	OPS:	.674
BA:	.258		

Teams

Chicago White Sox AL (1950–1955)
Cleveland Indians AL (1956–1958)
Kansas City Athletics AL (1958)
Baltimore Orioles AL (1959)

Phil Cavarretta

Chicago native Phil Cavarretta spent 20 years with the Cubs, winning the 1945 NL MVP Award and making three All-Star teams. In his first start on September 25, 1934, he smashed a game-winning home run. Cavarretta played in three World Series with the Cubs, losing all three, but batting .462 and .423 respectively in the 1938 and 1945 fall classics. In 1944, he had a league-high 197 hits, and in 1945, he led the NL with a .355 batting average and .449 OBP. As player-manager of the Cubs from 1951 to 1953, Cavarretta became the first Italian-American to manage a full season in MLB history. The first baseman/outfielder battled injuries, but batted over .300 six times, including .316 at age 37 for the ChiSox, where he ended his career in 1955. One of Wrigley Field's true legends, Cavarretta passed away in 2010 at age 94.

Career Stats

AB:	6,754	HR:	95
R:	990	RBI:	920
H:	1,977	OPS:	.788
BA:	.293		

Teams

Chicago Cubs NL (1934–1953)
Chicago White Sox AL (1954–1955)

1952 TOPPS
PHIL CAVARRETTA
#295
MINT
9
03025267
PSA

Ben Chapman

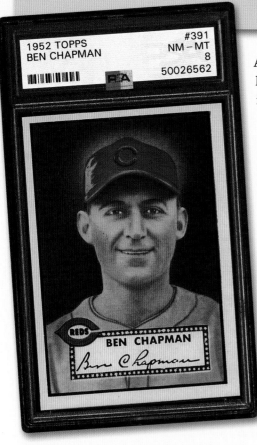

A career .302 hitter and four-time All-Star, Ben Chapman is more famous, or perhaps infamous, as the Phillies' manager who displayed outward racial prejudice toward Jackie Robinson when the Brooklyn Dodger broke baseball's color barrier in 1947. The fiery Chapman played for seven teams over 15 years. His best seasons were with the Yankees in the early 1930s, when he regularly topped the league in stolen bases and surpassed 100 RBI. Chapman batted .294 in the Yanks' 1932 World Series win vs. the Cubs. He played in the inaugural All-Star Game in 1933 and scored over 100 runs six times. As a manager, Chapman's competitive nature translated into abusive racial slurs toward Robinson when the Phillies met the Dodgers in 1947. His actions were his own undoing, as Chapman faced charges of racism and bigotry until his death in 1993 at the age of 84.

Career Stats

AB:	6,478	HR:	90
R:	1,144	RBI:	977
H:	1,958	OPS:	.823
BA:	.302		

Teams

New York Yankees AL (1930–1936)
Washington Senators AL (1936–1937, 1941)
Boston Red Sox AL (1937–1938)
Cleveland Indians AL (1939–1940)
Chicago White Sox AL (1941)
Brooklyn Dodgers NL (1944–1945)
Philadelphia Phillies NL (1945–1946)

Jerry Coleman

A decorated fighter pilot in both World War II and the Korean War, Jerry Coleman lived a rich, full life in baseball and in broadcasting. The California native spent nine seasons with the Yankees, from 1949 to 1957, playing in six World Series and winning four. He was an All-Star second baseman in 1950, batting .287 with 150 hits. In his final season, Coleman batted .364 in New York's World Series loss vs. Milwaukee. After his playing days, Coleman found his niche in the Yankees broadcast booth. One of the most beloved announcers in baseball history, Coleman called games for 51 years and 42 MLB seasons, including 33 consecutive years for the San Diego Padres. In 2005, he was honored by the Baseball Hall of Fame with the Ford C. Frick Award for his contributions to baseball. The affable Coleman passed away in 2014 at age 89.

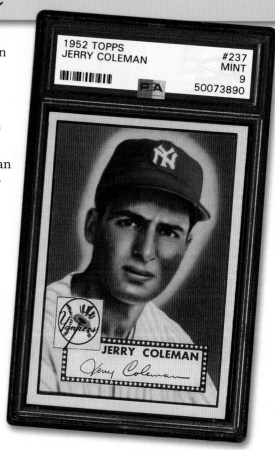

Career Stats

AB:	2,119	HR:	16
R:	267	RBI:	217
H:	558	OPS:	.680
BA:	.263		

Teams

New York Yankees AL (1949–1957)

Dale Coogan

A minor leaguer for most of his baseball career, Dale Coogan got the call-up for three months in 1950 with the Pittsburgh Pirates. At 6-foot-1 and 190 pounds, Coogan was a big first baseman but he didn't do much with the bat. During his brief MLB stint, Coogan batted just .240 with 31 hits. He fared better in his nine minor-league seasons, finishing in 1958 with a .277 BA and 73 homers. Coogan was not destined to wallow in the minors and then be forgotten. He studied in the offseason for his bachelor's degree and master's degree, and then earned his doctorate at the University of Southern California. As an educator, Coogan worked as a teacher and principal before he became the Superintendent of the Ocean View Elementary School District in California. Unfortunately, he died in 1989 from cancer at the age of 58.

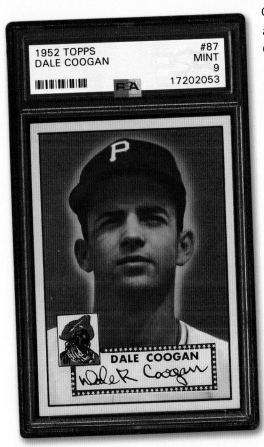

Career Stats

AB:	129	HR:	1
R:	19	RBI:	13
H:	31	OPS:	.663
BA:	.240		

Teams
Pittsburgh Pirates NL (1950)

Walker Cooper

At 6-foot-3 and 210 pounds, Walker Cooper was a physical anomaly at a position dominated by short and stocky talents. One of baseball's best catchers in the 1940s and 1950s, Cooper made his name with the Cardinals and Giants. In three World Series, Cooper batted .300. In 1942, his Cardinals beat the Yankees. The next season, New York got revenge, and in 1944, Cooper had his finest fall classic performance batting .318 as the Cards downed the cross-town rival Browns. During those St. Louis pennant seasons, Cooper's batterymate was his brother, 20-game winner Mort. Known for his game-calling skills, the durable Cooper played only the catcher position during his 18-year MLB career, which ended back in St. Louis with the Cardinals. The eight-time All-Star batted a career .285 and hit over .300 eight times. A valuable contributor to all of his clubs, Cooper died in 1991 at age 76.

Career Stats

AB:	4,702	HR:	173
R:	573	RBI:	812
H:	1,341	OPS:	.796
BA:	.285		

Teams
St. Louis Cardinals NL (1940–1945, 1956–1957)
New York Giants NL (1946–1949)
Cincinnati Reds NL (1949–1950)
Boston/Milwaukee Braves NL (1950–1953)
Pittsburgh Pirates NL (1954)
Chicago Cubs NL (1954–1955)

Billy Cox

A third sacker of the highest caliber, Billy Cox was respected by teammates and foes alike. He played the hot corner on three Brooklyn pennant winners in 1949, 1952, and 1953, enduring three World Series losses to the Yankees.

Adding to the despair, he was traded to the Orioles in December of 1954, just a few months before Brooklyn finally vanquished the Yanks for their first world championship. Cox began his career with the Pirates in 1941 and was inducted into the US Army in 1942. He returned to Pittsburgh for the 1946 season and, in 1947, smacked a career-high 15 homers for the Bucs. With Brooklyn, Cox delivered key hits and raised playing third base to an art form, making him a Dodger legend. The 1955 season with Baltimore was his last, and Cox returned to Pennsylvania. He succumbed to esophageal cancer in 1978 at age 58.

Career Stats

AB:	3,712	HR:	66
R:	470	RBI:	351
H:	974	OPS:	.698
BA:	.262		

Teams
Pittsburgh Pirates NL (1941, 1946–1947)
Brooklyn Dodgers NL (1948–1954)
Baltimore Orioles AL (1955)

Del Crandall

A stellar defensive catcher, Del Crandall was a four-time Gold Glove winner and played in 11 All-Star games. With the Braves for 13 seasons, Crandall was a great handler of pitchers, a team leader, and a field general. The batterymate of Warren Spahn and Lew Burdette, Crandall was named team captain in 1954 at 24 years old. Quick behind the plate with a bullet arm, he also had some power, posting three 20-home run seasons. In the 1957 World Series win vs. the Yankees, Crandall caught five games and launched an eighth-inning homer in Game Seven. In 1958, he was behind the dish for all seven games of the Series loss to the Yankees. Crandall later skippered the Brewers and Mariners, managed in the minors for 13 years, and was a broadcaster. The 2012 Braves Honor Roll inductee is 89 years old at the time of this writing.

Career Stats

AB:	5,026	HR:	179
R:	585	RBI:	657
H:	1,276	OPS:	.716
BA:	.254		

Teams
Boston/Milwaukee Braves NL (1949–1950, 1953–1963)
San Francisco Giants NL (1964)
Pittsburgh Pirates NL (1965)
Cleveland Indians AL (1966)

Frankie Crosetti

1952 TOPPS
FRANK CROSETTI
#384
MINT
9
09006657

The starting shortstop on one of baseball's greatest dynasties, Frankie Crosetti played in seven World Series and won six world championships with the Yankees. The two-time All-Star spent his entire career in the Bronx. Speedy and smart, Crosetti scored over 100 runs each year from 1936 to 1939 and led the American League in steals with 27 in 1938. Crosetti raised "taking one for the team" to an art form, leading the AL in getting hit-by-pitches for five straight seasons. He riled opposing pitchers with his equally constant motion and mouth. Crosetti transitioned to third-base coach for the Yanks, winning another nine World Series. He penned a book on baserunning and infield defense, and was part of lawsuits against baseball owners and MLB to increase pensions and payments for former players. In 2002, he died at age 91—truly a Yankee for life.

Career Stats

AB:	6,277	HR:	98
R:	1,006	RBI:	649
H:	1,541	OPS:	.695
BA:	.245		

Teams

New York Yankees AL (1932–1948)

George Crowe

A mountain of a man who became a real-life mountain man, George Crowe played nine big-league seasons, his best at the age of 36 when he hit 31 homers for Cincinnati in 1957. Crowe was Indiana's first-ever "Mr. Basketball," starring for Franklin High School. He was a civil rights champion and served his country as a WWII US Army lieutenant. Crowe played traveling hoops with the famed New York Rens, barnstormed with Willie Mays, and played winter ball with Roberto Clemente. In 1958, he nearly beat Stan Musial for the starting first-base slot in the All-Star Game, thanks to Cincinnati fans stuffing the ballot. As a result, fan voting was banned for several years. Crowe lived an equally unique post-baseball life, eventually disappearing from the mainstream and living off the land in New York's Catskill Mountains. He died in 2011 at 89 years old.

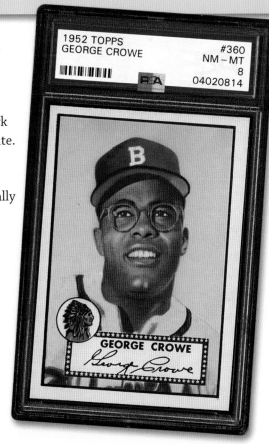

1952 TOPPS
GEORGE CROWE
#360
NM – MT
8
04020814

Career Stats

AB:	1,727	HR:	81
R:	215	RBI:	299
H:	467	OPS:	.799
BA:	.270		

Teams

Boston/Milwaukee Braves AL (1952–1953, 1955)
Cincinnati Redlegs NL (1956–1958)
St. Louis Cardinals NL (1959–1961)

Al Dark

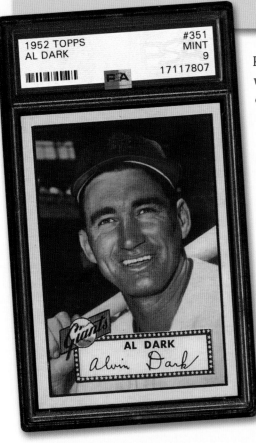

Perhaps better known as a manager with four teams, 994 wins, and a world championship with the A's, Al Dark enjoyed a 14-year playing career as a versatile infielder/outfielder. He even took to the mound in a game for the Giants in 1953. Dark was a doubles machine, leading the league in 1951, one of his three All-Star seasons. In 1954, he led the NL in games and at-bats. There was a certain symmetry to Dark's career. He broke in with the Boston Braves in 1946 and ended with the Milwaukee Braves in 1960. As an official rookie in 1948, Dark won the Rookie of the Year Award with 175 hits and a .322 average. He batted .323 in three World Series, winning with the Giants in 1954. The US Marine Corps veteran and LSU product was also drafted by the Philadelphia Eagles. He died in 2014 at age 92.

Career Stats

AB:	7,219	HR:	126
R:	1,064	RBI:	757
H:	2,089	OPS:	.744
BA:	.289		

Teams

Boston/Milwaukee Braves NL (1946, 1948–1949, 1960)
New York Giants NL (1950–1956)
St. Louis Cardinals NL (1956–1958)
Chicago Cubs NL (1958–1959)
Philadelphia Phillies NL (1960)

Dom DiMaggio

To most baseball fans, Dom DiMaggio was the younger brother of the "Yankee Clipper," Joe DiMaggio. In Boston, however, Dom was beloved as an exceptional ballplayer in his own right. Although he missed three key years during World War II, Dom returned to help the Red Sox to the 1946 AL pennant while forming a close and lasting friendship with teammates Ted Williams, Johnny Pesky, and Bobby Doerr. A seven-time All-Star, "The Little Professor" was one of the best leadoff hitters in the American League. An excellent outfielder and base stealer, he led the league in various categories over his notable career. Actually, Dom and Joe DiMaggio were considered among the best outfielders in baseball. After baseball, Dom owned a successful manufacturing business and was co-founder of the Boston Patriot's football franchise. The Red Sox Hall of Famer lived to the age of 92, passing away in 2009.

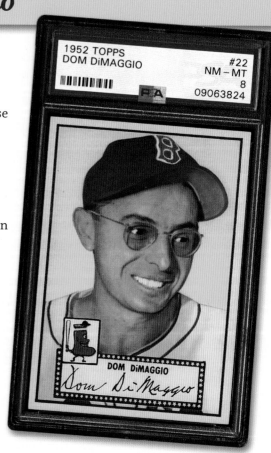

Career Stats

AB:	5,640	HR:	87
R:	1,046	RBI:	618
H:	1,680	OPS:	.802
BA:	.298		

Teams

Boston Red Sox AL (1940–1942, 1946–1953)

Joe Dobson

With a record of 106–72 in nine years with Boston, Joe Dobson ranks among the winningest pitchers in Red Sox history. He won 11 games or more in seven out of eight seasons between 1941 and 1950. In Boston's 1946 World Series loss to the Cardinals, Dobson pitched in three games and registered a 1–0 record, allowing no earned runs. Dobson had a sparkling 18–8 record and 2.95 ERA in 1947 but led the league in wild pitches. The next season, he went 16–10 and made the All-Star team. After a 15-win season in 1950, Dobson was traded to the White Sox where in 1952, at age 35, he logged a 14–10 record and 2.51 ERA. After baseball, the US Army veteran owned a general store, was a golf pro, and was GM of the Red Sox complex in Winter Haven, Florida. Dobson died in 1994 at age 77.

Career Stats

Record:	137–103
ERA:	3.62
IP:	2,170.0
Ks:	992
Threw:	RH

Teams

Cleveland Indians AL (1939–1940)
Boston Red Sox AL (1941–1943, 1946–1950, 1954)
Chicago White Sox AL (1951–1953)

Chuck Dressen

Born in Decatur, Illinois, in 1894, Chuck Dressen played seven years for the Reds and was a member of the 1933 World Champion Giants. Dressen batted a career .272, but his greatest performances came as a coach and manager. In 16 seasons as a manager spanning from 1934 to 1966, Dressen amassed a 1008–973 record and won pennants with Brooklyn in 1952 and 1953. He also managed the Reds, Senators, Braves, and Tigers. Dressen was third-base coach and pitching coach for the 1947 world champion Yankees, and he coached the 1959 world champion Dodgers. A master of stealing signs, Dressen brought confidence, intelligence, and statistical analysis to the game. While managing in Detroit, a minor heart attack caused Dressen to miss part of the 1965 season. Sadly, after returning to manage in 1966, Dressen suffered a fatal heart attack and died on August 10 at age 71.

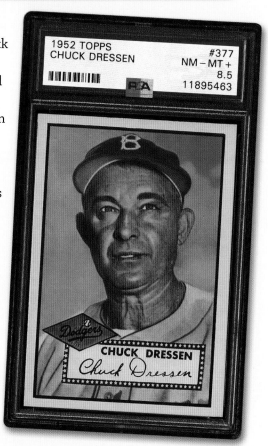

Career Stats

AB:	2,215	HR:	11
R:	313	RBI:	221
H:	603	OPS:	.711
BA:	.272		

Teams

Cincinnati Reds NL (1925–1931)
New York Giants NL (1933)

Walt Dropo

In 1950, Walt Dropo batted .322 with 34 home runs and a league-leading 144 RBI. He was Rookie of the Year and an All-Star. In 11 more big-league seasons, Dropo never again batted .300, hit 30 home runs, or knocked in 100 runs. At 6-foot-5 and 220 pounds, Dropo was the prototypical big, right-handed power hitter. He hit 29 homers, splitting time with Boston and Detroit in 1952 and had 152 dingers for his career. Dropo also spent time with the White Sox, Reds, and Orioles. The first baseman was a star in baseball, football, and basketball at UConn, and his post-baseball career was equally as varied. Dropo owned a fireworks company, worked in real estate, devoted time to charitable endeavors, and participated in Red Sox Fantasy Camps. The World War II US Army veteran settled in the Boston area and passed away in 2010 at age 87.

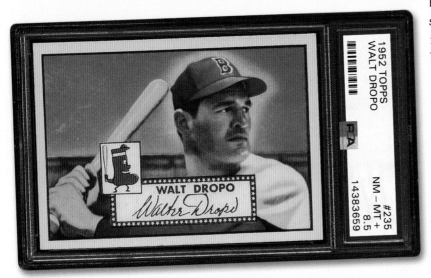

Career Stats

AB:	4,124	HR:	152
R:	478	RBI:	704
H:	1,113	OPS:	.757
BA:	.270		

Teams

Boston Red Sox AL (1949–1952)
Detroit Tigers AL (1952–1954)
Chicago White Sox AL (1955–1958)
Cincinnati Redlegs/Reds NL (1958–1959)
Baltimore Orioles AL (1959–1961)

Luke Easter

"Luscious" Luke Easter got a late start playing in the Major Leagues. He was 33 years old in 1949, his first season with the Cleveland Indians. That's an age when most players are contemplating retirement. For three of the six years he played for the Indians, Easter was a prodigious home run hitter. He became a fan favorite while stoically handling the on-the-field racism of that era. Before signing with the Indians, Easter starred for the Homestead Grays. Statistician Bill James rated him as the second-greatest Negro Leagues first baseman of all time. After his brief MLB career, Easter wowed fans in the minors for ten years, playing for Buffalo and Rochester in the International League until he was 48 years old. Sadly, in 1979, at age 63, Easter was murdered in an armed robbery while he was transporting money for his employer.

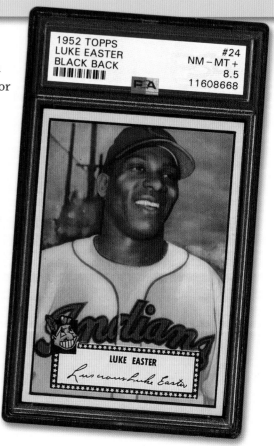

Career Stats

AB:	1,725	HR:	93
R:	256	RBI:	340
H:	472	OPS:	.830
BA:	.274		

Teams

Cleveland Indians AL (1949–1954)

Bob Elliott

Could an argument be made for Bob "Mr. Team" Elliott as a bubble candidate for the Hall of Fame? Maybe, maybe not. However, the seven-time All-Star certainly had an outstanding career. In 1947, Elliott batted .317 with 22 dingers earning the National League MVP Award. Then in 1948, Boston Braves fans rejoiced when his .283 BA, 100 RBI, and league-leading 131 walks helped the team to the National League pennant. Originally an outfielder, Elliott switched to the hot corner in 1942 while with Pittsburgh. The slick-fielding third baseman was an offensive force over his career with three 20-home run seasons and six 100-plus RBI seasons. Known for his team spirit and integrity, the California native coached and managed in both the minors and majors after his playing days came to an end in 1953. Sadly, Elliott passed away at the relatively young age of 49 in 1966.

Teams

Pittsburgh Pirates NL (1939–1946)

Boston Braves NL (1947–1951)

New York Giants NL (1952)

St. Louis Browns AL (1953)

Chicago White Sox AL (1953)

Career Stats

AB:	7,141	HR:	170
R:	1,064	RBI:	1,195
H:	2,061	OPS:	.815
BA:	.289		

Del Ennis

After serving in the US Navy on Guam, Philadelphia native Del Ennis made an impact in 1946, his rookie year, when he batted .313 for the Phillies and made the All-Star team. The power behind the "Whiz Kids," he batted .311 with 31 home runs and a league-leading 126 RBI in 1950. The three-time All-Star had a lifetime .284 BA, hit almost 300 home runs, and had seven 100-plus RBI seasons. He patrolled the Phillies outfield for 11 of his 14 Major League seasons, but the hometown Ennis was a marginal fielder and was unmercifully booed by Phillies fans despite his stellar offense. Ennis rose above the fray and was a major offensive contributor for years. In retirement, he owned a bowling alley, coached at Penn State, and bred greyhounds. A member of the Phillies Wall of Fame and the Phillies Centennial Team, Ennis died in 1996 at age 70.

Career Stats

AB:	7,254	HR:	288
R:	985	RBI:	1,284
H:	2,063	OPS:	.812
BA:	.284		

Teams

Philadelphia Phillies NL (1946–1956)

St. Louis Cardinals NL (1957–1958)

Cincinnati Reds NL (1959)

Chicago White Sox AL (1959)

Carl Erskine

1952 TOPPS #250
CARL ERSKINE
MINT 9
21099269

Born in Indiana, Carl Erskine became a favorite son of Brooklyn, playing for the Dodgers from 1948 to 1959, with his last two seasons in Los Angeles. Erskine went 20–6 with 187 Ks in 1953 and fashioned a career record of 122–78 with two no-hitters. In Brooklyn, he was on pitching staffs that included Sandy Koufax, Don Drysdale, and Don Newcombe among other greats. Erskine was an All-Star in 1954 winning 18 games. He played on five Dodgers pennant winners and was a member of the 1955 world championship team. A master of the curveball, Erskine served in the US Navy in Boston and worked out for the Braves, but Branch Rickey signed him for Brooklyn. After baseball, Erskine thrived in business and coached at Anderson College for several seasons. At the time of this writing, he is 93 years old and remains an iconic figure in Dodgers lore.

Career Stats

Record:	122–78
ERA:	4.00
IP:	1,718.2
Ks:	981
Threw:	RH

Teams
Brooklyn/Los Angeles Dodgers NL
(1948–1959)

Hoot Evers

Outfielder Walter "Hoot" Evers had some outstanding seasons for the Detroit Tigers between 1946 and 1952. Signed by Detroit in 1941, Evers played in the minors and with the US Army Air Force Waco Wolves before joining the Tigers in 1946. The oft-injured Evers had a banner year in 1950, batting .323 with 21 home runs while leading the league with 11 triples and his .997 fielding percentage, and he hit for the cycle in September. Evers batted over .300 three consecutive seasons from 1948 to 1950 and was an All-Star twice in that period. As his production declined due to injuries, Evers played for the Red Sox, Giants, Orioles, and Indians before he retired in 1956. Evers stayed in baseball as a scout and executive for the Indians and Tigers for many years. He passed away in 1991 at the age of 69.

Career Stats

AB:	3,801	HR:	98
R:	555	RBI:	565
H:	1,055	OPS:	.778
BA:	.278		

Teams
Detroit Tigers AL (1941, 1946–1952, 1954)
Boston Red Sox AL (1952–1954)
New York Giants NL (1954)
Baltimore Orioles AL (1955, 1956)
Cleveland Indians AL (1955–1956)

1952 TOPPS #222
HOOT EVERS
MINT 9
12022088

"HOOT" EVERS
Walter 'Hoot' Evers

Ferris Fain

One of the best defensive first baseman in the game, the fiery Ferris Fain was a two-time American League batting champ and five-time All-Star. In 1952, Fain led the league with 43 doubles, a .327 BA, and 150 assists. That's the good stuff. Unfortunately, the quick tempered, heavy-drinking Fain developed a reputation for both on-the-field and barroom brawls. Knee injuries and his brawling curtailed his MLB career in 1955. Fain then worked in construction, but he eventually found himself on the wrong side of the law. In the 1980s, the former infielder was caught in his own field, growing marijuana. Fain was arrested a few times and was sentenced to 18 months in prison. His reasoning for growing the weed? "I was good at it." After his release, Fain lived a reclusive life, staying under the radar. He passed away in 2001 at the age of 80.

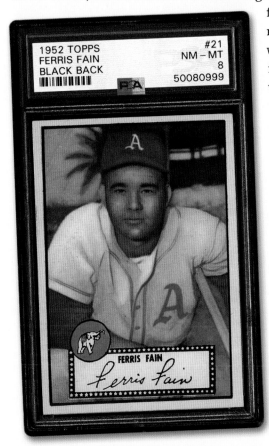

Career Stats

AB:	3,930	HR:	48
R:	595	RBI:	570
H:	1,139	OPS:	.820
BA:	.290		

Teams
Philadelphia Athletics AL (1947–1952)
Chicago White Sox AL (1953–1954)
Detroit Tigers AL (1955)
Cleveland Indians AL (1955)

Ed Fitz Gerald

Backup catcher Ed Fitz Gerald enjoyed a 12-year MLB career. The California native was drafted into the US Army in 1943 and served with the 597th AAA Battalion in World War II. He single-handedly captured two German soldiers while on guard duty on the German border. In 1947, Fitz Gerald batted an impressive .363 in the minors for Sacramento. He debuted in 1948 with Pittsburgh and hit a respectable .267 in 102 games. In 1954, Fitz Gerald

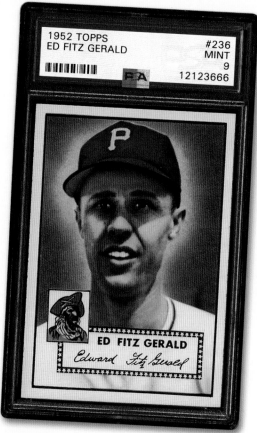

played in a career-high 115 games with Washington and batted .289. He also batted .304 for the Senators in 1956. Fitz Gerald played on some bad teams, but with some great players including Ralph Kiner and Harmon Killebrew. After his playing career ended in 1959, he coached for the Indians, Athletics, and Twins, and also managed in the minor leagues. At the time of this writing, he is 95 years old.

Career Stats

AB:	2,086	HR:	19
R:	199	RBI:	217
H:	542	OPS:	.659
BA:	.260		

Teams
Pittsburgh Pirates NL (1948–1953)
Washington Senators AL (1953–1959)
Cleveland Indians AL (1959)

Dee Fondy

Long and lean at 6-foot-3 and 195 pounds, Dee Fondy made his MLB bones with the Cubs, Pirates, and Reds. Fondy started in the Brooklyn organization, an eventual dead end with Gill Hodges manning first base for the Dodgers. A rock-solid first baseman for the Cubbies from 1952 through 1956, Fondy's best season was 1953 when he smashed 18 home runs to go along with 78 RBI and a .309 average. He was a free swinger who struck out often. Fondy was also a war hero, who served in the

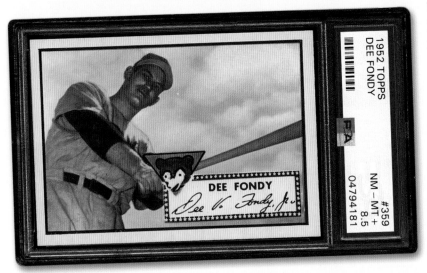

US Army artillery. In September of 1944, he landed at Utah Beach, Normandy, and was eventually awarded a Purple Heart. In retirement, Fondy worked as a scout and front office man until 1995.

He was instrumental in constructing the Milwaukee Brewers' World Series team of 1982. Dee Fondy died of pancreatic cancer in 1999 at age 74.

Career Stats

B:	3,502	HR:	69
R:	437	RBI:	373
H:	1,000	OPS:	.737
BA:	.286		

Teams

Chicago Cubs NL (1951–1957)
Pittsburgh Pirates NL (1957)
Cincinnati Redlegs NL (1958)

Bob Friend

Bob Friend pitched a lot of innings, gave up a lot of hits, and won and lost a lot of games in his 16-year career. In 1958, the three-time All-Star led the National League with 22 wins, but also lost 14 games. He led the league in games started, but surrendered the most hits and earned runs. Friend won 15 games or more five times, but twice lost 19, 18, and 17 games in a season. In 1960, when the Pirates won the World Series, the enigmatic Friend won 18 games, but was 0–2 in the World Series with a 13.50 ERA. In 16 seasons, he went 197–230 and never spent a moment on the disabled list. After baseball, Friend won election as Allegheny County, Pennsylvania, controller and was a delegate at several Republican National Conventions. The man known as "The Warrior" died in 2019 at age 88.

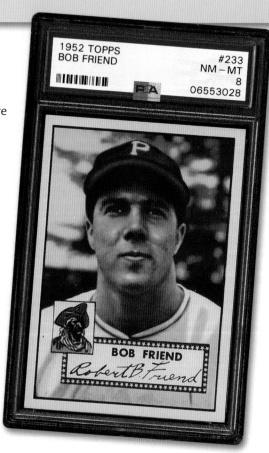

Career Stats

Record:	197–230
ERA:	3.58
IP:	3,611.0
Ks:	1,734
Threw:	RH

Teams

Pittsburgh Pirates NL (1951–1965)
New York Yankees AL (1966)
New York Mets NL (1966)

Joe Garagiola

1952 TOPPS #227
JOE GARAGIOLA
MINT 9
09007480

Primarily a backup catcher during his nine Major League seasons, Joe Garagiola's career started with the 1946 world champion St. Louis Cardinals, and he batted .316 in that fall classic. He finished his career with the 1954 world champion Giants, but did not play in the Series. Well-liked because of his self-deprecating humor, Garagiola's success came after his baseball career. For the next 30 years, he was a renowned television broadcaster. Garagiola was the color analyst for the *Game of the Week* with Curt Gowdy, Vin Scully, and Tony Kubek; co-hosted the *Today* show with Hugh Downs and Barbara Walters; and appeared on the *Tonight Show* with Johnny Carson on numerous occasions. He helped start the Baseball Assistance Team, advocated against the use of chewing tobacco, and authored the bestseller *Baseball is a Funny Game*. Garagiola passed away at the age of 90 in 2016.

Career Stats

AB:	1,872	HR:	42
R:	198	RBI:	255
H:	481	OPS:	.739
BA:	.257		

Teams
St. Louis Cardinals NL (1946–1951)
Pittsburgh Pirates NL (1951–1953)
Chicago Cubs NL (1953–1954)
New York Giants NL (1954)

Mike Garcia

With Cleveland for most of his career, Mike "The Big Bear" Garcia won 22 games in 1952 while posting an ERA of 2.37 ERA. The three-time All-Star posted a career mark of 142–97 and was part of Cleveland's pennant-winning team in 1954. Garcia hit batters and gave up home runs, but still managed to deliver a nifty 3.27 career ERA. He teamed with future Hall of Famers Bob Feller, Bob Lemon, and Early Wynn on one of the best pitching staffs in baseball history. A World War II veteran, Garcia blazed a trail for future big leaguers of Mexican heritage. He finished up with the White Sox and Senators but will forever be remembered as one of Cleveland's "Big Four." Before his death in 1986 at age 62, Garcia was a businessman in Cleveland who stayed close to the game playing softball and volunteering with Little League.

1952 TOPPS #272
MIKE GARCIA
NM – MT 8
40501568

Career Stats

Record:	142–97
ERA:	3.27
IP:	2,174.2
Ks:	1,117
Threw:	RH

Teams
Cleveland Indians AL (1948–1959)
Chicago White Sox AL (1960)
Washington Senators AL (1961)

Billy Goodman

It's a wonder that Billy Goodman made only two All-Star appearances considering his significant career accomplishments. The 1950 American League batting champ and MVP runner-up, Goodman batted over .300 six seasons and he banged out over 1,600 career hits. Solid both offensively and defensively, the North Carolina native was the quintessential utility player who was used at every infield and outfield position. A key member of the Red Sox for most of his career, Goodman later played with the 1959 pennant-winning White Sox. After his playing days, Goodman managed the Carolina League's Durham Bulls before working as a scout and instructor for the Red Sox, Athletics, Braves, and Royals. During that period, he moved to Sarasota, Florida, where he passed away in 1984 at the relatively young age of 58. He is a member of the North Carolina Sports Hall of Fame and the Red Sox Hall of Fame.

Career Stats

AB:	5,644	HR:	19
R:	807	RBI:	591
H:	1,691	OPS:	.754
BA:	.300		

Teams

Boston Red Sox AL (1947–1957)
Baltimore Orioles AL (1957)
Chicago White Sox AL (1958–1961)
Houston Colt .45s NL (1962)

Sid Gordon

Brooklyn-born Sid Gordon was a stellar outfielder and infielder for the cross-town rival New York Giants. Gordon smacked a career-high 30 homers in 1948 and would go on to eclipse the 20-homer plateau in each of the next four seasons. Over his career, he batted .283 with 202 home runs and 805 RBI in 13 seasons, but he lost the 1944 and 1945 seasons to US Coast Guard service. The two-time All-Star joined the Boston Braves in 1950 and tied a National League record with his four grand slams that year. He would also play for the Pirates before returning to the Giants in 1955 to end his career with them. Gordon was one of baseball's most popular players, respected by teammates and opponents alike. He remained close to the game, and sadly, passed away from a heart attack while playing softball in 1975. He was just 57 years old.

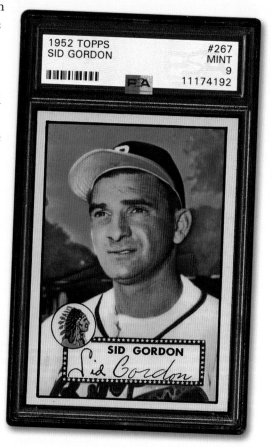

Career Stats

AB:	4,992	HR:	202
R:	735	RBI:	805
H:	1,415	OPS:	.843
BA:	.283		

Teams

New York Giants NL (1941–1943, 1946–1949, 1955)
Boston/Milwaukee Braves NL (1950–1953)
Pittsburgh Pirates NL (1954–1955)

Mickey Grasso

1952 TOPPS #90
MICKEY GRASSO
NM – MT
8
09082096

In January 1942, with one season of minor-league ball under his belt, Mickey Grasso enlisted in the US Army to defend his country. Sergeant Grasso was assigned to the 34th Infantry Division in Tunisia where his unit was captured by the Germans. For the next two years, Grasso was a prisoner of war. After three unsuccessful escape attempts, Grasso and several others finally made it to the Allied line. Back in the States, he regained the 60 pounds he lost as a POW and played briefly for the Giants in 1946. Grasso came up to the majors again in 1950 as the Senators backup catcher, and he started for them in 1952. In his seven Major League seasons, Grasso was weak offensively, but he was a fiery player who was very popular with the fans. He became a restaurateur in Florida and died in 1975 at the age of 55.

Career Stats

AB:	957	HR:	5
R:	78	RBI:	87
H:	216	OPS:	.558
BA:	.226		

Teams

New York Giants NL (1946, 1955)
Washington Senators AL (1950–1953)
Cleveland Indians AL (1954)

Dick Groat

Pennsylvania native Dick Groat fashioned a terrific 14-year MLB career. He broke in with the Pirates in 1952 but spent the next two years serving in the US Army. The five-time All-Star shortstop batted .325 to win the NL batting crown and MVP in 1960. His performance propelled the Bucs to a World Series title vs. the Yankees. A lifetime .286 hitter, Groat won another ring with the 1964 Cardinals. Groat could have played in both the NBA and MLB. An All-American in both basketball and baseball at Duke, Groat was coached by the legendary Red Auerbach. He was elected to the College Basketball Hall of Fame in 2007 and the College Baseball Hall of Fame in 2011. The Arnold Palmer Spirit of Hope Award recipient was inducted to the Missouri Sports Hall of Fame in 2012, and at the time of this writing is 89 years old.

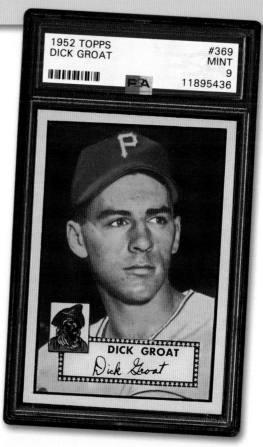

1952 TOPPS #369
DICK GROAT
MINT
9
11895436

Career Stats

AB:	7,484	HR:	39
R:	829	RBI:	707
H:	2,138	OPS:	.696
BA:	.286		

Teams

Pittsburgh Pirates NL (1952, 1955–1962)
St. Louis Cardinals NL (1963–1965)
Philadelphia Phillies NL (1966–1967)
San Francisco Giants NL (1967)

Granny Hamner

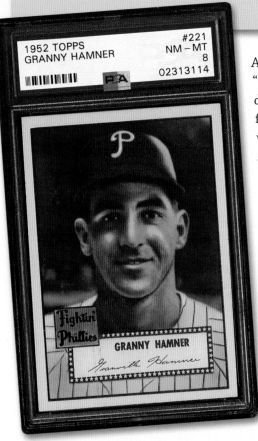

An integral part of the 1950 Phillies "Whiz Kids," Granny Hamner was a very dependable shortstop/second baseman for 17 seasons. The three-time All-Star was the starting shortstop in the 1952 All-Star Game and the starting second baseman in the 1954 All-Star Game. The longtime Phillies team captain had some pop in his bat with his best year in 1953 when he batted .276 with 21 home runs. Interestingly, in 1945, Granny played middle infield for a few months with his brother Garvin. Granny played at short and Garvin at second until the Phillies sent them back to the minors. At the end of his career, Hamner converted to pitcher without much success. In retirement, Hamner had various business interests and also managed and coached in the minors for the Phillies. In 1993, at age 66, he died from a heart attack while in Philadelphia for a team reunion.

Career Stats

AB:	5,839	HR:	104
R:	711	RBI:	708
H:	1,529	OPS:	.686
BA:	.262		

Teams

Philadelphia Phillies NL (1944–1959)
Cleveland Indians AL (1959)
Kansas City Athletics AL (1962)

Roy Hartsfield

Georgia native Roy Hartsfield was an outstanding three-sport star in high school. After serving in the US Navy in 1944 and 1945, the second baseman distinguished himself in the Boston Braves farm system. In 1950, he batted a respectable .277 as a Braves rookie. The 5-foot-9, 165-pound Hartsfield played hard and had a knack for delivering a big hit or defensive gem. His MLB career ended in 1952, but in 1956 he got his first minor-league managerial job, which put him on the road to baseball history. Hartsfield managed a total of 19 seasons in the minors, interrupted by a stint as coach for the Dodgers, and a stint as the first-ever manager of the expansion Toronto Blue Jays. In his three seasons as Toronto's manager, he compiled a 166–318 record. Hartsfield later scouted and was active in charities until his death at age 86 in 2011.

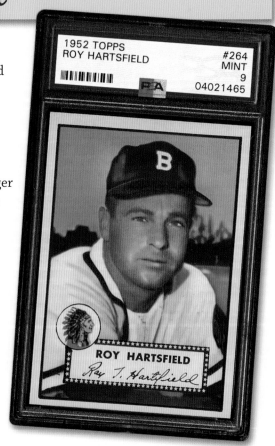

Career Stats

AB:	976	HR:	13
R:	138	RBI:	59
H:	266	OPS:	.682
BA:	.273		

Teams

Boston Braves NL (1950–1952)

Grady Hatton

Between playing, managing, coaching, and scouting, Grady Hatton devoted over 40 years to the game of baseball. A star for the University of Texas Longhorns, Hatton attracted Major League notice while playing ball in the US Army Air Force. Signed by Cincinnati in 1946, he purchased a ranch in his home state of Texas with his signing bonus. A pretty good infielder, he played third base for the Reds for most of his career and was also a player-representative. He was an All-Star in 1952 and played for six different teams during his 12-year career. Hatton then managed in the minors, spent 15

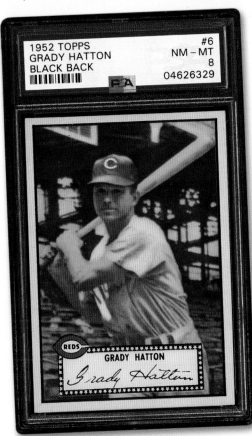

years as manager and executive with the Houston Colt .45s/Astros organization, and followed that with a 16-year run as scout for the San Francisco Giants. A solid baseball man who was known for his sterling character, Hatton passed away in 2013 at the age of 90.

Career Stats

AB:	4,206	HR:	91
R:	562	RBI:	533
H:	1,068	OPS:	.728
BA:	.254		

Teams

Cincinnati Reds NL (1946–1954)
Chicago White Sox AL (1954)
Boston Red Sox AL (1954–1956)
St. Louis Cardinals NL (1956)
Baltimore Orioles AL (1956)
Chicago Cubs NL (1960)

Joe Haynes

A starter and reliever, righty Joe Haynes enjoyed a 14-year Major League pitching career. He made his debut with the Senators in 1939, married owner Clark Griffith's daughter in 1941, and was traded to Chicago soon after. Initially a reliever for the Sox, Haynes led the league with 40 appearances and 35 games finished in 1942. A starter in 1947, Haynes went 14–6 with seven complete games, two shutouts, and a league-leading 2.42 ERA. He was an

All-Star in 1948, but arm woes hampered his performance. Haynes returned to the Senators in 1949 and finished with them in 1952. He continued with the Griffith family business in various capacities and served as Executive Vice President from 1958 to 1967, a period in which the Senators moved to Minnesota and became the Twins. Sadly, he died in 1967 at age 49 after suffering a heart attack while shoveling snow.

Career Stats

Record:	76–82
ERA:	4.01
IP:	1,581.0
Ks:	475
Threw:	RH

Teams

Washington Senators AL (1939–1940, 1949–1952)
Chicago White Sox AL (1941–1948)

Jim Hegan

Billy Hitchcock

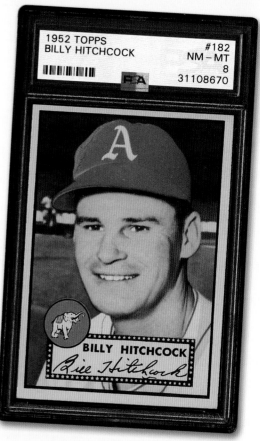

Hall of Famer Bob Feller once said that Jim Hegan was "the best defensive catcher I ever had." A whiz at calling games and handling pitchers, Hegan was a five-time All-Star despite his .228 lifetime batting average. The starting backstop for the Cleveland Indians from 1946 to 1956, Hegan's skill behind the plate was a big part of the Tribe's success. In 1948, the Indians pitching staff led the American League in ERA and Cleveland won the World Series. From 1951 through 1956, the Indians didn't finish lower than second place, and, in 1954, their stellar 111-win season, they captured the pennant but were shockingly swept in the Series. It should be noted that Hegan caught no-hitters by Bob Feller, Bob Lemon, and Don Black. He later coached for the Yankees and Tigers. In 1984, Jim Hegan died at age 63 after suffering a heart attack.

Infielder Billy Hitchcock was a decent utility guy who happened to have an excellent baseball IQ. The Alabama native was signed out of Auburn University where he played football and baseball while earning a Business Administration degree. He was starting shortstop for Detroit in 1942, his rookie season. Hitchcock spent the next three years in the US Army Air Force, served in the Pacific, and rose to the rank of major. He returned to play for the Tigers, Senators, Browns, Red Sox, and Athletics until 1953. Hitchcock then managed in the minors and coached before managing the Detroit Tigers, Baltimore Orioles, and Atlanta Braves in the 1960s. He was president of the prestigious Southern League from 1971 through 1980 and was very involved with his alma mater. Auburn University renamed their baseball field Hitchcock Field in his honor. He died in 2006 at the age of 89.

Career Stats

AB:	4,772	HR:	92
R:	550	RBI:	525
H:	1,087	OPS:	.639
BA:	.228		

Career Stats

AB:	2,249	HR:	5
R:	231	RBI:	257
H:	547	OPS:	.609
BA:	.243		

Teams

Cleveland Indians AL (1941–1942, 1946–1957)
Detroit Tigers AL (1958)
Philadelphia Phillies NL (1958–1959)
San Francisco Giants NL (1959)
Chicago Cubs NL (1960)

Teams

Detroit Tigers AL (1942, 1946, 1953)
Washington Senators AL (1946)
St. Louis Browns AL (1947)
Boston Red Sox AL (1948–1949)
Philadelphia Athletics AL (1950–1952)

Gil Hodges

Given his impressive stats, it's a head scratcher why Gil Hodges is not in Cooperstown. An eight-time All-Star, Hodges won three Gold Gloves, played on seven NL pennant winners, two World Series champions, clubbed 370 home runs, and managed the New York "Miracle Mets" to the most improbable World Series Championship in 1969. In 1950, Hodges hit four home runs in one game against the Boston Braves. Along with teammate, Duke Snider, Hodges was one of the most feared hitters in the National League. He is still second on the Dodgers all-time home run list, right behind Snider. One of the most beloved players in Dodgers history, Hodges was an outstanding first baseman, with a career .992 fielding percentage. The Mets manager and US Marine Corps veteran was only 47 years old when he died in 1972 from a massive heart attack while playing golf with some of his baseball friends.

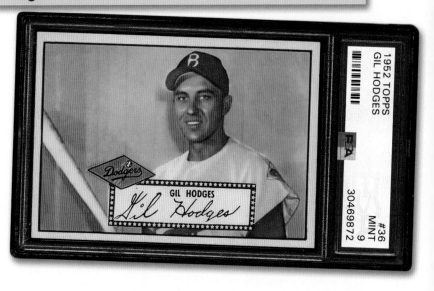

Career Stats

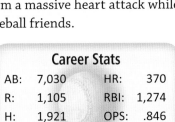

AB:	7,030	HR:	370
R:	1,105	RBI:	1,274
H:	1,921	OPS:	.846
BA:	.273		

Teams
Brooklyn/Los Angeles Dodgers NL (1943, 1947–1961)
New York Mets NL (1962–1963)

Tommy Holmes

Brooklyn-born Tommy Holmes had one of the greatest seasons in baseball history with the Boston Braves in 1945. Unable to serve in World War II due to a sinus condition, he batted .352 with a league-leading 224 hits, 47 doubles, and 28 home runs. He led the league in slugging and OPS, and had a NL record 37-game hitting streak that stood until Pete Rose's 44-game streak in 1978. Holmes hit over .300 five times in his career and bashed over 190 hits four times. The 1948 All-Star spent ten seasons with the Braves, managing the team parts of 1951 and 1952, before ending his career with the 1952 Dodgers NL pennant winners. A fan favorite in Boston, the popular outfielder batted .302 for his career. Holmes managed in the minors before his 30-year career with the Mets organization. He passed away in 2008 at age 91.

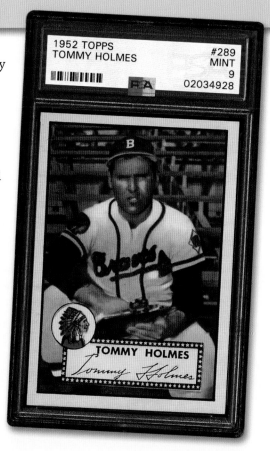

Career Stats

AB:	4,992	HR.	88
R:	698	RBI:	581
H:	1,507	OPS:	.798
BA:	.302		

Teams
Boston Braves NL (1942–1951)
Brooklyn Dodgers NL (1952)

Johnny Hopp

Outfielder and first baseman Johnny Hopp was a key member of the World War II era St. Louis Cardinals teams that won three consecutive NL pennants and the World Series in 1942 and 1944. He joined the Cards in 1939 and started to make his mark in 1941, batting .303 with 15 stolen bases. In 1944, Hopp batted .336 with 177 hits and 15 steals while leading league outfielders with his .997 fielding percentage. An All-Star with the Boston Braves in 1946, Hopp batted .333 with 148 hits and 21 stolen bases. A contributor to all of his teams, Hopp joined the Yankees toward the end of his 14-year career and helped them to World Series championships in 1950 and 1951. He later coached for the Cardinals and Tigers, worked for Kansas-Nebraska Energy, held baseball clinics, and was a motivational speaker. Hopp died in 2003 at age 86.

Career Stats

AB:	4,260	HR:	46
R:	698	RBI:	458
H:	1,262	OPS:	.782
BA:	.296		

Teams

St. Louis Cardinals NL (1939–1945)
Boston Braves NL (1946–1947)
Pittsburgh Pirates NL (1948–1949, 1950)
Brooklyn Dodgers NL (1949)
New York Yankees AL (1950–1952)
Detroit Tigers AL (1952)

Ralph Houk

A Yankees backup catcher with great baseball IQ, Ralph "Major" Houk made his mark on baseball as a manager. With the Yankees his entire playing career, Houk won championships in 1947, 1952, and 1953. Before baseball, he served in the US Army in Europe and rose to the rank of major. Houk won another ring as coach of the 1958 Yankees, and then replaced Casey Stengel as manager in 1961. Houk led the likes of Mantle, Ford, Berra, and Maris to World Series championships in 1961 and 1962, and to the AL pennant in 1963. Well-liked by his players and known for his fiery temper, Houk eventually moved up to the front office as general manager of the Yanks, and later managed the Detroit Tigers and Boston Red Sox. He won a final World Series championship as VP of the 1987 Minnesota Twins. Houk died in 2010 at age 90.

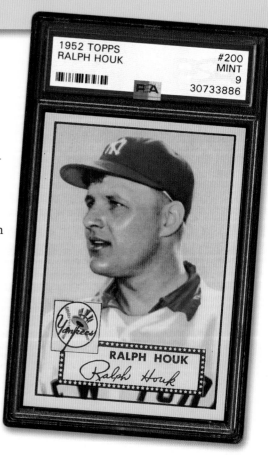

Career Stats

AB:	158	HR:	0
R:	12	RBI:	20
H:	43	OPS:	.650
BA:	.272		

Teams

New York Yankees AL (1947–1954)

Fred Hutchinson

The name Fred Hutchinson will always be remembered outside of baseball. A dependable pitcher for the Detroit Tigers throughout his career, Hutchinson compiled a tidy 95–71 record over ten seasons. A sub-.500 pitcher in his early years, the young righty matured while serving four years in the military and returned to post double-digit wins for six consecutive seasons. The 1951 All-Star went on to manage the Tigers, Cardinals, and Reds from 1952 through 1964, and his 1961 Reds took the NL pennant. Diagnosed with cancer in December 1963, Hutchinson resigned as Cincinnati's manager in August 1964, finishing with a 830–827 record compiled in 12 seasons. Sadly, he passed away that November at the age of 45. In honor of a wonderful guy who had an impact on his players and on the game, the highly regarded Fred Hutchinson Cancer Research Center was established in Seattle in 1975.

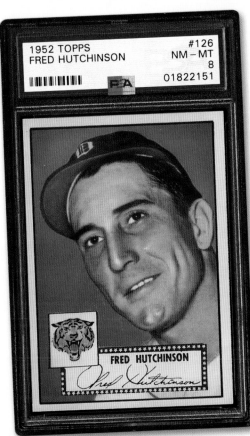

Career Stats

Record:	95–71
ERA:	3.73
IP:	1,464
Ks:	591
Threw:	RH

Teams

Detroit Tigers AL (1939–1940, 1946–1953)

Larry Jansen

A darn good pitcher, Larry Jansen was a starter for the New York Giants for eight seasons. His Major League career took off in 1947 when he finished second to future Hall of Famer Jackie Robinson in Rookie of the Year votes. A two-time 20-game winner, Jansen was a two-time All-Star and led the league with 23 wins in 1951. Interestingly, that 23rd win was the famous Bobby Thomson "Shot Heard 'Round the World" game. Regrettably, back and arm problems prevented Jansen from extending his pitching career. As pitching coach for the Giants from 1961 through 1971, Jansen developed pitchers like Juan Marichal and Gaylord Perry. After retiring, Jansen authored *The Craft of Pitching*. He also dabbled in real estate and enjoyed golfing, fishing, hunting, and spending time with his wife and ten children. He died in 2009 at the age of 89.

Career Stats

Record:	122–89
ERA:	3.58
IP:	1,765.2
Ks:	842
Threw:	RH

Teams

New York Giants NL (1947–1954)
Cincinnati Redlegs NL (1956)

Jackie Jensen

A Boston fan favorite, Red Sox Hall of Famer Jackie Jensen was a three-time All-Star who led the league in RBI three-times. The 1954 AL stolen bases leader and 1956 AL triples leader, Jenson was voted American League MVP in 1958 when he batted .286 with 122 RBI and 35 bombs. A terrific right fielder, the 1959 Gold Glove Award winner paced the league in multiple defensive categories over his career. A rookie with the 1950 world champion Yankees, Jensen also played for the Senators before finding a home with the Red Sox. Unfortunately, he cut short his career because of his fear of flying. He tried therapy to overcome his anxiety, but it finally caught up with him. Jensen then worked as a broadcaster and coach before retiring to run his Christmas tree farm. He passed away in 1982 at age 55 from an apparent heart attack.

Career Stats

AB:	5,236	HR:	199
R:	810	RBI:	929
H:	1,463	OPS:	.829
BA:	.279		

Teams

New York Yankees AL (1950–1952)
Washington Senators AL (1952–1953)
Boston Red Sox AL (1954–1959, 1961)

Sam Jethroe

A Negro Leagues All-Star and batting champ, Sam Jethroe played three seasons with the Boston Braves. Known as "The Jet" because of his great speed, he was signed by the Brooklyn Dodgers in 1948 and traded to the Boston Braves in late 1949. The first black player on the Braves roster, Jethroe electrified Boston fans with his base-stealing ability. The *Boston Herald* reported Jethroe was "regarded as the greatest base runner since Ty Cobb in his prime." In 1950, the 33-year-old centerfielder led the National League with 35 stolen bases and was named NL Rookie of the Year. In 1951, he again led the league with 35 steals. After one at-bat with Pittsburgh in 1954, Jethroe played for Toronto in the minors until 1958. Jethroe then owned a successful restaurant/bar in Erie, Pennsylvania, but he had financial woes later on. Sam Jethroe died in 2001 at age 84.

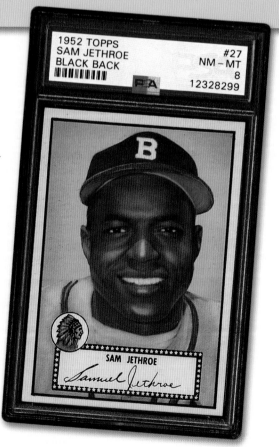

Career Stats

AB:	1,763	HR:	49
R:	280	RBI:	181
H:	460	OPS:	.755
BA:	.261		

Teams

Boston Braves NL (1950–1952)
Pittsburgh Pirates NL (1954)

Sam Jones

On May 12, 1955, Sam Jones became the first African American to toss a no-hitter in MLB history. The Cubs hurler, who also starred in the Negro Leagues and Latin America, fired his gem vs. Pittsburgh. Three years earlier, Jones joined catcher Quincy Trouppe as the first African American battery in American League history. Jones credited Satchel Paige for perfecting his breaking ball and flirted with two more no-hitters during a 12-year MLB career. Despite losing 20 games in 1955, the Ohio native was an All-Star and led the NL in strikeouts. Jones topped the league in Ks three times and in walks four times. In 1959, he was again an All-Star, posting a career-high 21 wins, an ERA of 2.83, and 209 strikeouts. Jones wrapped things up with the Orioles in 1964 and played for the AAA level Columbus Jets through 1967. He succumbed to cancer in 1971 at just 45 years-old.

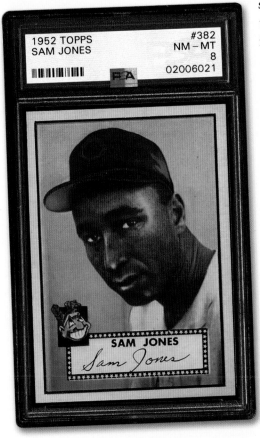

Career Stats

Record:	102–101
ERA:	3.59
IP:	1,643.1
Ks:	1,376
Threw:	RH

Teams

Cleveland Indians AL (1951–1952)
Chicago Cubs NL (1955–1956)
St. Louis Cardinals NL (1957–1958, 1963)
San Francisco Giants NL (1959–1961)
Detroit Tigers AL (1962)
Baltimore Orioles AL (1964)

Willie Jones

Arguably the best-fielding National League third baseman of the 1950s, Willie "Puddin' Head" Jones was as solid as they come. The two-time All-Star batted .267, with 25 home runs and 163 hits as a member of the fabulous "Whiz Kids" Phillies team of 1950. With an average age of 26, they won the Phillies first pennant since 1915, only to be swept by the Yankees in the Series. The following year, Jones batted .285 with 22 homers and 161 hits. A career .258 hitter, Jones also had power, hitting 190 home runs over his 15-year career. The slick-fielding third baseman often led the league in fielding percentage, putouts, assists, and double plays. His 2,045 career putouts as third baseman rank eleventh in MLB history. One of the greatest third sackers in Phillies history, Willie Jones died of cancer in 1983 at the age of 58.

Career Stats

AB:	5,826	HR:	190
R:	786	RBI:	812
H:	1,502	OPS:	.753
BA:	.258		

Teams

Philadelphia Phillies NL (1947–1959)
Cleveland Indians AL (1959)
Cincinnati Reds NL (1959–1961)

Eddie Kazak

1952 TOPPS #165
EDDIE KAZAK
NM – MT 8
40525165

Third baseman Eddie Kazak was as tough as they come. In 1944, the US Army Air Force paratrooper suffered a bayonet wound to his left arm, and his right elbow was shattered by shrapnel. Hospitalized for 18 months, Kazak was released in December 1945 with a plastic patch in his elbow and was advised not to play ball again. Eddie defied the odds. He returned to the minors in 1946 and played through the pain. The determined Kazak came up to the Cardinals in 1948 and as starting third sacker in 1949, his first full MLB season, he batted .304 and made the All-Star team. Kazak broke his ankle sliding into base and was primarily a pinch-hitter and utility man after that. His MLB days ended in 1952, but he played in the minors until 1960, retiring at 40 years old. Kazak died in 1999 at age 79.

Career Stats

AB:	605	HR:	11
R:	69	RBI:	71
H:	165	OPS:	.716
BA:	.273		

Teams

St. Louis Cardinals NL (1948–1952)
Cincinnati Reds NL (1952)

Bob Kennedy

Chicago native Bob Kennedy signed with his hometown White Sox at 16 years old. He developed into a respectable outfielder and third baseman but made a name for himself as a manager and executive in Major League Baseball. Kennedy played for five different teams over his 16-year career. His best year as a player was 1950 when he batted .291 with 157 hits for the Indians. Good defensively, Kennedy was known for his rifle of an arm. After his retirement as a player, Kennedy served more than 30 years in various capacities for several teams. He managed the Chicago Cubs and Oakland A's, was director of player development and assistant GM for the St. Louis Cardinals, GM for the Cubs, and assistant GM for both the Houston Astros and San Francisco Giants. The WWII and Korean War veteran died in 2005 at the age of 84.

1952 TOPPS #77
BOB KENNEDY
NM – MT 8
08021508

Career Stats

AB:	4,624	HR:	63
R:	514	RBI:	514
H:	1,176	OPS:	.665
BA:	.254		

Teams

Chicago White Sox AL (1939–1942, 1946–1948, 1955–1956, 1957)
Cleveland Indians AL (1948–1954)
Baltimore Orioles AL (1954–1955)
Detroit Tigers AL (1956)
Brooklyn Dodgers NL (1957)

Ellis Kinder

One of the more dominant American League pitchers, Ellis "Old Folks" Kinder was a 31-year-old rookie with the St. Louis Browns in 1946. A humorous incident involving Kinder took place in Fenway Park in 1947. He was on the mound pitching for St. Louis when a seagull flew over and dropped a fish on him. Kinder wound up with the Red Sox in 1948 and was a solid pitcher for Boston for eight years. His most successful season was 1949 when he went 23–6 with a 3.36 ERA and a league-leading six shutouts. Later on, Ellis was a very successful closer for the Sox. He paced the league with 16 saves in 1951 and 27 saves in 1953. In his 12 Major League seasons, Kinder compiled a career 102–71 record with a sparkling 3.43 ERA and 104 saves. He died in 1968 at the age of 54.

Career Stats

Record:	102–71
ERA:	3.43
IP:	1,479.2
Ks:	749
Threw:	RH

Teams

St. Louis Browns AL (1946–1947)
Boston Red Sox AL (1948–1955)
St. Louis Cardinals NL (1956)
Chicago White Sox AL (1956–1957)

Clyde King

Although hampered by arm woes and injury, Clyde King was a respectable pitcher for the Dodgers for most of his seven-year career. Used primarily as a reliever, King played on the 1947 and 1952 Brooklyn Dodgers pennant winners. However, his contribution to our National Pastime came over the next 60 years as a coach, manager, general manager, and baseball executive. King was a successful minor-league manager before moving up to manage the San Francisco Giants, Atlanta Braves, and New York Yankees to a combined record of 234–229 in five seasons. He also served as a coach with the Reds, Cardinals, Pirates, and Yankees at various points. King was general manager of the Yankees in the mid-1980s before serving as longtime special advisor to Yankees owner George Steinbrenner. He helped launch the Baseball Assistance Team to assist retired ballplayers. King passed away in 2010 at the age of 86.

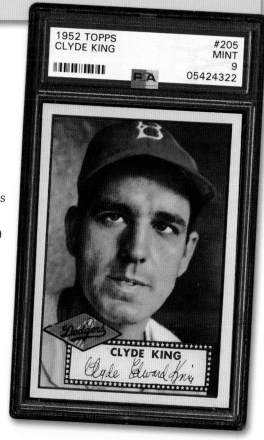

Career Stats

Record:	32–25
ERA:	4.14
IP:	496.0
Ks:	150
Threw:	RH

Teams

Brooklyn Dodgers NL (1944–1945, 1947, 1948, 1951–1952)
Cincinnati Reds NL (1953)

Ted Kluszewski

1952 TOPPS   **#29**
TED KLUSZEWSKI   **MINT**
    9
90103204

Known as "Big Klu," Ted Kluszewski was a power-hitting first baseman for the Cincinnati Reds. The four-time All-Star had a banner season in 1954 when he hit 49 home runs, batted .326, and knocked in 141 runs. Couple that with his .996 fielding percentage for an outstanding season. One of the strongest players in Major League Baseball, Klu hit 171 home runs in four years, from 1953 to 1956. Because he felt the sleeves of his uniform restricted his biceps, he wore sleeveless baseball jerseys. Late in his career, Kluszewski was traded to the Chicago White Sox where he helped them in the 1959 World Series, batting .391 with three home runs and ten RBI. After his playing career, Klu was hitting coach for Sparky Anderson's Big Red Machine Reds throughout the 1970s. He passed away in 1988 at age 63 after suffering a heart attack.

Career Stats

AB:	5,929	HR:	279
R:	848	RBI:	1,028
H:	1,766	OPS:	.850
BA:	.298		

Teams
Cincinnati Reds/Redlegs NL (1947–1957)
Pittsburgh Pirates NL (1958–1959)
Chicago White Sox AL (1959–1960)
Los Angeles Angels AL (1961)

Clem Labine

Clem Labine was a key member of the pitching staff that helped the Brooklyn/Los Angeles Dodgers to four pennants and two world championships between 1953 and 1959. He also pitched for the 1960 world champion Pirates. One of the NL's best rookies in 1951, Labine pitched a shutout in the pennant race that year. The two-time All-Star led the league in games pitched in 1955 and saves in 1956 and 1957. In Game Six of the 1956 World Series, Labine pitched a ten-inning shutout. Brooklyn's top bullpen workhorse, his Dodgers records for games and saves were eventually broken by Don Drysdale and Ron Perranoski. Labine employed the curveball and sinker to carve a niche as a true money pitcher, and he came up big when it counted most. After baseball, Labine was GM and designer for a sports apparel company. He died in 2007 at age 80.

1952 TOPPS
CLEM LABINE

#342
NM–MT
8
31513966

Teams
Brooklyn/Los Angeles Dodgers NL (1950–1960)
Detroit Tigers AL (1960)
Pittsburgh Pirates NL (1960–1961)
New York Mets NL (1962)

Career Stats

Record:	77–56
ERA:	3.63
IP:	1,079.2
Ks:	551
Threw:	RH

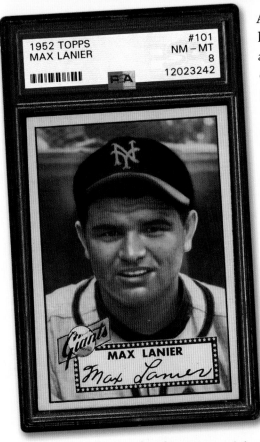

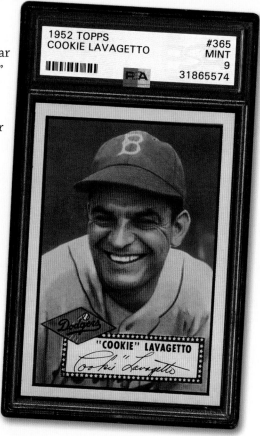

A lefty because he broke his right arm twice as a child, Max Lanier played for the Cardinals most of his career. In his two All-Star seasons, he went 15–7 and led the NL with 1.90 ERA in 1943 and went 17–12 with 2.65 ERA in 1944. He won the 1942 and 1944 Series, and the 1943 NL pennant with the Cards. Lanier got the win in Game Six, the deciding game of the 1944 Series vs. the Browns. He served part of 1945 in the military and was suspended in 1946 for jumping to the Mexican League for more money. Reinstated in 1949, Lanier had a few decent MLB seasons before retiring in 1953 with a career 108–82 record and a tidy 3.01 ERA. He later scouted and coached for the Giants and managed in the minors. Lanier was 91 years old when he died in 2007.

Four-time All-Star, Harry "Cookie" Lavagetto was a popular player for "Dem Bums" of Brooklyn. The Oakland, California, native began his career with the Pirates in 1934. In Brooklyn, he became, arguably, the National League's best third baseman. With a keen eye at the plate, Lavagetto batted a career-best .300 in 1939. His nickname came from being signed by the Oakland Oaks minor-league owner, Cookie DiVincenzi, in 1933. Lavagetto missed four seasons to service in the US Navy where he also managed a team that included Stan Musial. He later coached for the Dodgers, managed the Senators, and was the first manager of the Twins after they moved from Washington in 1961. Lavagetto died in 1990 at the age of 77, but he will forever be remembered by Dodgers fans for his game-winning pinch hit in Game Four of the 1947 World Series vs. the Yankees.

Career Stats

Record:	108–82
ERA:	3.01
IP:	1,619.1
Ks:	821
Threw:	LH

Teams

St. Louis Cardinals NL (1938–1946, 1949–1951)
New York Giants NL (1952–1953)
St. Louis Browns AL (1953)

Career Stats

AB:	3,509	HR:	40
R:	487	RBI:	486
H:	945	OPS:	.737
BA:	.269		

Teams

Pittsburgh Pirates NL (1934–1936)
Brooklyn Dodgers NL (1937–1941, 1946–1947)

Vern Law

Known as "The Deacon," Vern Law, played for the Pirates for his entire 16-year career. A devout Mormon, Law got the nickname because he was, in fact, a deacon in the Mormon church. Steady and dependable, Law had nine double-digit win seasons, but 1960 was the pinnacle. That year Law won 20 games, paced the league with 18 complete games, played in both All-Star games, won the Cy Young Award, and was the catalyst on the mound for the world champion Pirates. Playing with an injured ankle, Law won Game One and Game Four of the Series vs. the Yankees and left Game Seven in the sixth inning with a 4–1 lead. After retiring, Law coached in the majors and minors and for Brigham Young University. The 1965 Lou Gehrig Award recipient is 89 years old at the time of this writing.

Career Stats

Record:	162–147
ERA:	3.77
IP:	2,672.0
Ks:	1,092
Threw:	RH

Teams

Pittsburgh Pirates NL (1950–1951, 1954–1967)

Dutch Leonard

Durable knuckleballer Emil "Dutch" Leonard had a productive 20-year MLB career, pitching until he was 44 years old. The five-time All-Star's best years were with Clark Griffith's Washington Senators where he was encouraged to use his knuckleball. As a matter of fact, Griffith put together a four-man knuckleballer pitching rotation in 1945 and the Senators made a serious run at the pennant, finishing second to the Tigers. A dependable workhorse, Leonard pitched more than 200 innings nine times. Although Leonard's lifetime record is only ten games over .500, his 3.25 ERA is a good indication of his pitching ability. Jackie Robinson once said Leonard was one of the toughest pitchers he ever faced. After his playing career ended, Leonard coached for the Cubs and later worked for the Illinois Youth Commission. He died of congestive heart failure in 1983 at the age of 74.

Career Stats

Record:	191–181
ERA:	3.25
IP:	3,218.1
Ks:	1,170
Threw:	RH

Teams

Brooklyn Dodgers NL (1933–1936)
Washington Senators AL (1938–1946)
Philadelphia Phillies NL (1947–1948)
Chicago Cubs NL (1949–1953)

Billy Loes

A bit eccentric to say the least, in his early career with Brooklyn, Billy Loes compiled a 50–26 record. During those seasons, the Dodgers won two pennants and the 1955 World Series. With the Orioles, Loes had 12 wins in 1957, earning All-Star status. Noted more for his wacky quips than pitching, Loes once remarked he did not want to win 20 games because, "I'd be expected to do it every year." Before the 1952 Series, Loes caused controversy by predicting the Yanks would win over the Dodgers in six games. The Yankees won in seven games. In Game Six, Loes was charged with a balk when the ball slipped out of his hand onto the mound. When asked to explain, he replied, "too much spit on it." Simply said, Loes was a character, but one solid pitcher. He passed away in 2010 at the age of 80.

Teams
Brooklyn Dodgers NL (1950, 1952–1956)
Baltimore Orioles AL (1956–1959)
San Francisco Giants NL (1960–1961)

Career Stats
Record:	80–63
ERA:	3.89
IP:	1,190.1
Ks:	645
Threw:	RH

Sherm Lollar

Sherm Lollar and Yogi Berra were arguably the two best catchers during the decade of the 1950s. Although Berra was a better hitter, Lollar held his own offensively. His lifetime .264 batting average and 155 home runs were considered very good for a catcher. Lollar batted a combined .308 in the postseason for the 1947 Yankees World Series champs, and the 1959 "Go-Go" White Sox AL pennant winners. He played in nine All-Star games, won three Gold Gloves, and led the league in double plays and fielding percentage several times. The durable backstop played 18 MLB seasons, debuting in 1946 at age 21 and retiring in 1963 at age 38. Adept at handling pitchers and regarded as another manager on the field, Lollar went on to coach in the majors and manage in the minors through 1974. He succumbed to cancer at the age of 53 in 1977.

Career Stats
AB:	5,351	HR:	155
R:	623	RBI:	808
H:	1,415	OPS:	.759
BA:	.264		

Teams
Cleveland Indians AL (1946)
New York Yankees AL (1947–1948)
St. Louis Browns AL (1949–1951)
Chicago White Sox AL (1952–1963)

Eddie Lopat

A model of consistency, "Steady Eddie" Lopat was a perennial winner throughout his excellent career. A double-digit winner for the White Sox and Yankees from 1944 through 1954, the lefty was not overpowering, but he had outstanding command. Part of the Yankees "Big Three" starting rotation with Allie Reynolds and Vic Raschi, Lopat played on five consecutive World Series champion teams between 1949 and 1953. The All-Star won a career-high 21 games in 1951, and his 2.42 ERA led the league in 1953. Also called "The Junkman," Lopat finished up with the Orioles in 1955. He managed in the minors and coached for the Yankees and Athletics. As Kansas City's manager in 1963 and part of 1964, Lopat compiled a 90–124 record. He then scouted for years, never leaving baseball. A Polish-American Sports Hall of Fame member, Ed Lopat passed away at the age of 73 in 1992.

Career Stats

Record:	166–112
ERA:	3.21
IP:	2,439.1
Ks:	859
Threw:	LH

Teams

Chicago White Sox AL (1944–1947)
New York Yankees AL (1948–1955)
Baltimore Orioles AL (1955)

Hank Majeski

One of the best-fielding third baseman of the 1950s, Hank Majeski was near the top of the heap defensively during his Major League career. The dependable third baseman played for six different teams over his 13 MLB seasons. He came up to the Boston Bees in 1939 and worked for Uncle Sam from 1943 through 1945. With the Philadelphia Athletics, he led the AL with his .988 fielding percentage in 1947, and in 1948 he batted .310 with 120 RBI and 183 hits. Majeski was a member of the 1954 Cleveland Indians AL pennant-winning team that was swept by the Giants in the Series. Known for his defense, Majeski's career .968 fielding percentage still ranks in the Top 20 for third basemen in the American League. In retirement, Majeski managed in the minor leagues, scouted, and coached for Wagner College. He succumbed to cancer in 1991 at the age 74.

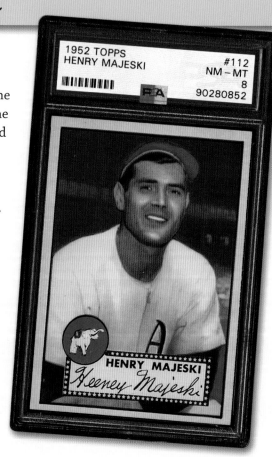

Career Stats

AB:	3,421	HR:	57
R:	404	RBI:	501
H:	956	OPS:	.740
BA:	.279		

Teams

Boston Braves NL (1939–1941)
New York Yankees AL (1946)
Philadelphia Athletics AL (1946–1949, 1951–1952)
Chicago White Sox AL (1950–1951)
Cleveland Indians AL (1952–1955)
Baltimore Orioles AL (1955)

Connie Marrero

Colorful, cigar-smoking Conrado "Connie" Marrero was already a baseball legend in his native Cuba before he made it to the MLB in 1950 at the age of 39. He became an All-Star posting an ERA of 3.90 with 11 wins for the Senators in 1951 and followed that with another 11-win season in 1952. The 5-foot-5, 158-pound Marrero wielded a wicked curveball and slider emanating from a windmill windup that baffled hitters. Known as "El Curveador" in Cuba and "Conrado the Conqueror" in the United States, Marrero's wild delivery led to more walks than strikeouts in 1951, but he baffled some of baseball's greats including Joe DiMaggio and Ted Williams. A baseball lifer, Marrero continued to pitch and coach in Cuba into his 80s, becoming the ultimate baseball elder statesman. Marrero was the oldest living former Major Leaguer when he died in 2014 at the age of 102.

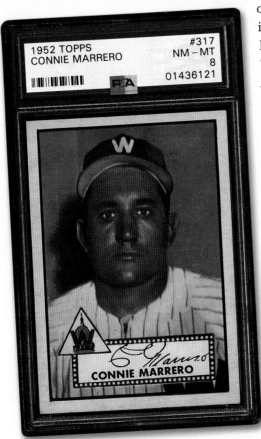

Career Stats

Record:	39–40
ERA:	3.67
IP:	735.1
Ks:	297
Threw:	RH

Teams
Washington Senators AL (1950–1954)

Willard Marshall

When Virginia native Willard Marshall joined the New York Giants in 1942, manager Mel Ott made him a regular outfielder from day one. Marshall made the All-Star team as a rookie but lost the next three seasons to service in the US Marines during World War II. A consistent outfielder with a good arm, Marshall batted a tidy .291 and socked 36 home runs with 107 RBI in 1947. That year, he slammed three home runs in one game, which tied the National League record at the time. The three-time All-Star batted a career-best .307 in 1949. With the Boston Braves in 1951, the stellar outfielder led the NL with his perfect 1.000 fielding percentage. After a stop with Cincinnati, Marshall ended his MLB journey in 1955 with the White Sox. The 1990 Virginia Sports Hall of Fame inductee died in 2000 at the age of 79.

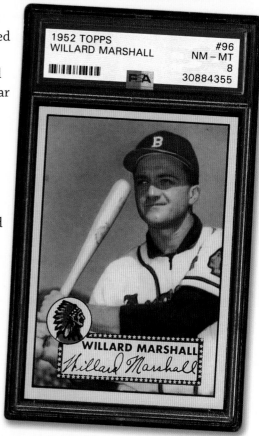

Career Stats

AB:	4,233	HR:	130
R:	583	RBI:	604
H:	1,160	OPS:	.770
BA:	.274		

Teams
New York Giants NL (1942, 1946–1949)
Boston Braves NL (1950–1952)
Cincinnati Reds NL (1952–1953)
Chicago White Sox AL (1954–1955)

Billy Martin

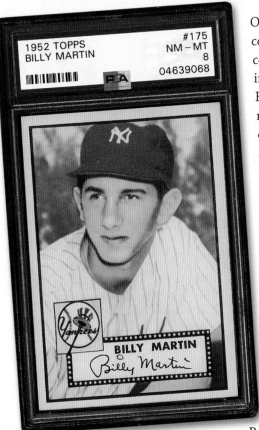

One of the most colorful and controversial players in baseball history, Billy Martin played, managed, fought, and drank hard. The 1956 All-Star played on seven different teams and won five World Series championships as second sacker for the Yankees. He managed the Yankees on five different occasions and led them to a world championship in 1977. Besides managing the Yanks, he skippered the Twins, Tigers, Rangers, and Athletics, and was named MLB Manager of the Year in 1981. Martin's off-field activities with his friend Mickey Mantle were legendary. They both loved the New York nightlife and the New York bars. Brawls and arguments with players and owners were commonplace for Martin. The only constant was that Billy Martin was an excellent player and manager. After a night of drinking, Martin was killed in an auto accident at the age of 61 in 1989.

Career Stats

AB:	3,419	HR:	64
R:	425	RBI:	333
H:	877	OPS:	.669
BA:	.257		

Teams

New York Yankees AL (1950–1953, 1955–1957)
Kansas City Athletics AL (1957)
Detroit Tigers AL (1958)
Cleveland Indians AL (1959)
Cincinnati Reds NL (1960)
Milwaukee Braves NL (1961)
Minnesota Twins AL (1961)

Morrie Martin

Morrie "Lefty" Martin had a ten-year career in the majors, but his backstory is very interesting. A member of the First Army 49th Combat Engineers, Martin saw action in North Africa and was also part of the D-Day landing in Normandy and the Battle of the Bulge. He suffered shrapnel wounds in his hand and frostbite in his feet, but in 1945, in Bonn, Germany, he was shot in the leg and the wound became infected. Thankfully a nurse discovered that Martin was a baseball player, and she convinced the doctors to treat Martin with a new experimental drug called penicillin rather than amputate his leg. The penicillin worked and thanks to that kind nurse, Martin went on to enjoy a respectable MLB pitching career, playing for seven different teams. The decorated World War II veteran lived to the age of 87 and passed away in 2010.

Career Stats

Record:	38–34
ERA:	4.29
IP:	604.2
Ks:	245
Threw:	LH

Teams

Brooklyn Dodgers NL (1949)
Philadelphia Athletics AL (1951–1954)
Chicago White Sox AL (1954–1956)
Baltimore Orioles AL (1956)
St. Louis Cardinals NL (1957–1958)
Cleveland Indians AL (1958)
Chicago Cubs NL (1959)

Phil Masi

A Boston Bees and Braves mainstay from 1939 to 1949, Phil Masi batted over .300 just once, but he made three consecutive All-Star teams from 1946 to 1948. A fine defensive catcher, Masi played on the Braves NL title team in 1948, but went just 1-for-8 in Boston's World Series loss to Cleveland. In Game One of that fall classic, a controversial pickoff attempt of Masi prevented Indians ace Bob Feller from getting the win. Masi was traded to Pittsburgh in 1949 and spent his last three MLB seasons in his native Chicago with the White Sox. In addition to his 1,101 career games as a catcher, he also played first base, third base, and the outfield. Adept at handling pitchers, Masi caught future Hall of Famer Warren Spahn and 20-game winner Johnny Sain while with Boston. He succumbed to cancer in 1990 at age 74.

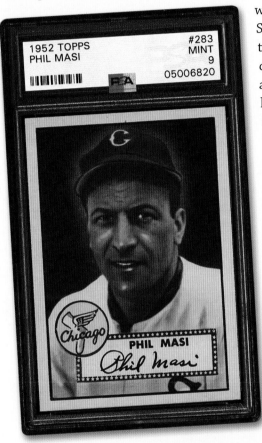

Career Stats

AB:	3,468	HR:	47
R:	420	RBI:	417
H:	917	OPS:	.714
BA:	.264		

Teams
Boston Bees/Braves NL (1939–1949)
Pittsburgh Pirates NL (1949)
Chicago White Sox AL (1950–1952)

Charlie Maxwell

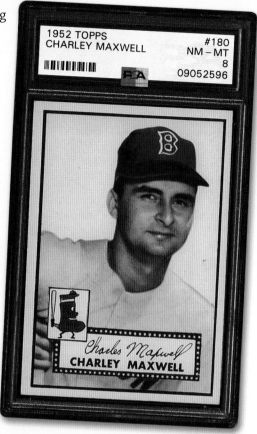

Known for entertaining fans before games by hitting fungoes to kids and clowning with them, Charlie Maxwell had a solid 14-year career but is known for his time with the Tigers from 1955 to 1962. Maxwell broke out in 1956 when he batted .326 and went yard 28 times, and the two-time All-Star blasted 31 homers while batting .251 in 1959. Nicknamed "Paw Paw" after his hometown of Paw Paw, Michigan, Maxwell had power, slamming 20-plus home runs four times. The fleet-footed left fielder led the league in fielding percentage on four occasions, and in range factor, putouts, and assists at various times. After a brief stint with the White Sox, he left baseball in 1964 to start a sales career. Maxwell was inducted into the Michigan Sports Hall of Fame in 1997. At the time of this writing, he is 92 years old.

Career Stats

AB:	3,245	HR:	148
R:	480	RBI:	532
H:	856	OPS:	.811
BA:	.264		

Teams
Boston Red Sox AL (1950–1952, 1954)
Baltimore Orioles AL (1955)
Detroit Tigers AL (1955–1962)
Chicago White Sox AL (1962–1964)

Barney McCosky

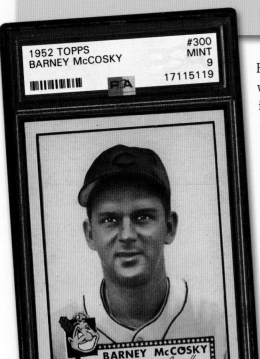

Barney McCosky broke into the majors with style, batting .311 as a Tigers rookie in 1939. He followed that up with a .340 average and a league-leading 200 hits and 19 triples in 1940. Detroit won the AL Championship that season, and McCosky batted .304 in the World Series loss to the Reds. In 1941, McCosky batted .324, but his road to stardom was halted by a three-year stint in the US Navy. Upon his return in 1946, McCosky batted .318 and followed that with averages of .328 and .326 with the Athletics in 1947 and 1948 respectively. Back injuries derailed the speedy outfielder, and, after stops in Cincinnati and Cleveland, his career ended in 1953. The affable McCosky was popular with fans and teammates. He was inducted into the Michigan Sports Hall of Fame in 1995 and passed away a year later at age 79.

Career Stats

AB:	4,172	HR:	24
R:	664	RBI:	397
H:	1,301	OPS:	.801
BA:	.312		

Teams

Detroit Tigers AL (1939–1942, 1946)
Philadelphia Athletics AL (1946–1951)
Cincinnati Reds NL (1951)
Cleveland Indians AL (1951–1953)

Gil McDougald

The 1951 American League Rookie of the Year, Gil McDougald played ten seasons for the Yankees and was a five-time All-Star. The infielder played in eight World Series and won five rings, batting .321 in New York's 1958 Series win vs. Milwaukee. His rookie season was his best, when he batted .306 with 14 homers and 63 RBI. McDougald had another solid season in 1957, but that year will forever be marked by his May 7 line drive that hit Indians pitcher Herb Score in the face, tragically altering the young hurler's promising career. Two years earlier, McDougald himself was struck by a batting practice liner which later caused debilitating hearing loss. After baseball, McDougald coached at Fordham University, embraced charitable causes, and underwent successful cochlear implant surgery to aid his hearing. A true champion in all ways, McDougald died in 2010 at the age of 82.

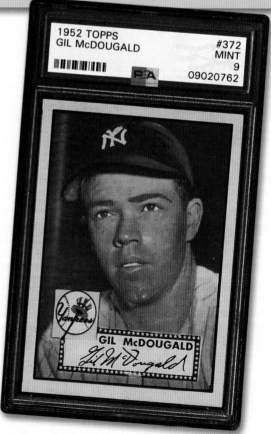

Career Stats

AB:	4,676	HR:	112
R:	697	RBI:	576
H:	1,291	OPS:	.766
BA:	.276		

Teams

New York Yankees AL (1951–1960)

Roy McMillan

Known for his slick fielding, Roy McMillan carved out a good career as both a player and manager. One of the best defensive shortstops of the era, McMillan was a two-time All-Star and three-time Gold Glove winner. The 1956 Reds MVP led the league in many defensive categories multiple times during his 16-year MLB career. Not a dynamo offensively, McMillan was not an embarrassment either. McMillan had a long ten-year run playing for the Cincinnati Reds/Redlegs, followed by stints with the Milwaukee Braves and the New York Mets. He wrapped it up in 1966 and continued on to manage in the majors and minors, coach, and scout until 1997. He was the interim manager for the 1972 Milwaukee Brewers and 1975 Mets. The Cincinnati Reds Hall of Famer passed away from a heart attack in 1997 at the age of 68.

Career Stats

AB:	6,752	HR:	68
R:	739	RBI:	594
H:	1,639	OPS:	.635
BA:	.243		

Teams

Cincinnati Reds/Redlegs NL (1951–1960)

Milwaukee Braves NL (1961–1964)

New York Mets NL (1964–1966)

Sam Mele

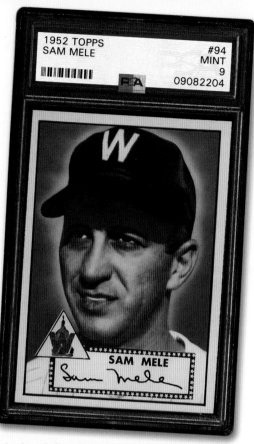

Not a star by any means, Sam Mele was an effective ballplayer and even better manager. The lanky right fielder batted .302 with 12 home runs for the Boston Red Sox in 1947, his rookie season. In 1951, he batted .274 for the Senators and led the American League with 36 doubles. A defensive force, the three-time league-leader in fielding percentage as a right fielder retired in 1956 with a lifetime .990 fielding percentage. Mele then coached for the Senators and moved with the club to Minnesota in 1961. As the Twins manager from 1961 through 1967, Mele posted a 524–436 record. He led the Twins to their first AL pennant in 1965 and was recognized with *The Sporting News* Manager of the Year Award. Mele then scouted for the Red Sox for 25 years. The WWII US Marine Corps veteran died in 2017 at the age of 95.

Career Stats

AB:	3,437	HR:	80
R:	406	RBI:	544
H:	916	OPS:	.736
BA:	.267		

Teams

Boston Red Sox AL (1947–1949, 1954–1955)

Washington Senators AL (1949–1952)

Chicago White Sox AL (1952–1953)

Baltimore Orioles AL (1954)

Cincinnati Redlegs NL (1955)

Cleveland Indians AL (1956)

George Metkovich

George "Catfish" Metkovich broke in with the Boston Red Sox in 1943 and was a member of their 1946 AL title team. A solid doubles man for the BoSox, his stats fizzled as Metkovich moved through a 10-year career. He got his nickname during spring training 1940 when he was cut by a fin while trying to remove the hook from a catfish. During and after his career, Metkovich ran with some lofty company. The outfielder was signed by Casey Stengel as a Boston Bee in 1940, was traded by Cleveland owner Bill Veeck to the Browns in 1947, and he was part of the trade that sent Ralph Kiner from Pittsburgh to the Cubs in 1953. A California native, Metkovich also had bit roles in several movies, acting with the likes of Elizabeth Taylor, Doris Day, and future President Ronald Reagan. He died in 1995 at age 74.

Career Stats

AB:	3,585	HR:	47
R:	476	RBI:	373
H:	934	OPS:	.689
BA:	.261		

Teams

Boston Red Sox AL (1943–1946)
Cleveland Indians AL (1947)
Chicago White Sox AL (1949)
Pittsburgh Pirates NL (1951–1953)
Chicago Cubs NL (1953)
Milwaukee Braves NL (1954)

Cass Michaels

Two-time All-Star Cass Michaels broke into the majors in 1943 with the Chicago White Sox. In 1949, he batted .308 with 83 RBI for Chicago. Patient at the plate, Michaels walked 101 times that year. In 1950, he was batting .312 at the end of May when the Sox traded him to the Senators. From that point on, Michaels' glory years were behind him. A dependable infielder for several teams, Michaels came back to Chicago in 1954 and the 28-year-old seemed to regain his form, but on August 27, 1954, it was all over. That day a vicious beaning by the A's Marion Fricano fractured Michaels' skull, leaving him in a coma. He slowly recovered but dizzy spells and impaired vision ended his baseball career. Michaels returned home to Detroit and owned a popular bar which he operated until he died at age 56 in 1982.

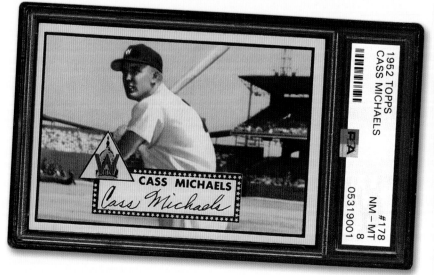

Career Stats

AB:	4,367	HR:	53
R:	508	RBI:	501
H:	1,142	OPS:	.702
BA:	.262		

Teams

Chicago White Sox AL (1943–1950, 1954)
Washington Senators AL (1950–1952)
St. Louis Browns AL (1952)
Philadelphia Athletics AL (1952–1953)

Minnie Minoso

One of the most popular players in White Sox history, left fielder Minnie Minoso could do it all. A nine-time All-Star, three-time Gold Glove winner, three-time stolen base and triples leader, and a power threat, the "Cuban Comet" was a pleasure to watch. Minoso came up through the Cuban and Negro Leagues to become a superstar and batted over .300 eight seasons. He could literally take one for the team, leading the league in hit-by-pitches ten times. While coaching for the Sox, he made a Major League appearance with a base hit at age 50. At the time of this writing, Minoso is still being considered for entry into the Hall of Fame. The White Sox retired Minoso's number "9" and honored him with a statue at US Cellular Field. The first black player for the White Sox, Minoso died in 2015 at age 89.

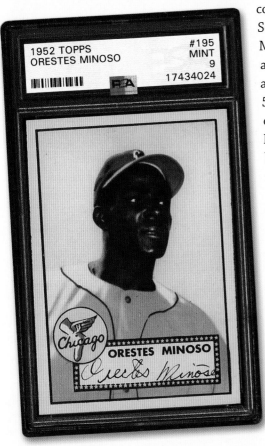

Career Stats

AB:	6,579	HR:	186
R:	1,136	RBI:	1,023
H:	1,936	OPS:	.848
BA:	.298		

Teams
Cleveland Indians AL (1949, 1951, 1958–1959)
Chicago White Sox AL (1951–1957, 1960–1961, 1964, 1976, 1980)
St. Louis Cardinals NL (1962)
Washington Senators AL (1963)

Dale Mitchell

A star high school and college athlete and a US Army Air Force veteran, Dale Mitchell joined the Cleveland Indians in 1946 at age 24. The prototypical contact hitter, he had some outstanding years with Cleveland, with his best being 1948 when he batted .336 with 204 hits and led the Tribe to a World Series championship. As regular left fielder for a seven-year stretch, Mitchell was the offensive catalyst for the Indians, and was near or at the top of several hitting categories. The two-time All-Star helped the Indians to an 111-win season and the AL pennant in 1954. Mentored by Tris Speaker, Mitchell was an excellent outfielder, with a career .985 fielding percentage and .312 lifetime batting average. A successful businessman after baseball, Mitchell died in 1987 at the age of 65. The baseball stadium at the University of Oklahoma, his alma mater, bears his name.

Career Stats

AB:	3,984	HR:	41
R:	555	RBI:	403
H:	1,244	OPS:	.784
BA:	.312		

Teams
Cleveland Indians AL (1946–1956)
Brooklyn Dodgers NL (1956)

Vinegar Bend Mizell

1952 TOPPS
WILMER MIZELL
#334
NM – MT
8
09007469

Mississippi native Wilmer "Vinegar Bend" Mizell got his nickname from a nearby Alabama town, which got its name from an historic vinegar-spilling train accident. Mizell played nine big league seasons, interrupted by military service in 1954 and 1955. He broke in with the Cardinals in 1952 and won 69 games for them over seven seasons. Both a starter and reliever, the 1959 All-Star had the ability to strike out the side but also the wildness to walk the ballpark. He played for the world champion Pirates in 1960 and the hapless expansion Mets in 1962. Mizell was out of baseball in 1963, but five years later, he was elected to the U.S. House of Representatives from North Carolina and served three terms. He later served in the administrations of Gerald Ford, Ronald Reagan, and George H.W. Bush. Mizell died of a heart attack in 1999 at the age of 68.

Career Stats

Record:	90–88
ERA:	3.85
IP:	1,538.2
Ks:	918
Threw:	LH

Teams

St. Louis Cardinals NL (1952–1953, 1956–1960)
Pittsburgh Pirates NL (1960–1962)
New York Mets NL (1962)

Don Mueller

Dubbed "Mandrake the Magician" for his uncanny ability to place his hits, Don Mueller was a very good hitter and a very tough out. With the New York Giants for most of his career, Mueller was outstanding in 1954. That year his 212 hits paced the NL, his .342 BA was second only to teammate Willie Mays (who won the NL batting title), and he batted a robust .389 with seven hits in the World Series as the Giants swept the Indians. The two-time All-Star and .296 lifetime hitter was involved in several memorable games. Mueller's single helped set up Bobby Thomson's pennant-winning "Shot Heard 'Round the World" in 1951, and he played in Game One of the 1954 Series when Willie Mays made "The Catch." After his career, Mueller scouted for the Giants and worked in the insurance business. He was 84 years old when he died in 2011.

1952 TOPPS
DON MUELLER
#52
NM – MT
8
09045392

Teams

New York Giants NL (1948–1957)
Chicago White Sox AL (1958–1959)

Career Stats

AB:	4,364	HR:	65
R:	499	RBI:	520
H:	1,292	OPS:	.712
BA:	.296		

Bill Nicholson

A five-time All-Star with six 20-home run seasons, Bill "Swish" Nicholson was an imposing figure at the plate. The nickname? When Nicholson took his practice swings, the fans chanted "swish." With the Cubs most of his career, Nicholson batted .309 and led the league with 128 RBI and 29 homers in 1943. The next year, he led the NL with 122 RBI, 33 home runs, and 116 runs. He played every game in the 1945 World Series. Nicholson was such a threat that he is one of only six MLB players to be walked with the bases loaded. A great right fielder, Nicholson led the league in putouts, assists, and fielding percentage several times. Soon after joining the Phillies, he was diagnosed with diabetes and missed the "Whiz Kids" 1950 pennant run. After baseball, he returned home to Chestertown, Maryland, where he died in 1996 at the age of 81.

Career Stats

AB:	5,546	HR:	235
R:	837	RBI:	948
H:	1,484	OPS:	.830
BA:	.268		

Teams
Philadelphia Athletics AL (1936)
Chicago Cubs NL (1939–1948)
Philadelphia Phillies NL (1949–1953)

Joe Nuxhall

On June 10, 1944, 15-year-old Reds pitcher Joe Nuxhall took the hill against St. Louis and became the youngest player ever to participate in a Major League game. The Reds were behind 13–0 in the top of the ninth. Nuxhall faced ten batters, allowed five runs, and was pulled by manager Bill McKechnie. After graduating high school and honing his craft in the minors, Nuxhall rejoined the Reds in 1952. The two-time All-Star led the league with five shutouts in 1955. Nuxhall pitched for a total of 16 MLB seasons, 15 of them with the Reds, and finished in 1966 with 135 career wins and a 3.90 ERA. His fiery personality and folksy manner made the "Ol' Lefthander" a beloved fixture in the Reds broadcast booth from 1967 to 2004. The 1968 Reds Hall of Fame inductee died in 2007 at the age of 79.

Career Stats

Record:	135–117
ERA:	3.90
IP:	2,302.2
Ks:	1,372
Threw:	LH

Teams
Cincinnati Reds/Redlegs NL (1944, 1952–1960, 1962–1966)
Kansas City Athletics AL (1961)
Los Angeles Angels AL (1962)

Andy Pafko

1952 TOPPS #1
ANDY PAFKO NM – MT 8
03008347

A very good player who stayed under the radar, "Handy Andy" Pafko was a five-time All-Star outfielder and third baseman who helped the Cubs win the NL pennant in 1945. Known for his ability in the outfield and with the bat, the versatile Pafko saw World Series play again with the Brooklyn Dodgers in 1952. After joining the Milwaukee Braves in 1953, the Wisconsin native became a fan favorite. There he played in two World Series, winning his ring in 1957 vs. the Yankees. With his 213 bombs, and lifetime .285 batting average, Andy Pafko was a solid player for all three organizations. He later managed for the Braves in the minors and scouted for the Expos and the Braves. Pafko was named to the Cubs All-Century Team in 1999 and passed away in 2013 at the age of 92.

Career Stats

AB:	6,292	HR:	213
R:	844	RBI:	976
H:	1,796	OPS:	.799
BA:	.285		

Teams

Chicago Cubs NL (1943–1951)
Brooklyn Dodgers NL (1951–1952)
Milwaukee Braves NL (1953–1959)

Joe Page

Joe "The Fireman" Page is one of the templates for today's modern-day closer. An imposing figure, the 6-foot-3, 200-pound relief pitcher relied on his fastball and spitter to put batters away. Unfortunately, Page played as hard as he worked, to the chagrin of his manager. A three-time All-Star and member of the 1947, 1949, and 1950 Yankees' World Series champion teams, Page's 57–49 record does not jump out at you. However, his 76 saves over his eight-year career really jump-started the role of the closer and changed how the Yankees handled their pitchers. Released by the Yankees in 1951 after he developed arm troubles, Page unsuccessfully tried a comeback with the Pittsburgh Pirates in 1954. After retiring, he opened up a couple of bars in Pennsylvania that were fairly successful. He died in 1980, at the age of 62, after suffering a heart attack.

1952 TOPPS #48
JOE PAGE
CORRECT BIO – BLACK BACK NM – MT 8
04042003

Career Stats

Record:	57–49
ERA:	3.53
IP:	790.0
Ks:	519
Threw:	LH

Teams

New York Yankees AL (1944–1950)
Pittsburgh Pirates NL (1954)

Mel Parnell

One of the greatest left-handed pitchers in Boston Red Sox history, Mel Parnell dominated the American League from 1948 through 1953. Parnell enjoyed his best season in 1949, earning the AL pitching title with his 25–7 record and 2.77 ERA. In 1956, his last season, he tossed a no-hitter in July at Fenway Park against the White Sox. That feat was not accomplished again at Fenway by a Red Sox leftie until John Lester did it 52 years later in 2008. Sadly, a torn muscle in his elbow cut short Parnell's great career. After his playing days, Parnell managed in the minors before joining the Red Sox as both a radio and television broadcaster. Mel "Dusty" Parnell was elected to the Red Sox Hall of Fame in 1997. The two-time All-Star known for his inside slider was 89 years old when he died in 2012.

Career Stats

Record:	123–75
ERA:	3.50
IP:	1,752.2
Ks:	732
Threw:	LH

Teams
Boston Red Sox AL (1947–1956)

Johnny Pesky

"Mr. Red Sox," Johnny Pesky was an outstanding shortstop and third baseman for Boston. He led the American League with 205 hits and finished third in MVP voting in 1942, his rookie season. Pesky lost three seasons to military service and returned in 1946 to have an All-Star season. The starting shortstop for the Sox in the 1946 World Series, Pesky developed a close, lifelong friendship with teammates Ted Williams, Bobby Doerr, and Dom DiMaggio. He finished his career with the Tigers and the Senators but returned to Boston in 1961, working as coach, manager, color commentator, and special instructor until his death in 2012 at age 93. Still beloved in Beantown, the right-field foul pole in Fenway Park is called the "Pesky Pole." He was presented with World Series rings after the Sox won the fall classic in 2004 and 2007, and Pesky's number "6" was retired by the Red Sox in 2008.

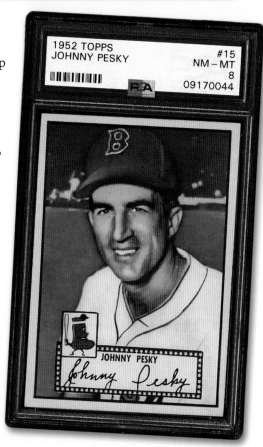

Career Stats

AB:	4,475	HR:	17
R:	867	RBI:	404
H:	1,455	OPS:	.780
BA:	.307		

Teams
Boston Red Sox AL (1942, 1946–1952)
Detroit Tigers AL (1952–1954)
Washington Senators AL (1954)

Billy Pierce

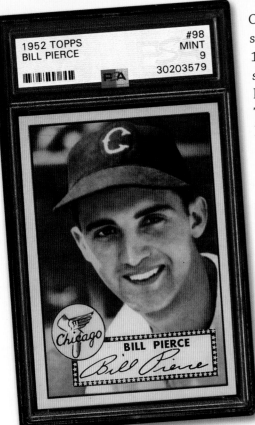

One of the best southpaws of the 1950s, Billy Pierce signed with his hometown Detroit Tigers right out of high school in 1945, but his glory years were with the "Go-Go" White Sox. Belying his slight build, Pierce dominated with his fastball, changeup, curve, and slider. The seven-time All-Star led the American League with 186 strikeouts in 1953. He won the AL pitching title with his 1.97 ERA in 1955 and led the league with 20 wins in 1957. Twice named *The Sporting News* Pitcher of the Year, Pierce won pennants with the 1959 White Sox and the 1962 San Francisco Giants. After baseball, he returned to Chicago, where he had played for most of his career. The White Sox retired his number "19" in 1987 and unveiled a statue of Pierce in the center-field concourse in 2007. Pierce passed away in 2015 at the age of 88.

Career Stats

Record:	211–169
ERA:	3.27
IP:	3,306.2
Ks:	1,999
Threw:	LH

Teams

Detroit Tigers AL (1945, 1948)
Chicago White Sox AL (1949–1961)
San Francisco Giants NL (1962–1964)

Howie Pollet

After a promising start in the majors, Howie Pollet's career was interrupted by two years of service in World War II. The crafty left-hander returned to St. Louis with a vengeance in 1946, leading the league with 21 wins, a 2.10 ERA, and 266 innings pitched. He helped lead the Cardinals to the National League pennant and a victory over the Red Sox in the 1946 World Series. After a few mediocre seasons due to injuries, Howie won 20 games in 1949 while leading the league with his five shutouts. Plagued by injuries, the three-time All-Star was traded to the Pirates, Cubs, White Sox, and back to the Pirates, but never regained his form. Pollet coached for the Cardinals and Astros from 1959 through 1965 and retired to work in the insurance business. Howie Pollet passed away in 1974 at the age of 53.

Career Stats

Record:	131–116
ERA:	3.51
IP:	2,107.1
Ks:	934
Threw:	LH

Teams

St. Louis Cardinals NL (1941–1943, 1946–1951)
Pittsburgh Pirates NL (1951–1953, 1956)
Chicago Cubs NL (1953–1955)
Chicago White Sox AL (1956)

Wally Post

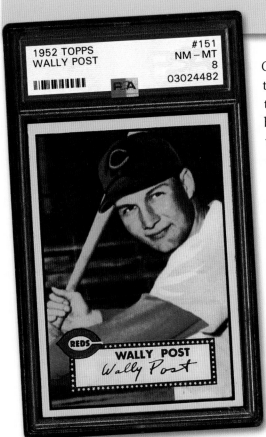

1952 TOPPS #151
WALLY POST
NM – MT 8
03024482

Outfielder Wally Post had a very strong arm and could track down a fly ball with the best of them. He spent 12 years of his 15-year Major League career patrolling the outfield for Cincinnati. Post's best year was in 1955 with the Redlegs when he batted .309 and swatted 40 home runs. A member of the 1961 Reds NL pennant winners, Post played in all five games of the World Series and batted .333 in the disappointing loss to the Yankees. Over his long career, Post had five 20-home run seasons and smacked a total of 210 home runs. After baseball, Post was an executive in the family business, Minster Canning Company, and he started the annual Wally Post Golf Outing to benefit the cancer society. A member of the Cincinnati Reds Hall of Fame, Post died of cancer in 1982 at the young age of 52.

Career Stats

AB:	4,007	HR:	210
R:	594	RBI:	699
H:	1,064	OPS:	.808
BA:	.266		

Teams

Cincinnati Reds/Redlegs NL (1949, 1951–1957, 1960–1963)
Philadelphia Phillies NL (1958–1960)
Minnesota Twins AL (1963)
Cleveland Indians AL (1964)

Jerry Priddy

A slick-fielding second baseman and decent hitter, Jerry Priddy looked like a "can't miss" in the minors. There was a lot of buzz about the formidable Priddy–Phil Rizzuto double-play tandem in the Yankees farm system, but when Priddy arrived in New York in 1941 his big ego and fiery temper got in the way. After two seasons of limited play, Priddy moved on to the Senators, Browns, and Tigers, maturing into a dependable player. From 1947 through 1951, he regularly led the league in putouts, assists, and double plays turned at second base. After retiring, Priddy tried his hand at the movie business, professional golf, and various business ventures. In 1973, in a bizarre twist, he was sentenced to nine months in prison for trying to extort $250,000 from a cruise ship company. Jerry Priddy died from a heart attack in 1980 at age 60.

1952 TOPPS
JERRY PRIDDY
BLACK BACK
#28 MINT 9
09033540

Career Stats

AB:	4,720	HR:	61
R:	612	RBI:	541
H:	1,252	OPS:	.725
BA:	.265		

Teams

New York Yankees AL (1941–1942)
Washington Senators AL (1943, 1946–1947)
St. Louis Browns AL (1948–1949)
Detroit Tigers AL (1950–1953)

Pete Reiser

1952 TOPPS
PETE REISER
#189
NM – MT
8
04626391

Had "Pistol Pete" Reiser not been so injury-prone, the sky would have been the limit. An excellent hitter who played the outfield with reckless abandon, Reiser suffered skull fractures, concussions, shoulder injuries, and various broken bones. Playing before ballpark walls were padded, the competitive Reiser was carried off the field on a stretcher 11 times. In an amazing 1941 season, Reiser batted .343 for the league crown and led the league with 117 runs, 32 doubles, and 17 triples. The three-time All-Star played in the 1941 and 1947 World Series and led the league with 20 stolen bases in 1942 and 34 steals in 1946. In between, he lost three quality years to World War II. After ten MLB seasons, Reiser managed, coached, and scouted until his death at age 62 in 1981. Baseball historian Lawrence Ritter included Reiser in his Top 100 players of all time.

Career Stats

AB:	2,662	HR:	58
R:	473	RBI:	368
H:	786	OPS:	.829
BA:	.295		

Teams

Brooklyn Dodgers NL (1940–1942, 1946–1948)
Boston Braves NL (1949–1950)
Pittsburgh Pirates NL (1951)
Cleveland Indians AL (1952)

Allie Reynolds

A member of the Creek Nation, Allie Reynolds, honed his great skills with Cleveland, but exploded with the Yankees, playing on six world championship teams. For eight straight seasons, Reynolds was one of the most dominant pitchers in the American League. In 1951 he led the league with seven shutouts and became the first AL hurler to pitch two no-hitters in one season, earning the nickname "Super Chief." The next season, at age 35, Reynolds led the league with 160 Ks, six shutouts, and his 2.06 ERA. The six-time All-Star was so resilient that he was sometimes used between starts as a reliever. In those six World Series, Reynolds had a 7–2 record with four saves, two shutouts, and a .308 BA. After baseball, he operated his Oklahoma oil business and was involved in civic, charitable, and Native American cultural organizations. Reynolds passed away in 1994 at age 77.

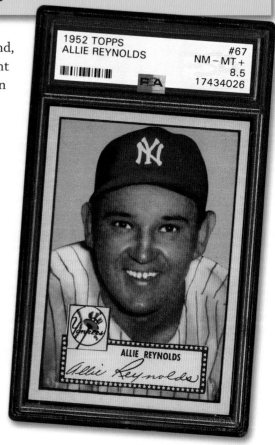

1952 TOPPS
ALLIE REYNOLDS
#67
NM – MT +
8.5
17434026

Career Stats

Record:	182–107
ERA:	3.30
IP:	2,492.1
Ks:	1,423
Threw:	RH

Teams

Cleveland Indians AL (1942–1946)
New York Yankees AL (1947–1954)

Paul Richards

He broke in with Brooklyn in 1932, but only played three games in Dodger blue. A light-hitting catcher, Paul Richards batted .211 in Detroit's 1945 World Series win vs. the Cubs. Offensively, Richards' playing career was of little note, but the Texas native went on to manage for 12 MLB seasons split between the White Sox and Orioles. While he never won a pennant, Richards won 923 games, righted the ship for some downtrodden franchises, and developed many young stars. He also chewed out numerous umpires with his fiery temper.

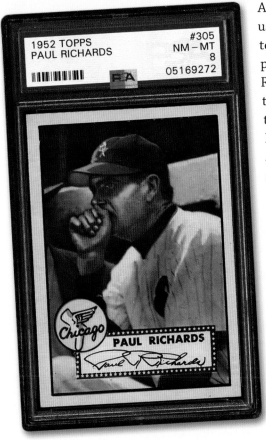

An innovator in using statistics to evaluate player talent, Richards became the first GM of the expansion Houston Colt .45s in 1961 and was later an executive with the Atlanta Braves. The ultimate "baseball man," Paul Richards was a scout and advisor until he died of a heart attack on the golf course at age 77 in 1986.

Career Stats

AB:	1,417	HR:	15
R:	140	RBI:	155
H:	321	OPS:	.606
BA:	.227		

Teams

Brooklyn Dodgers NL (1932)
New York Giants NL (1933–1935)
Philadelphia Athletics AL (1935)
Detroit Tigers AL (1943–1946)

Bill Rigney

A decent infielder, Bill Rigney was a dependable starter for the New York Giants for eight years, but his second career as a Major League manager lasted much longer. The 1948 All-Star with a career .259 batting average won the National League pennant with the 1951 Giants and batted a combined .250 in four games of that 4–2 Series loss to the Yankees. Starting in 1956, Rigney had managerial stints with the New York/San Francisco Giants, Los Angeles/California Angels, and the Minnesota Twins, before he wrapped it up with the Giants in 1976 with an 18-season 1239–1321 managerial record. Some of Rigney's teams were stuck in the second division and some were contenders. The 1970 Twins team was his most successful. They won the American League West but eventually fell to the Baltimore Orioles. Also a coach and scout, Bill Rigney died in 2001 at the age of 83.

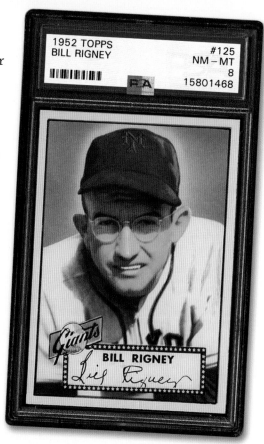

Career Stats

AB:	1,966	HR:	41
R:	281	RBI:	212
H:	510	OPS:	.710
BA:	.259		

Teams

New York Giants NL (1946–1953)

Eddie Robinson

1952 TOPPS #32
EDDIE ROBINSON
NM – MT 8
90187688

A fine first baseman, Eddie Robinson had one heck of a run in Major League Baseball. The four-time All-Star had his greatest success with the Senators and White Sox. Robinson had four 20-home run seasons and often led the league in various defensive categories. He played on the 1948 Indians World Series championship team, batting .300 with six hits in the Series.

After his playing career, Robinson spent 22 years as an executive for the Orioles, Colt .45s, A's, Braves, and Rangers. He then spent 23 years scouting for ten different teams before leaving the game in 2004. In retirement, Robinson was instrumental in getting partial pensions for former players who were not eligible for MLB pensions because they played less than four seasons. He also authored his autobiography *Lucky Me: My Sixty-five Years in Baseball*. At the time of this writing, he is 99 years old.

Career Stats

AB:	4,282	HR:	172
R:	546	RBI:	723
H:	1,146	OPS:	.793
BA:	.268		

Teams
Cleveland Indians AL (1942, 1946–1948, 1957)
Washington Senators AL (1949–1950)
Chicago White Sox AL (1950–1952)
Philadelphia Athletics AL (1953)
New York Yankees AL (1954–1956)
Kansas City Athletics AL (1956)
Detroit Tigers AL (1957)
Baltimore Orioles AL (1957)

Preacher Roe

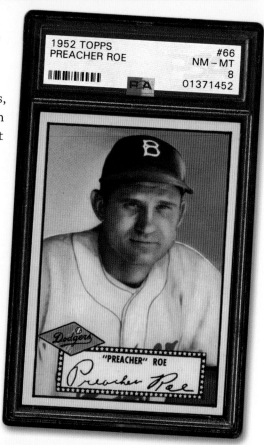

1952 TOPPS #66
PREACHER ROE
NM – MT 8
01371452

One of Brooklyn's "Boys of Summer," Elwin "Preacher" Roe started with the 1938 Cardinals, had a nice run with the Pirates, and hit his stride with the Dodgers. The five-time All-Star took his sweet time on the mound and used a repertoire of fastball, slider, and the illegal spitter. With the Pirates, Roe led the National League with 148 strikeouts in 1945, and he won 22 games for the 1951 Dodgers at age 35. He pitched a gem in Game Two of the 1949 World Series against the Yankees—a complete game six-hit shutout. Roe helped Brooklyn to three pennants and compiled a 2–1 record and 2.54 ERA in the three Series. In retirement, Roe created controversy when he admitted using the spitball, in hopes of getting it legalized. The math teacher, youth baseball coach, and fantasy camp instructor died in 2008 at the age of 92.

Career Stats

Record:	127–84
ERA:	3.43
IP:	1,914.1
Ks:	956
Threw:	LH

Teams
St. Louis Cardinals NL (1938)
Pittsburgh Pirates NL (1944–1947)
Brooklyn Dodgers NL (1948–1954)

Red Rolfe

A New Hampshire native and Dartmouth College grad, Red Rolfe combined brains and baseball throughout his career. Rolfe played ten seasons with the Yankees and was an All-Star from 1937 through 1940. He led the American League in runs, hits, and doubles in 1939, and batted .400 in the 1936 World Series, leading New York to a championship vs. the Giants. Overall, he would win five rings with the Yanks and bat .284 in the postseason. The third baseman and shortstop was part of some of the greatest teams in baseball history, but his battles with colitis cut short a brilliant career in 1942. In 1949, he became manager of the Detroit Tigers and was voted Manager of the Year in 1950. Rolfe returned to Dartmouth College as athletic director in 1954. He settled back home in the Granite State and died in 1969 at age 60.

Career Stats

AB:	4,827	HR:	69
R:	942	RBI:	497
H:	1,394	OPS:	.773
BA:	.289		

Teams

New York Yankees AL (1931, 1934–1942)

Al Rosen

One heck of a ballplayer, Al "The Hebrew Hammer" Rosen left his mark both on the field and in the front office. The four-time All-Star and 1953 AL MVP twice led the league in home runs and was a defensive standout. In 1953, his watershed season, Rosen barely missed winning the Triple Crown, batting .336 with 43 bombs, 145 RBI, and over 200 hits. After injuries cut short Rosen's promising career in 1956, he became a stockbroker. Rosen returned to baseball as President/COO of the 1978 world champion Yankees. He later took the helm of the Houston Astros and was named Major League Executive of the Year in 1987 while President/GM of the San Francisco Giants. Before his baseball career, Lieutenant Rosen saw combat in the Pacific arena during World War II. He retired from the game in 1992 and died in 2015 at age 91.

Career Stats

AB:	3,725	HR:	192
R:	603	RBI:	717
H:	1,063	OPS:	.879
BA:	.285		

Teams

Cleveland Indians AL (1947–1956)

Pete Runnels

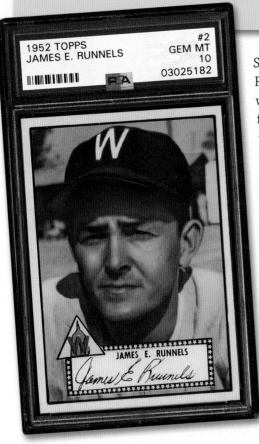

Slap-hitting, All-Star infielder, Pete Runnels was the epitome of a quiet guy who went about his business playing for the Senators, Red Sox, and finally the Colts. A two-time American League batting champ and .291 lifetime hitter, Runnels credited Boston teammate Ted Williams for helping him perfect his hitting stroke. During his five seasons in Boston, Runnels batted .320 and played every infield position. A steady singles hitter, the affable Runnels never hit for power, but he made up for it with his bat control and slick fielding. With his soft Texas drawl and laid-back personality, Pete was well-liked by fellow players and fans. Runnels coached for Boston after his playing days and then returned to Pasadena, Texas, where he owned a successful sporting goods store and gas station. Runnels died of a heart attack in 1991 at age 63, while playing a round of golf.

Career Stats

AB:	6,373	HR:	49
R:	876	RBI:	630
H:	1,854	OPS:	.753
BA:	.291		

Teams

Washington Senators AL (1951–1957)
Boston Red Sox AL (1958–1962)
Houston Colt .45s NL (1963–1964)

Johnny Sain

"Spahn and Sain, and pray for rain" was the mantra in Boston during the Braves' drive to the 1948 pennant. Warren Spahn won 15 games that year, but Johnny Sain dominated, with a league-leading 24 wins and 314 innings pitched. Although he lost three prime years to WWII military service, the 28-year-old Sain returned to post four 20-win seasons between 1946 and 1950 for the Braves. After his days as a starter, the three-time All-Star was a successful relief pitcher with the Yankees. Upon retirement, Sain was a pitching coach for six different teams over a span of nearly 30 years. Renowned for developing talent, Sain coached 16 pitchers to 20-win seasons, and the Tigers' Denny McLain to a 31-win season. Between pitching and coaching, he was involved in six World Series championships. Johnny Sain passed away at the age of 89 in 2006.

"First we'll use Spahn, then we'll use Sain,
Then an off day, followed by rain.
Back will come Spahn, followed by Sain,
And followed, we hope, by two days of rain."

—Gerry Hern, *Boston Post*,
September 14, 1948

Career Stats

Record:	139–116
ERA:	3.49
IP:	2,125.2
Ks:	910
Threw:	RH

Teams

Boston Braves NL (1942, 1946–1951)
New York Yankees AL (1951–1955)
Kansas City Athletics AL (1955)

Hank Sauer

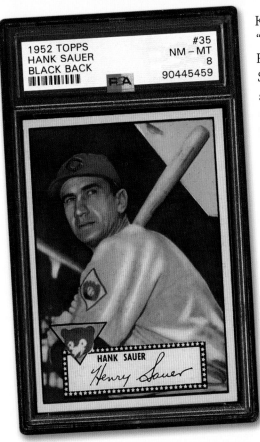

Known as the "Mayor of Wrigley Field," Hank Sauer spent seven seasons with the Chicago Cubs. Those Cubs teams were woeful but Sauer was one of the bright spots, along with future Hall of Famer, Ernie Banks. After switching to a 40-ounce bat in the minors, Sauer got a shot as regular left fielder for Cincinnati in 1948, when he was 31 years old. The power-hitting slugger was NL MVP in 1952, when he led the league with 37 home runs and 121 RBI. A two-time All-Star, he blasted a career-high 41 homers in 1954. Although his glory years were with the Cubs, Sauer also played for the Reds, Cardinals, and Giants, and his 288 career home runs made him a fan favorite. After retiring as a player, Sauer coached and scouted for the Giants until 1993. He died of a heart attack while golfing in 2001 at age 84.

Career Stats

AB:	4,796	HR:	288
R:	709	RBI:	876
H:	1,278	OPS:	.843
BA:	.266		

Teams
Cincinnati Reds NL (1941–1942, 1945, 1948–1949)
Chicago Cubs NL (1949–1955)
St. Louis Cardinals NL (1956)
New York/San Francisco Giants NL (1957–1959)

Andy Seminick

A lunch-pail type of player who hustled every day and laid it on the line for his team, catcher Andy Seminick came up with the Phillies in 1943 and was an All-Star in 1949. In 1950, he delivered his best season, batting .288 with 24 home runs and 68 RBI. More importantly, he led the "Whiz Kid" Phillies to a National League title. In December 1951, Seminick was traded to Cincinnati for Smoky Burgess, among others. In 1955, he was traded back to the Phillies for Smoky Burgess, among others. By fighting through injuries and standing strong as a backstop over 15 seasons, Seminick endeared himself to the baseball faithful. Named the catcher on the Phillies' all-time team in a 1969 fans' vote, Seminick later managed in the minors, coached in the majors, scouted, and was assistant athletic director at Florida Tech. He passed away in 2004 at age 83.

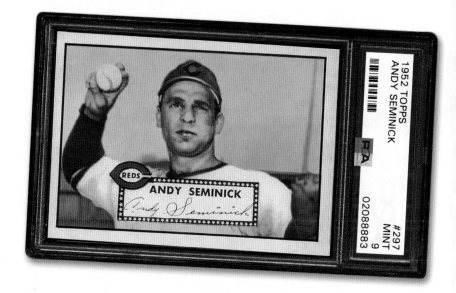

Career Stats

AB:	3,921	HR:	164
R:	495	RBI:	556
H:	953	OPS:	.764
BA:	.243		

Teams
Philadelphia Phillies NL (1943–1951, 1955–1957)
Cincinnati Reds/Redlegs NL (1952–1955)

Bobby Shantz

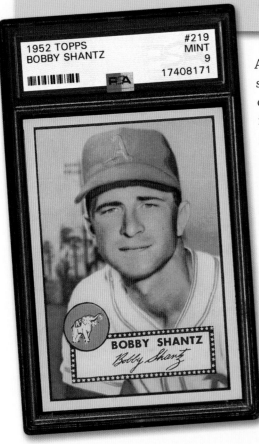

1952 TOPPS
BOBBY SHANTZ
#219
MINT
9
17408171

At 5-foot-6 Bobby Shantz was short on stature but long on talent. He started out with the Athletics, posted 18 wins in 1951, and a league-leading 24 wins in 1952. The three-time All-Star and 1952 American League MVP suffered a shoulder injury in 1953 which hampered him for several seasons. After joining the Yankees, Shantz led the league with his 2.45 ERA in 1957. He appeared in the 1957 and 1960 World Series, but missed the 1958 contest due to injury. The lefty converted to relief pitcher in mid-career and continued to baffle batters with an array of pitches including a pretty nasty knuckleball. A great defensive pitcher, Shantz won eight Gold Gloves during his 16-year career. He is a member of the Philadelphia Baseball Wall of Fame and the Philadelphia Sports Hall of Fame. At the time of this writing, Shantz is 94 years old.

Career Stats

Record:	119–99
ERA:	3.38
IP:	1,935.2
Ks:	1,072
Threw:	LH

Teams

Philadelphia/Kansas City Athletics AL (1949–1956)
New York Yankees AL (1957–1960)
Pittsburgh Pirates NL (1961)
Houston Colt .45s NL (1962)
St. Louis Cardinals NL (1962–1964)
Chicago Cubs NL (1964)
Philadelphia Phillies NL (1964)

Roy Sievers

The 1949 American League Rookie of the Year, Roy Sievers played five seasons for the St. Louis Browns. After moving to the Washington Senators in 1954, Sievers really broke out. He led the AL with 42 home runs and 114 RBI in 1957, and was third in the AL MVP voting behind Mickey Mantle and Ted Williams that year. In 1958, the outfielder and first baseman had another great year, batting .295 and swatting 39 homers. The four-time All-Star had terrific power-hitting seasons with the Senators and White Sox, and while with the Phillies he slammed his 300th home run. He finished up in Washington with the new expansion Senators and retired in 1965. One of those Hall of Fame bubble guys who had great talent, but just not enough to get into Cooperstown, Roy Sievers passed away at the age of 90 in 2017.

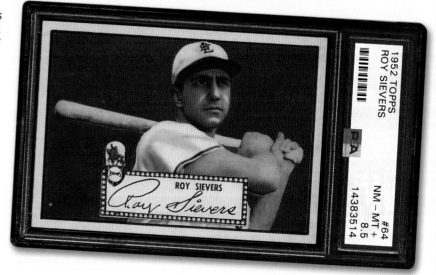

1952 TOPPS
ROY SIEVERS
#64
NM – MT +
8.5
14383514

Career Stats

AB:	6,387	HR:	318
R:	945	RBI:	1,147
H:	1,703	OPS:	.829
BA:	.267		

Teams

St. Louis Browns AL (1949–1953)
Washington Senators AL (1954–1959)
Chicago White Sox AL (1960–1961)
Philadelphia Phillies NL (1962–1964)
Washington Senators AL (1964–1965)

Curt Simmons

A schoolboy star from Egypt, Pennsylvania, Curt Simmons got a $65,000 bonus when the Phillies signed him out of high school. The lefty became an anchor on the Phils teams of the 1950s along with future Hall of Famer, Robin Roberts. Simmons went 17–8 with a 3.40 ERA for the "Whiz Kids" in 1950, but missed the Series because his National Guard unit was activated in August. The three-time All-Star posted an 18–9 record with a 3.43 ERA for the 1964 world champion St. Louis Cardinals and pitched alongside Bob Gibson in the World Series. A tough pitcher and a real workhorse, Curt Simmons pitched successfully for 20 seasons. He retired in 1967 to restore and manage a golf course he bought with Robin Roberts. The 2011 Philadelphia Sports Hall of Fame inductee is 90 years old at the time of this writing.

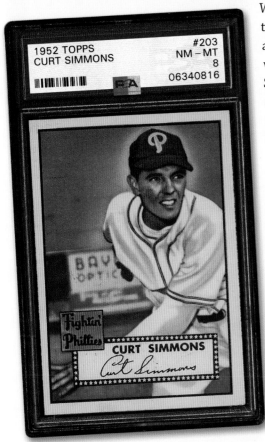

Career Stats

Record:	193–183
ERA:	3.54
IP:	3,348.1
Ks:	1,697
Threw:	LH

Teams

Philadelphia Phillies NL (1947–1950, 1952–1960)
St. Louis Cardinals NL (1960–1966)
Chicago Cubs NL (1966–1967)
California Angels AL (1967)

Gerry Staley

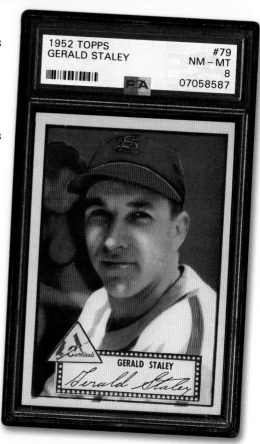

A stalwart pitcher for the St. Louis Cardinals in the late 1940s and early 1950s, Gerry Staley's sinkerball was his "go-to" pitch. His best year for the Cards was 1953, when he went 18–9. Not afraid to brush back hitters, Staley led the league in hit batsmen in 1952 and 1953. After joining the Chicago White Sox in 1956, Staley experienced a rebirth as a reliever. In 1959, he led the American League with 67 appearances, 37 games finished, and 15 saves for the "Go-Go" White Sox, and he pitched in the World Series. An All-Star as both a starter and reliever, Staley compiled a 134–111 record with a tidy 3.70 ERA in 15 MLB seasons. After baseball, he was superintendent of Clark County Parks and Recreation in his home state of Washington for 17 years. He passed away in 2008 at the age of 87.

Career Stats

Record:	134–111
ERA:	3.70
IP:	1,981.2
Ks:	727
Threw:	RH

Teams

St. Louis Cardinals NL (1947–1954)
Cincinnati Redlegs NL (1955)
New York Yankees AL (1955–1956)
Chicago White Sox AL (1956–1961)
Kansas City Athletics AL (1961)
Detroit Tigers AL (1961)

Eddie Stanky

A fiery player, Eddie "The Brat" Stanky used every tactic to win. The scrappy second sacker harassed pitchers, ran the bases aggressively, and argued with umpires while leading the league in walks and hit-by-pitches. Although not a fan of baseball integration, Stanky stood up for teammate Jackie Robinson when he was taunted by racial slurs in 1947. A three-time All-Star, Stanky's aggressive play sparked the 1947 Dodgers, 1948 Braves, and 1951 Giants to National League pennants. As a strict, hard-nosed manager, he delivered 467 combined wins for the Cardinals, White Sox, and Rangers. In his 14 years as head coach for the University of Southern Alabama, Stanky posted a 488–193 record and never had a losing season. Leo Durocher once said, "He can't hit, can't run, can't field. He's no nice guy...all the little SOB can do is win." Stanky died in 1999 at the age of 83.

Career Stats

AB:	4,301	HR:	29
R:	811	RBI:	364
H:	1,154	OPS:	.758
BA:	.268		

Teams

Chicago Cubs NL (1943–1944)
Brooklyn Dodgers NL (1944–1947)
Boston Braves NL (1948–1949)
New York Giants NL (1950–1951)
St. Louis Cardinals NL (1952–1953)

Vern Stephens

Has Red Sox Hall of Famer Vern "Junior" Stephens been overlooked by Cooperstown? The debate continues to this day. A power-hitting shortstop, Stephens' 20 homers and 109 RBI helped the Browns to the 1944 pennant. He led the AL with 24 homers in 1945. After joining Boston in 1948, Stephens slammed a career-high 39 dingers in 1949 and his 159 RBI that year is a single-season record by a shortstop. The eight-time All-Star had six 20-home runs seasons, and paced the league in RBI three times. Very good defensively with a powerful arm, Stephens reputedly enjoyed the nightlife, but he was always ready to play to his potential. Dependable, popular, and well-respected by management, Vern retired in 1955 with 247 career home runs and a .286 BA. A top amateur golfer, Vern died suddenly of a heart attack at the age of 48 in 1968.

Career Stats

AB:	6,497	HR:	247
R:	1,001	RBI:	1,174
H:	1,859	OPS:	.815
BA:	.286		

Teams

St. Louis Browns/Baltimore Orioles AL (1941–1947, 1953–1955)
Boston Red Sox AL (1948–1952)
Chicago White Sox AL (1953, 1955)

Snuffy Stirnweiss

Infielder George "Snuffy" Stirnweiss was called up to the Yankees in 1943 to fill in for Phil Rizzuto and Joe Gordon, who were serving in the military. As starting second sacker in 1944, Stirnweiss batted .319 and led the league in runs, hits, triples, stolen bases, putouts, assists, and fielding percentage. He was league batting champ in 1945 with his .309 BA, again led the AL in runs, hits, triples and stolen bases, and was named an All-Star. When Rizzuto and Gordon returned, Stirnweiss's star started to fade, although he did make the All-Star team in 1946. Stirnweiss played in the 1943, 1947, and 1949 World Series, and won three rings with the Yanks. After retiring in 1952, he managed in the minors, ran a youth baseball program, and worked in banking. Tragically he was killed in a train wreck in 1958, just weeks before his 40th birthday.

Career Stats

AB:	3,695	HR:	29
R:	604	RBI:	281
H:	989	OPS:	.733
BA:	.268		

Teams

New York Yankees AL (1943–1950)
St. Louis Browns AL (1950)
Cleveland Indians AL (1951–1952)

Milt Stock

Infielder Milt Stock enjoyed a 14-year career with the Giants, Phillies, Cardinals, and the Brooklyn Robins. He batted .289, highlighted by four consecutive seasons hitting over .300 (1919–1922). Stock was a key cog in bringing the Phillies to the 1915 World Series, where they lost to the Red Sox. Thirty-five years later, Stock again assisted Philadelphia's drive to the pennant. As the Dodgers third-base coach, Stock sent Cal Abrams home in the ninth inning of the season's pennant-deciding final game. Abrams was tagged out and the Phillies eventually beat Brooklyn for the National League flag. As a boy, Stock also excelled at boxing, basketball, and hockey. When his playing career ended in 1926, he managed for 16 seasons in the minors before taking his vast sports knowledge to the coach's box. Stock died in 1977 at age 84 following coaching stops in the Cubs organization, Brooklyn, and Pittsburgh.

Career Stats

AB:	6,249	HR:	22
R:	839	RBI:	696
H:	1,806	OPS:	.700
BA:	.289		

Teams

New York Giants NL (1913–1914)
Philadelphia Phillies NL (1915–1918)
St. Louis Cardinals NL (1919–1923)
Brooklyn Robins NL (1924–1926)

Clyde Sukeforth

1952 TOPPS
CLYDE SUKEFORTH
#364
MINT
9
17773307

Maine native Clyde Sukeforth broke in with the Reds in 1926 and batted .354 in part-time duty in 1929. Sukeforth was a catcher who understood the big picture of baseball—a strength that benefited him as a groundbreaking scout. In 1931, he suffered severe eye damage in a hunting accident. He was dealt to Brooklyn and his playing career ended in 1934, sort of. In 1945, with MLB rosters depleted by military service, Sukeforth suited up for the Dodgers for 18 games and batted .294 at age 43. With Brooklyn, Sukeforth thrived as a manager, coach, and scout for Branch Rickey. He scouted and mentored Jackie Robinson, and was Brooklyn's interim manager in 1947 when Robinson broke the color barrier. He also signed Roberto Clemente for the Pirates. Sukeforth passed away in 2000 at 98 years old, a grand old baseball man who helped change the game.

Career Stats

AB:	1,237	HR:	2
R:	122	RBI:	96
H:	326	OPS:	.650
BA:	.264		

Teams

Cincinnati Reds NL (1926–1931)
Brooklyn Dodgers NL (1932–1934, 1945)

Birdie Tebbetts

After joining the Tigers in 1936, Birdie Tebbetts worked his way to All-Star status in 1941 and 1942. He then lost three prime big-league seasons to military service. When he returned in 1946, Tebbetts regained his form and made two more All-Star teams in 1948 and 1949 with the Red Sox. The New England native flourished at Fenway, batting .287 in his four years with the BoSox. A sturdy, hard-nosed catcher during his 14 Major League seasons, Tebbetts ended his career with Cleveland in 1952, finishing with a .270 career average and 1,000 hits. The brainy backstop with a philosophy degree from Providence College went on to manage the Redlegs, Braves, and Indians, compiling a 748–705 record over 11 seasons at the helm. A baseball man for life, Tebbetts then managed in the minors and scouted until his retirement in 1992. He died in 1999 at age 86.

1952 TOPPS
BIRDIE TEBBETTS
#282
MINT
9
03025237

Career Stats

AB:	3,704	HR:	38
R:	357	RBI:	469
H:	1,000	OPS:	.700
BA:	.270		

Teams

Detroit Tigers AL (1936–1942, 1946–1947)
Boston Red Sox AL (1947–1950)
Cleveland Indians AL (1951–1952)

Wayne Terwilliger

Wayne "Twig" Terwilliger had an average career offensively, but defensively he was a solid second baseman in his nine Major League seasons. Twig also had a successful run as a minor-league manager, working for several different organizations and finishing with a 1224–1089 record. He took a couple of lengthy breaks in his managing career to work as third-base coach for the Washington Senators/Texas Rangers and as first-base coach for the Minnesota Twins. There he won two World Series championships (1987 and 1991). Along the way, he coached for the likes of Ted Williams, Don Zimmer, and Bobby Valentine. A real baseball guy, Wayne Terwilliger worked more than 60 years in the game, managing well into his 80s. A 2003 inductee to the Texas Baseball Hall of Fame, Terwilliger published his autobiography entitled *Terwilliger Bunts One* in 2006. At the time of this writing, he is 94 years old.

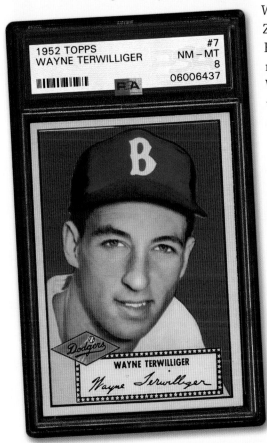

Career Stats

AB:	2,091	HR:	22
R:	271	RBI:	162
H:	501	OPS:	.648
BA:	.240		

Teams

Chicago Cubs NL (1949–1951)
Brooklyn Dodgers NL (1951)
Washington Senators AL (1953–1954)
New York Giants NL (1955–1956)
Kansas City Athletics AL (1959–1960)

Hank Thompson

One of the pioneers to transition from the Negro Leagues to the Major Leagues, Hank Thompson became a steady, reliable player for the New York Giants after his "cup of coffee" with the St. Louis Browns. The first African American to play for the Browns and the Giants, Thompson was also the first African American to play in both the American League and the National League. In fact, Thompson, along with Monte Irvin and Willie Mays, comprised the first all-black outfield in Major League history. Not just a trailblazer, Thompson was a good ballplayer, with the highlight of his career being the 1954 Giants championship season. After his career, Thompson fell on hard times, spent time in prison for armed robbery, and turned his life around to work with troubled kids as a playground director. He died suddenly from a heart attack in 1969 at the young age of 43.

Career Stats

AB:	3,003	HR:	129
R:	492	RBI:	482
H:	801	OPS:	.825
BA:	.267		

Teams

St. Louis Browns AL (1947)
New York Giants NL (1949–1956)

Bobby Thomson

Most people would not like to have their lives defined by one moment, but most people did not win the 1951 National League pennant against an arch-rival team with one colossal swing of a bat. Bobby Thomson's three-run bottom of the ninth "Shot Heard 'Round the World" off Brooklyn's Ralph Branca at the Polo Grounds remains a seminal baseball moment, but Thomson himself did much more. Born in Glasgow, Scotland, Thomson's family eventually settled in Staten Island. He played for five teams and was a three-time All-Star, clouting 264 career homers. In 1954, Thomson had a Wally Pipp moment when an ankle injury allowed a rookie named Henry Aaron to break into the Milwaukee Braves lineup. A sales executive after baseball, Thomson sadly lost both his wife and son in 1993, but he continued to make personal appearances, many with Branca. Thomson died in 2010 at age 86.

Career Stats

AB:	6,305	HR:	264
R:	903	RBI:	1,026
H:	1,705	OPS:	.794
BA:	.270		

Teams

New York Giants NL (1946–1953, 1957)

Milwaukee Braves NL (1954–1957)

Chicago Cubs NL (1958–1959)

Boston Red Sox AL (1960)

Baltimore Orioles AL (1960)

Dizzy Trout

A two-time All-Star, Dizzy Trout had some darn good seasons with the Tigers. He won 82 games in four seasons (1943–1946), with the high water mark being his 27 wins in 1944. That year, Trout led the league with his sparkling 2.12 ERA, 352 innings pitched, 33 complete games, and seven shutouts. In 1943, he paced the NL with 20 wins. Trout pitched in both the 1940 and 1945 World Series. In Game Four of the 1945 Series, he nailed a 4–1 complete game win, helping Detroit to the championship. Trout also had a good stick for a pitcher, socking 20 career home runs. After posting nine wins for the Red Sox in 1952, Trout retired. His 1957 comeback attempt in Baltimore was not successful. He became a Tigers broadcaster and later ran the White Sox speakers bureau. Dizzy Trout passed away in 1972 at age 56.

Career Stats

Record:	170–161
ERA:	3.23
IP:	2,725.2
Ks:	1,256
Threw:	RH

Teams

Detroit Tigers AL (1939–1952)

Boston Red Sox AL (1952)

Baltimore Orioles AL (1957)

Virgil Trucks

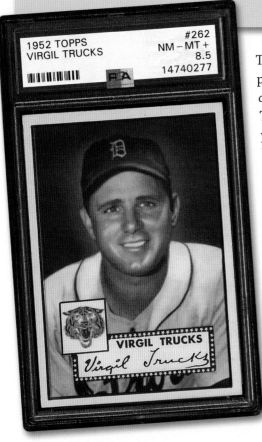

The ultimate workhorse, Virgil Trucks played 17 seasons for five teams. His career highlight was with Detroit in 1952. Trucks posted a dismal 5–19 record that year, but on August 25, he no-hit the Yankees for his second no-hitter of the season. The hard-throwing Alabama native pitched over 2,600 innings and saw the ups and downs of mound life. He won 16 games in 1943, lost 13 in 1948, and won 20 in 1953. Trucks joined the US Navy in 1944 and just days after his 1945 release, he won the pennant-clinching game for Detroit. He won Game Two of the 1945 Series helping the Tigers to the championship. The 1949 All-Star made the All-Star team again with the White Sox in 1954 at age 37. In retirement, Trucks pitched Pirates batting practice, coached, scouted, and had various business interests. He passed away in 2013 at age 95.

Career Stats

Record:	177–135
ERA:	3.39
IP:	2,682.1
Ks:	1,534
Threw:	RH

Teams

Detroit Tigers AL (1941–1943,
1945–1952, 1956)
St. Louis Browns AL (1953)
Chicago White Sox AL (1953–1955)
Kansas City Athletics AL (1957–1958)
New York Yankees AL (1958)

Mickey Vernon

One of the true gentlemen of the game, seven-time All-Star Mickey Vernon was a solid, durable first baseman who played 20 MLB seasons, 14 of them with the Washington Senators. He joined the Senators in 1939 and missed 1944 and 1945 to US Navy service. When he returned to Washington in 1946, Vernon batted .353 with 207 hits to win his first batting title. Seven years later, in 1953, he batted .337 with 205 hits to earn his second batting crown. The skillful first sacker led the league in doubles three times and in fielding percentage four times. In 1961, Vernon became the first manager of the expansion Washington Senators, posting a 135–227 record in nearly three seasons. He coached, managed in the minors, and scouted until retiring in 1988 after 50 years in the game. Vernon passed away in 2008 at the age of 90.

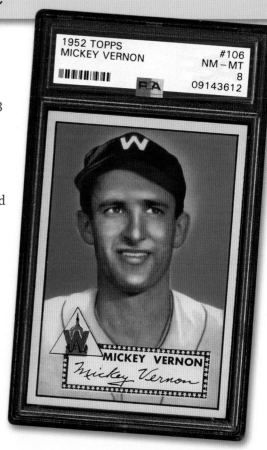

Career Stats

AB:	8,731	HR:	172
R:	1,196	RBI:	1,311
H:	2,495	OPS:	.787
BA:	.286		

Teams

Washington Senators AL (1939–1943, 1946–1948,
1950–1955)
Cleveland Indians AL (1949–1950, 1958)
Boston Red Sox AL (1956–1957)
Milwaukee Braves NL (1959)
Pittsburgh Pirates NL (1960)

Eddie Waitkus

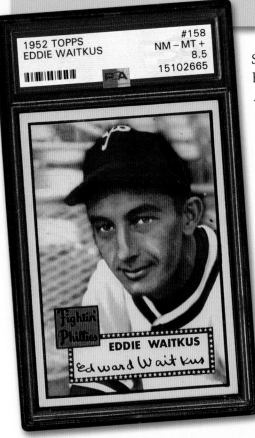

1952 TOPPS #158
EDDIE WAITKUS NM – MT + 8.5
15102665

Slick-fielding first baseman Eddie Waitkus batted .295 for the Cubs and made the All-Star team in 1948. The handsome man about town was an All-Star again in 1949 when he batted .306 for the Phillies, but an event on June 14 changed everything. That evening, Waitkus was shot in the chest by an obsessed female fan. Severely wounded, it took four operations and hard work on his part to fully recover. Unbelievably, he returned to the Phillies as starting first sacker in 1950. Waitkus was a big part of the "Whiz Kids" NL pennant-winning season and played in all four games of the Series loss to the Yankees. His experience was the inspiration for the Roy Hobbs character in the movie *The Natural*. After baseball, Waitkus worked in sales and taught at the Ted Williams Baseball Camp. The WWII US Army veteran died from cancer at the age of 53.

Career Stats

AB:	4,254	HR:	24
R:	528	RBI:	373
H:	1,214	OPS:	.718
BA:	.285		

Teams

Chicago Cubs NL (1941, 1946–1948)
Philadelphia Phillies NL (1949–1953, 1955)
Baltimore Orioles AL (1954–1955)

Rube Walker

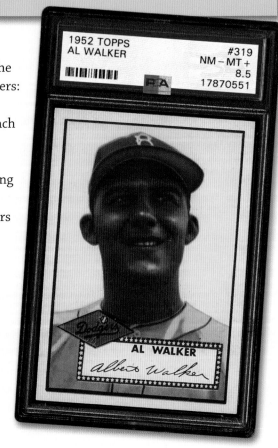

1952 TOPPS
AL WALKER #319
NM – MT + 8.5
17870551

It could be said that in baseball lore, one of the smartest guys on the field was a Rube. A steady 6-foot, 175-pound catcher, Rube Walker played 11 seasons with the Cubs and Dodgers. A so-so hitter, Walker served as backup to two excellent catchers: All-Star Mickey Owen, in Chicago, and future Hall of Famer Roy Campanella, in Brooklyn. After his playing days, he managed in the minors, and was pitching coach for the Senators, Mets, and Braves. Hired by his old Dodgers buddy Gil Hodges, Walker developed the pitching staff of the Amazin' 1969 World Champion Mets, mentoring the young arms of Tom Seaver, Jerry Koosman, and Nolan Ryan, among others. Called "a pitcher's pitching coach" by Seaver, Walker initiated a five-man rotation, and imparted baseball wisdom that belied his first name. He was 66 years old when he died of lung cancer in 1992.

Career Stats

AB:	1,585	HR:	35
R:	114	RBI:	192
H:	360	OPS:	.635
BA:	.227		

Teams

Chicago Cubs NL (1948–1951)
Brooklyn/Los Angeles Dodgers NL (1951–1958)

Bob Wellman

With the Philadelphia A's for the proverbial cup of coffee, Bob Wellman had a grand total of 25 at-bats as a Major League ballplayer. However, Wellman's career as a manager was quite different. Over his 25-year span as a minor-league manager, Wellman ripped off more than 1,600 victories. He managed in the Cincinnati Reds farm system for five years, from 1955 through 1959. Wellman then managed minor-league teams for the Philadelphia Phillies from 1961 through 1976, and the New York Mets from 1977 through 1980. His 1966 Spartanburg Phillies won 25 games in a row and were league champs.

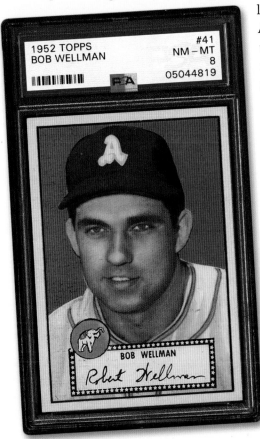

After wrapping up his successful minor-league management career, Bob became a scout for the New York Mets. Although his days as a player were not very successful, his contribution to developing young players was outstanding. Bob Wellman passed away in 1994 at the age of 69.

Career Stats

AB:	25	HR:	1
R:	2	RBI:	1
H:	7	OPS:	.837
BA:	.280		

Teams
Philadelphia Athletics AL (1948, 1950)

Vic Wertz

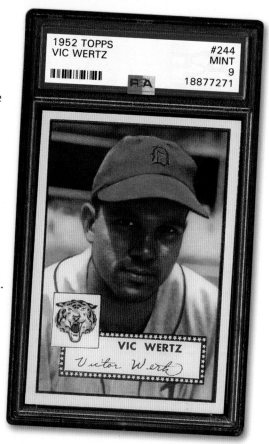

Four-time All-Star Vic Wertz played 17 seasons and hit .277 with 266 home runs and 1,178 RBI, but he is most remembered for something that someone else did. Playing for Cleveland in Game One of the 1954 World Series vs. the Giants, Wertz smashed a fly ball to the Polo Grounds' cavernous centerfield. Giants centerfielder Willie Mays made an impossible over the shoulder catch, today known simply as "The Catch." Wertz actually had four hits in that game, but Mays got the glory, New York won the Series, and Wertz unfairly became a footnote. The right fielder and first baseman hit over 20 homers six times, had more than 100 RBI five times, and was consistently productive into his mid-30s. A US Army veteran, Wertz settled in Michigan, prospered in the beer distributor business, and volunteered with Special Olympics. He died during heart surgery in 1983 at age 58.

Career Stats

AB:	6,099	HR:	266
R:	867	RBI:	1,178
H:	1,692	OPS:	.833
BA:	.277		

Teams
Detroit Tigers AL (1947–1952, 1961–1963)
St. Louis Browns/Baltimore Orioles AL (1952–1954)
Cleveland Indians AL (1954–1958)
Boston Red Sox AL (1959–1961)
Minnesota Twins AL (1963)

Wes Westrum

1952 TOPPS #75
WES WESTRUM
NM – MT 8
05052406

One of the best defensive backstops of the era, Wes Westrum caught 902 games for the New York Giants over his 11-year career. With his .999 fielding percentage in 1950, Westrum set a record for National League catchers which stood until 1997. Despite his .217 lifetime batting average, Westrum had some power, banging out 23 homers in 1950 and 20 in 1951. Because of his outstanding defensive skills and leadership abilities, the two-time All-Star was an integral part of the Giants' 1951 and 1954 NL pennant wins. Westrum was behind the plate for all six games of the 1951 Series loss to the crosstown Yankees and all four games of the 1954 Series sweep of Cleveland. After his brilliant career, Westrum remained part of Major League Baseball for many years as coach, manager, and scout. He passed away in 2002 at the age of 79.

Career Stats

AB:	2,322	HR:	96
R:	302	RBI:	315
H:	503	OPS:	.729
BA:	.217		

Teams

New York Giants NL (1947–1957)

Sammy White

Sammy White was steady and consistent as a Red Sox catcher from 1951 through 1959. The 1953 All-Star's best season was 1954 when he batted .282 with 14 homers and 75 RBI. One of the best catchers in baseball, White was respected by teammates and opponents alike. He framed pitches brilliantly and was a true field general. Before his MLB days, White served in the Naval Reserve and was a University of Washington baseball and hoops star. In 1952, he famously hit a walk-off grand slam off of the legendary Satchel Paige.

1952 TOPPS #345
SAM WHITE
MINT 9
16674280

While with Boston, White tried to start a touring basketball team of Major Leaguers and even owned a bowling alley. After short stints with the Braves and Phillies, White left baseball in 1962. He worked as a golf pro in Hawaii with his former batterymate, Frank Sullivan, and died there in 1991 at age 64.

Career Stats

AB:	3,502	HR:	66
R:	324	RBI:	421
H:	916	OPS:	.682
BA:	.262		

Teams

Boston Red Sox AL (1951–1959)
Milwaukee Braves NL (1961)
Philadelphia Phillies NL (1962)

Gene Woodling

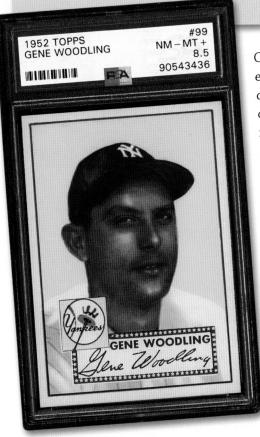

1952 TOPPS
GENE WOODLING
#99
NM – MT +
8.5
90543436

One of the best journeyman ballplayers ever, Gene Woodling played for six different teams over his 17-year MLB career. After a call-up by Cleveland in 1943, the Ohio native honed his baseball skills for two seasons in the US Navy. A clutch hitter, the one-time All-Star played on five consecutive world championship Yankees teams (1949–1953), batting .318 in the postseason. His best season, however, was 1957 when Woodling batted a lofty .321 with 19 home runs for the Cleveland Indians. With his excellent offensive and defensive skills, the left fielder hit over .300 five times in his career and led the league in several defensive categories. A member of the Baltimore Orioles Hall of Fame, Woodling later coached for the Orioles, scouted for the Yankees and the Indians, and had a sales career outside of baseball. Gene Woodling died in 2001 at the age of 78.

Career Stats

AB:	5,587	HR:	147
R:	830	RBI:	830
H:	1,585	OPS:	.817
BA:	.284		

Teams

Cleveland Indians AL (1943, 1946, 1955–1957)
Pittsburgh Pirates NL (1947)
New York Yankees AL (1949–1954)
Baltimore Orioles AL (1955, 1958–1960)
Washington Senators AL (1961–1962)
New York Mets NL (1962)

Johnny Wyrostek

Two-time All-Star Johnny Wyrostek had a solid career as both a ballplayer and later as a politician. The popular outfielder always went about his business in a professional, quiet manner. Signed by the Cardinals right out of high school, Wyrostek played in their farm system until the Pirates acquired him in 1941. He saw Major League action for the Pirates, playing 60 games in two seasons. A decent hitter and fielder, Wyrostek had some good seasons with the Phillies and Reds and lasted in the majors for 11 seasons. After being released in 1954, Wyrostek returned to his hometown of Fairmont City, Illinois. There he was deputy sheriff, a union carpenter, and president of the local union. He served on the city council and was then elected mayor for five terms. He was serving as mayor when he passed away in 1986 at age 67.

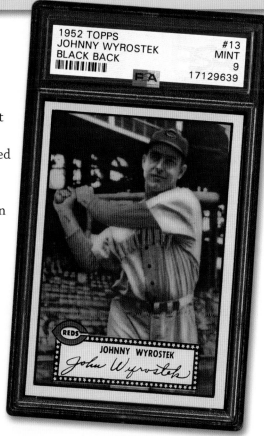

1952 TOPPS
JOHNNY WYROSTEK
BLACK BACK
#13
MINT
9
17129639

Career Stats

AB:	4,240	HR:	58
R:	525	RBI:	481
H:	1,149	OPS:	.731
BA:	.271		

Teams

Pittsburgh Pirates NL (1942–1943)
Philadelphia Phillies NL (1946–1947, 1952–1954)
Cincinnati Reds NL (1948–1952)

Eddie Yost

1952 TOPPS #123
EDDIE YOST MINT 9
04042024

In addition to "The Walking Man," Eddie Yost could have been nicknamed "Steady Eddie." A fine third baseman, Yost spent 14 years of his 18-year career with the Washington Senators. The green 17-year-old rookie joined the Senators in 1944, served in the US Navy, settled back in at age 20, and never looked back. Patient at the plate, "The Walking Man" led the league in walks six times, and he still ranks in the top 15 on the all-time walks list. The 1952 All-Star was an excellent leadoff man and defensive third baseman. Yost led the league in putouts eight times and paced the league in assists, double plays, and fielding percentage several times. After his playing career, Yost coached 22 years for the Senators, Mets, and Red Sox, winning a ring with the 1969 Miracle Mets. Eddie Yost passed away in 2012 at the age of 86.

Career Stats

AB:	7,346	HR:	139
R:	1,215	RBI:	682
H:	1,863	OPS:	.765
BA:	.254		

Teams

Washington Senators AL (1944, 1946–1958)
Detroit Tigers AL (1959–1960)
Los Angeles Angels AL (1961–1962)

Gus Zernial

A solid player from the 1952 Topps group, Gus "Ozark Ike" Zernial was a feared home run hitter who was initially referred to as the "New Joe DiMaggio." Even though Zernial never quite reached that level, he was an outstanding player for the White Sox and Athletics. Zernial led the American League with 33 home runs and 129 RBI in 1951 but interestingly did not make the All-Star team that year. His best year offensively was 1953 when he socked 42 homers with 108 RBI and made his only All-Star appearance. No slouch defensively, Zernial was an extremely aggressive outfielder who made such spectacular catches that he actually injured himself on several occasions. After retiring, he was a broadcaster for the Fresno Grizzlies and Fresno State University. Zernial was elected to the Philadelphia Baseball Wall of Fame in 2001. He died in 2011 at age 87.

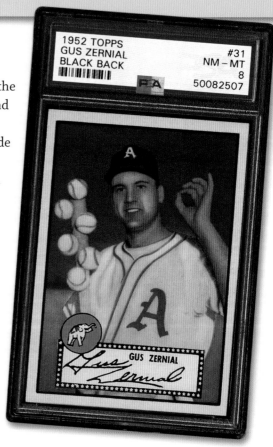

1952 TOPPS #31
GUS ZERNIAL
BLACK BACK NM – MT 8
50082507

Career Stats

AB:	4,131	HR:	237
R:	572	RBI:	776
H:	1,093	OPS:	.815
BA:	.265		

Teams

Chicago White Sox AL (1949–1951)
Philadelphia/Kansas City Athletics AL (1951–1957)
Detroit Tigers AL (1958–1959)

The Commons

In this great country, the foundation of our very economic existence revolves around the common worker. Whether it is the laborer, office worker, truck driver, middle manager, or restaurant server, no business would exist without the backbone of America's great workforce. The same holds true in the game of baseball. Without the "Commons," the players who went about their jobs without much fanfare, there would be no National Pastime. These were the utility players, unheralded starters, and the pitchers and position players, many of whom came up for the proverbial cup of coffee. Some of them had good seasons, some not so good. Without them, Major League Baseball would not exist. Meet the "Commons" of the 1952 Topps Collection.

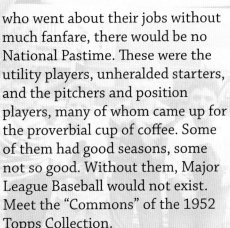

Cal Abrams

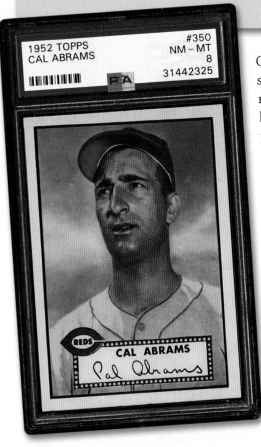

1952 TOPPS #350
CAL ABRAMS
NM – MT 8
31442325

Outfielder Cal Abrams played eight seasons in the Bigs and batted a respectable .269, but in Dodgers annals, he will always be remembered for one play. On the final day of the 1950 season, the Dodgers and Phillies were knotted at 1–1 with Brooklyn in need of a win to force a one-game playoff for the pennant. Abrams was the first batter in the bottom of the ninth and walked. He was sent home on a subsequent single by Duke Snider and was pegged at the plate by outfielder Richie Ashburn. The Dodgers eventually lost the game and pennant to the Whiz Kids. Born in Philly, Abrams grew up in Brooklyn, and was signed by the Dodgers out of high school. A decorated WWII US Army veteran before his Major League debut, Abrams died in 1997, at age 72, and was buried in his Dodgers uniform.

Career Stats

AB:	1,611	HR:	32
R:	257	RBI:	138
H:	433	OPS:	.778
BA:	.269		

Teams

Brooklyn Dodgers NL (1949–1952)
Cincinnati Reds NL (1952)
Pittsburgh Pirates NL (1953–1954)
Baltimore Orioles AL (1954–1955)
Chicago White Sox AL (1956)

Bobby Adams

Infielder Bobby Adams played 14 seasons in the majors and led the National League in games played and at-bats in 1952. That season, he batted .283 with 48 RBI for the Reds. Adams played ten years in Cincy, from 1946 to 1955, followed by stints with the White Sox, Orioles, and Cubs. He had 188 career doubles and a career batting average of .269. Adams served in the US Army Air Force during World War II and played military ball with future Hall of Famers Joe DiMaggio and Enos Slaughter. His brother Dick and son Mike were also Major Leaguers. After his MLB career ended in 1959, Bobby Adams joined the Cubs as a coach, managed in the minors, and later became the president of the Pacific Coast League's Tacoma Cubs. The California native spent his life in baseball and passed away at the age of 75 in 1997.

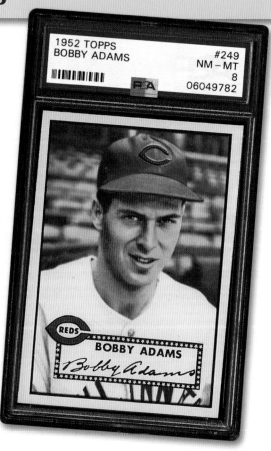

1952 TOPPS
BOBBY ADAMS
#249
NM – MT 8
06049782

Career Stats

AB:	4,019	HR:	37
R:	591	RBI:	303
H:	1,082	OPS:	.708
BA:	.269		

Teams

Cincinnati Reds/Redlegs NL (1946–1955)
Chicago White Sox AL (1955)
Baltimore Orioles AL (1956)
Chicago Cubs NL (1957–1959)

Bob Addis

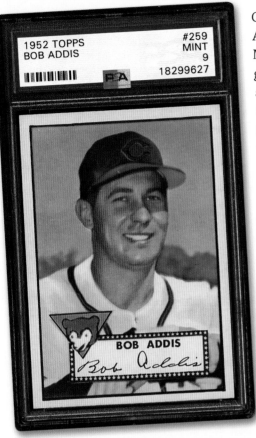

Outfielder Bob Addis played 208 Major League games in four seasons, but he is best known for one single play. Late in the 1951 season, the Dodgers and Giants were engaged in an historic pennant race. Addis, playing for the Boston Braves against Brooklyn, raced home on teammate Earl Torgeson's grounder to second base.

Addis slid past Roy Campanella's tag, beating Jackie Robinson's throw home. The controversial safe call by umpire Frank Dascoli led the Dodgers to an eventual playoff with the Giants, who won the pennant on Bobby Thomson's famous home run. Addis went on to play for the Cubs and Pirates. While he contributed to one of baseball's greatest postseasons, Addis himself never saw the light of a World Series. He became a teacher, coach, and athletic director at Euclid High School in Ohio. The WWII veteran passed away in Mentor, Ohio, in 2016 at age 91.

Career Stats

AB:	534	HR:	2
R:	70	RBI:	47
H:	150	OPS:	.668
BA:	.281		

Teams

Boston Braves NL (1950–1951)

Chicago Cubs NL (1952–1953)

Pittsburgh Pirates NL (1953)

Luis Aloma

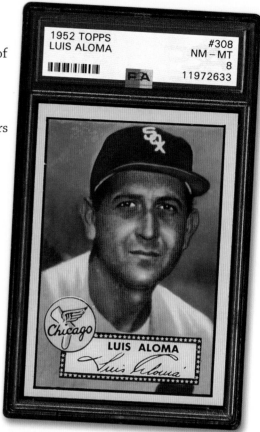

Havana, Cuba, native Luis Aloma compiled an impressive record of 18–3 for the Chicago White Sox in four seasons. Originally drafted by the Senators in 1944, Aloma pitched in their farm system until 1949, when he was shipped to Detroit and then to the ChiSox, where he made his debut in 1950 at age 26. Aloma posted a perfect 6–0 mark in 1951 with an ERA of 1.82 and three saves. His solid career ERA of 3.44 was tempered with a mediocre strikeout-to-walk ratio of 115 to 111. Aloma could also swing the lumber, batting .350 for the White Sox in 1951. Bursitis caused his retirement after the 1953 season. In the end, Aloma's career was like a low-cost cigar from his native Cuba. He took a while to ignite, had some nice moments along the way, but burned out too soon. He died in 1997 at age 73.

Career Stats

Record:	18–3
ERA:	3.44
IP:	235.1
Ks:	115
Threw	RH

Teams

Chicago White Sox AL (1950–1953)

Hank Arft

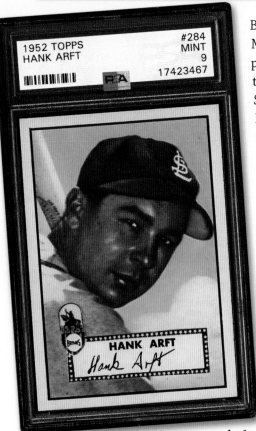

Born and bred in Missouri, Hank Arft played five seasons for the lowly hometown St. Louis Browns. His career began in fantastic fashion in 1948—a triple and homer in his debut vs. the Yanks, a 12-game hitting streak, and 23-game on-base streak, pretty heady stuff for a rookie. The part-time first baseman batted .268 in 1950 with 32 RBI and 16 doubles. A US Navy veteran, Arft bounced around the minors before and after his stint in St. Louis. The Browns never finished higher than sixth place with Arft on the roster, often approaching or surpassing the 100-loss mark, but his time with the lifeless franchise was fitting preparation for his post-baseball career. He and his wife became co-owners of a funeral home in Ballwin, Missouri. Arft remained active with MLB Alumni events and numerous civic organizations until his death in 2002 at age 80.

Career Stats

AB:	906	HR:	13
R:	116	RBI:	118
H:	229	OPS:	.727
BA:	.253		

Teams
St. Louis Browns AL (1948–1952)

Joe Astroth

Catcher Joe Astroth played ten MLB seasons, all with the Athletics. He made his debut in 1945 and accompanied the team when they moved to Kansas City a decade later. Before professional baseball, he played football, baseball, and basketball at the University of Illinois, and served in the US Coast Guard from 1942 to 1945. A solid backup catcher with a keen eye at the plate, Astroth batted .327 with 18 RBI in 39 games in 1950. Three years later, he hit .296 with a career-high three home runs and 15 doubles. Astroth was managed by a pair of Hall of Famers: Connie Mack in Philadelphia and Lou Boudreau in Kansas City. After baseball, he owned a bowling alley and a dairy bar, and he also worked in sales for General Copper & Brass Company. He remained active in numerous charity golf events until his death in 2013 at age 90.

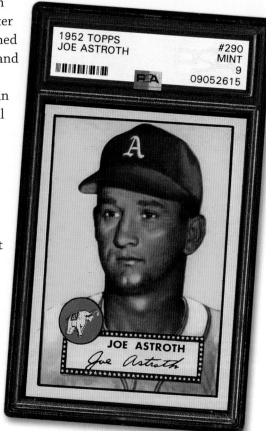

Career Stats

AB:	1,579	HR:	13
R:	163	RBI:	156
H:	401	OPS:	.658
BA:	.254		

Teams
Philadelphia/Kansas City Athletics AL
(1945–1956)

Toby Atwell

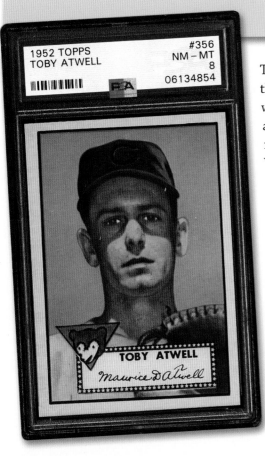

1952 TOPPS #356
TOBY ATWELL NM – MT 8
06134854

Toby Atwell was a rookie All-Star with the Cubs in 1952, batting .290. He would never again reach those heights although he did bat .289 in 96 games for the Pirates in 1954. The Leesburg, Virginia, native and quarterback for Virginia Polytechnic Institute served three years in the US Army Air Force before Brooklyn signed him in 1946. He languished in the Dodgers farm system until the Cubs acquired the 28-year-old catcher in 1952. The next year, Atwell was traded to Pittsburgh for, among others, future Hall of Famer Ralph Kiner, and future baseball broadcasting icon, Joe Garagiola. Atwell also played for the Milwaukee Braves. In his five-year Major League career, the backup catcher batted .260 with just nine home runs and 110 RBI. His statistics in life were much more prolific, with ten children, 19 grandchildren, and several great-grandchildren. Toby Atwell died in 2003 at age 78.

Career Stats

AB:	1,117	HR:	9
R:	116	RBI:	110
H:	290	OPS:	.688
BA:	.260		

Teams

Chicago Cubs NL (1952–1953)
Pittsburgh Pirates NL (1953–1956)
Milwaukee Braves NL (1956)

Floyd Baker

In his 13-year big-league career, Virginia native Floyd Baker had nearly 2,300 at-bats and exactly one home run. That singular dinger came on May 4, 1949. Playing for the White Sox, Baker slugged a two-run shot in the fourth inning off of Senator Sid Hudson. The blast gave Chicago a 7–0 lead, but they lost the game 8–7. A solid infielder, Baker's best hitting season was in 1950, when he batted .317 in 83 games. He broke in with the Browns in 1943 and would also play for the Senators, Red Sox, and Phillies. Baker had two at-bats in the 1944 World Series for the Browns but struck out, and the Browns eventually lost the Series to the rival Cardinals. After baseball, Baker coached and scouted until 1995. He was active in numerous organizations in Youngstown, Ohio, until his death in 2004 at age 88.

1952 TOPPS #292
FLOYD BAKER MINT 9
07024211

Career Stats

AB:	2,280	HR:	1
R:	285	RBI:	196
H:	573	OPS:	.658
BA:	.251		

Teams

St. Louis Browns AL (1943–1944)
Chicago White Sox AL (1945–1951)
Washington Senators AL (1952–1953)
Boston Red Sox AL (1953–1954)
Philadelphia Phillies NL (1954–1955)

Tony Bartirome

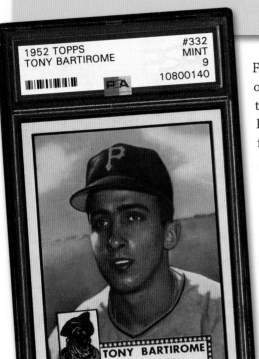

1952 TOPPS #332
TONY BARTIROME
MINT 9
10800140

First baseman Tony Bartirome, a native of Pittsburgh, began at the wet-behind-the-ears age of 19 with his hometown Pirates in 1952. He played in 124 games for the Bucs, but hit just .220 in his only Major League season. Discovered by Hall of Famer Pie Traynor, Bartirome plied his trade on the hardscrabble fields and vacant lots of the Steel City. After that one season, Bartirome served in the US Army until 1955 and returned to play in the minors through 1963. He was the Pirates trainer for nearly two decades, helping them to World Series wins in 1971 and 1979. Bartirome coached for the Atlanta Braves from 1986 through 1988 and then retired to Bradenton, Florida, where he passed away in 2018 at 86 years old. His obituary hailed him as perhaps the only man in MLB history to serve as a player, coach, and trainer.

Career Stats

AB:	355	HR:	0
R:	32	RBI:	16
H:	78	OPS:	.538
BA:	.220		

Teams
Pittsburgh Pirates NL (1952)

Monty Basgall

Second baseman Romanus "Monty" Basgall only played 200 games in the majors and hovered just above the Mendoza line as a hitter. However, Monty Basgall the coach was quite another story. In addition to his three Major League seasons, Basgall spent 13 years in the minors, the last three as player-manager. He then scouted for the Los Angeles Dodgers and managed in their farm organization before starting his notable coaching career in 1973. As assistant coach, bench coach, and first-base coach under both Walter Alston and Tommy Lasorda, Basgall was involved in two National League Championship Series and four World Series, with the Dodgers winning the World Series Championship in 1981. After more than 40 years in baseball, Basgall retired to the golf course in 1986. He passed away at the age of 83 in 2005.

Career Stats

AB:	512	HR:	4
R:	52	RBI:	41
H:	110	OPS:	.561
BA:	.215		

Teams
Pittsburgh Pirates NL (1948–1949, 1951)

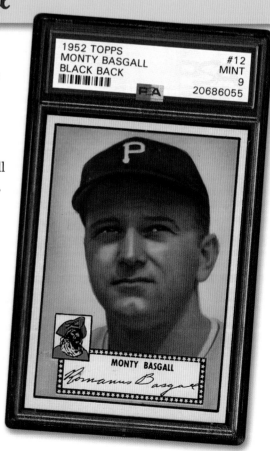

1952 TOPPS
MONTY BASGALL
BLACK BACK
#12
MINT 9
20686055

Matt Batts

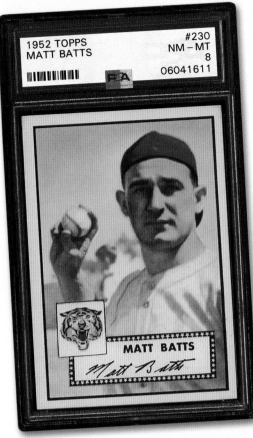

With one of the greatest baseball names in history, Matt Batts played a decade in the majors with the Red Sox, Browns, Tigers, White Sox, and Redlegs. Perhaps he moved around so much because of his value. Batts was a sturdy backup catcher who could handle a pitching staff and contribute key hits. He batted .269 for his career. Batts broke in with the Red Sox in 1947, batting .500 in 16 at-bats. The next year, he hit .314 in 46 games. The 5-foot-11, 200-pound Texan was the son of a firefighter and set the Texas high-school record in javelin. Batts was a sergeant in the US Army and served stateside during World War II. After his baseball career ended in 1956, he settled in Baton Rouge, Louisiana, counseled juvenile offenders, and ran the family printing business. Batts passed away in 2013 at age 91.

Career Stats

AB:	1,605	HR:	26
R:	163	RBI:	219
H:	432	OPS:	.720
BA:	.269		

Teams
Boston Red Sox AL (1947–1951)
St. Louis Browns AL (1951)
Detroit Tigers AL (1952–1954)
Chicago White Sox AL (1954)
Cincinnati Redlegs NL (1955–1956)

Ted Beard

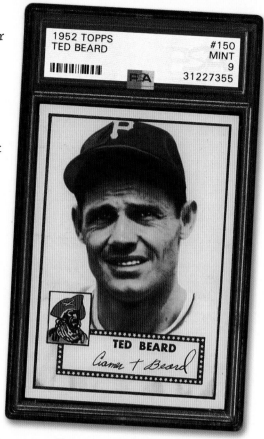

Between the majors and minors, outfielder Ted Beard played professional baseball for 19 seasons. After one minor-league season, Beard served three years as a medic in the US Army, spending part of that time in active service in the Pacific. He made it to the Bigs in 1948 with the Pirates but had limited success in his seven big-league seasons. He retired in 1958 with 474 MLB at-bats and never got over the Mendoza line as a Major Leaguer. A minor-league player for most of his pro career, Beard spent the majority of that time with the AAA Indianapolis Indians, where he was also a player-manager in 1960. After his playing days, Beard settled in Indiana, coached several years for Indianapolis, and later worked for the State of Indiana Highway Department. He lived to the age of 90 and passed away in 2011.

Career Stats

AB:	474	HR:	6
R:	80	RBI:	35
H:	94	OPS:	.600
BA:	.198		

Teams
Pittsburgh Pirates NL (1948–1952)
Chicago White Sox AL (1957–1958)

Vern Bickford

1952 TOPPS #252
VERN BICKFORD
NM – MT 8
11221326
P.S.A.

US Army veteran Vern Bickford made his debut in 1948 with the National League champion Boston Braves. The rookie went 0–1 in the World Series loss to Cleveland. Bickford was an All-Star in 1949, posting a 16–11 record despite surrendering 20 home runs and more hits than innings pitched. The ultimate workhorse and innings-eater, Bickford had a career-high 19 wins in 1950, highlighted by a no-hitter against the Dodgers. That season, he led the NL in games started, complete games, and innings pitched, and came in a close third to teammates Warren Spahn and Johnny Sain, who won 21 and 20 games respectively. Born in Kentucky and raised in Virginia, Bickford specialized in the changeup and slider. He moved to Milwaukee with the Braves in 1953 and finished his career the next season with Baltimore. After baseball, Bickford worked several jobs and sadly succumbed to cancer at age 39 in 1960.

Career Stats

Record:	66–57
ERA:	3.71
IP:	1,076.1
Ks:	450
Threw:	RH

Teams

Boston/Milwaukee Braves NL (1948–1953)
Baltimore Orioles AL (1954)

Steve Bilko

At 6-foot-1 and 230 pounds, Steve Bilko was the prototypical power-hitting first baseman. As a Pacific Coast Leaguer playing for Los Angeles, he won a Triple Crown in 1956 and became legendary for his prodigious home runs. Hollywood took note, giving actor Phil Silvers Bilko's last name for his humorous *Sergeant Bilko* TV show. Unfortunately, during his ten-year MLB career, Bilko showed only flashes of power. With the 1953 Cardinals, he slugged 21 dingers but struck out a league-high 125 times. Eight years later, Bilko became a fan favorite, smashing 20 homers for the expansion Los Angeles Angels. Known during his playing days for his ability to polish off a case of beer in record time, Bilko worked in sales for a perfume manufacturer after baseball. The 2003 Pacific Coast League Hall of Fame inductee passed away in 1978 at the young age of 49.

1952 TOPPS
STEVE BILKO
P.S.A.
#287
MINT 9
90119414

Career Stats

AB:	1,738	HR:	76
R:	220	RBI:	276
H:	432	OPS:	.780
BA:	.249		

Teams

St. Louis Cardinals NL (1949–1954)
Chicago Cubs NL (1954)
Cincinnati Redlegs NL (1958)
Los Angeles Dodgers NL (1958)
Detroit Tigers AL (1960)
Los Angeles Angels AL (1961–1962)

Ed Blake

St. Louis native Ed Blake had his biggest MLB moment before he was signed by the Cardinals in 1944. The 17-year-old prospect got to pitch batting practice for the Cards in the 1943 World Series. Blake soon ended up with the 40th Infantry Division in the Pacific and was wounded in the Philippines. After recovering, he pitched at the AAA minor-league level until 1959, posting a 143–122 record in 15 seasons. During that time, Blake had a few brief looks in the majors with the Reds and the Athletics, pitching a total of 8.2 innings in relief over parts of four seasons. With a major-league record of 0–0 and an 8.31 ERA, it is understandable that Blake's MLB career was short and fast. After baseball, he owned a successful plumbing business for 50 years. He passed away in 2009 at the age of 83.

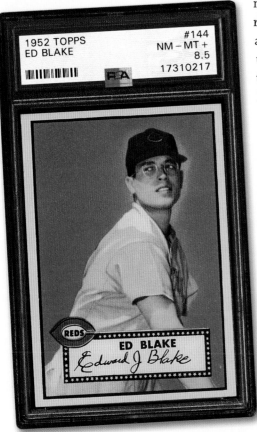

Career Stats

Record:	0–0
ERA:	8.31
IP:	8.2
Ks:	1
Threw:	RH

Teams

Cincinnati Reds NL (1951, 1952, 1953)
Kansas City Athletics AL (1957)

Don Bollweg

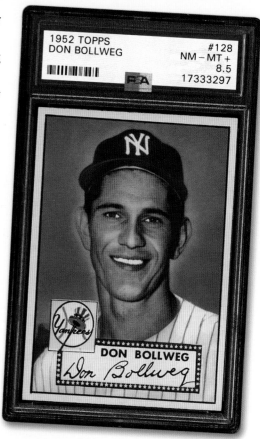

Strictly a bench player in the majors, first baseman Don Bollweg was a 29-year-old rookie when he finally made the big leagues. The US Army veteran enjoyed his best year in 1953, when he batted .297 in 155 at-bats for the World Champion Yankees. Bollweg pinch-hit in Game Three and Game Four and was a ninth-inning defensive replacement for Johnny Mize in Game Six of that fall classic to help the Yankees win the title. During his productive ten-season career in the minors, before and after his five Major League seasons, Bollweg was the American Association MVP in 1952. That year he batted .325 with 23 dingers for the AAA Yankees affiliate Kansas City Blues. After baseball, he worked in real estate and insurance and was an election board official in his hometown of Wheaton, Illinois, before he died in 1996 at age 75.

Career Stats

AB:	452	HR:	11
R:	62	RBI:	53
H:	110	OPS:	.733
BA:	.243		

Teams

St. Louis Cardinals NL (1950–1951)
New York Yankees AL (1953)
Philadelphia/Kansas City Athletics AL (1954–1955)

Bob Borkowski

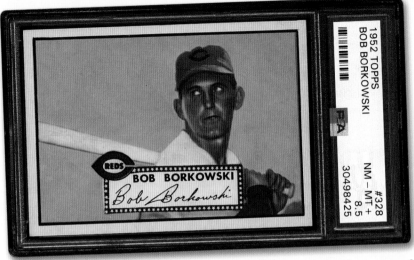

A native of Dayton, Ohio, Bob "Bush" Borkowski enjoyed a six-year big-league career with the Cubs, Reds, and Dodgers. He was the ultimate part-time player, never a star, but one of those valuable professional players that filled out Major League rosters during American wartime. A solid singles and doubles man, Borkowski played all three outfield positions, as well as first base, and rubbed elbows with some great players. Borkowski was traded to the Reds with Smoky Burgess and to the Dodgers for Joe Black. His greatest claim to fame was playing nine games for the 1955 World Champion Dodgers, filling in for injured future Hall of Famer Duke Snider. He then played three more seasons in the minors before hanging it up and returning home to Dayton where he working for a printing press manufacturing company. He died in 2017 at age 91.

Career Stats

AB:	1,170	HR:	16
R:	126	RBI:	112
H:	294	OPS:	.644
BA:	.251		

Teams

Chicago Cubs NL (1950–1951)
Cincinnati Reds/Redlegs NL (1952–1955)
Brooklyn Dodgers NL (1955)

Cloyd Boyer

Missouri native Cloyd Boyer played four of his five big league seasons with his hometown Cardinals. The right-handed pitcher went 7–7 for the 1950 Cards with a respectable 3.52 ERA and posted a career mark of 20–23. Boyer's stumbling block to stardom was twofold. He had a penchant for surrendering home runs—15 in 1950 and 21 in 1955—and he came from a family of incredible ballplayers, often playing in the shadows of younger brothers, Ken and Clete. Over two generations, nine members of the Boyer family signed pro-baseball contracts. After four seasons in St. Louis, Boyer ended his MLB career with the 1955 Kansas City Athletics and continued in the minors through 1961. In retirement, he was a successful pitching coach, scout, and manager until 1992. A US Navy veteran, Cloyd Boyer is 92 years old at the time of this writing.

Career Stats

Record:	20–23
ERA:	4.73
IP:	395.2
Ks:	198
Threw:	RH

Teams

St. Louis Cardinals NL (1949–1952)
Kansas City Athletics AL (1955)

Rocky Bridges

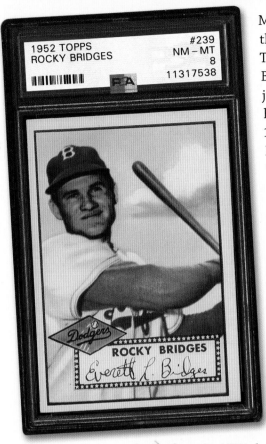

More about fun than figures, Texas-born Rocky Bridges batted just .247 with 16 home runs and 187 RBI in 11 MLB seasons. The light-hitting infielder was an All-Star in 1958 with the Senators despite some pedestrian statistics: .263 batting average, five home runs, and 28 RBI. Known for his down-home wit and one-liners, Bridges broke in with the Dodgers in 1951, backing up future Hall of Famers Jackie Robinson and Pee Wee Reese. He went on to play for the Reds, Senators, Tigers, Indians, Cardinals, and Angels. When asked about that he quipped, "I've had more numbers on my back than a bingo board." Bridges was a Major League coach and spent 21 seasons managing in the minors, making baseball fun for his teams. "The umpire says 'Play ball,' right?" A true baseball character, Rocky Bridges left a legacy of laughter when he died at age 87 in 2015.

Career Stats

AB:	2,272	HR:	16
R:	245	RBI:	187
H:	562	OPS:	.623
BA:	.247		

Teams

Brooklyn Dodgers NL (1951–1952)
Cincinnati Reds/Redlegs NL (1953–1957)
Washington Senators AL (1957–1958)
Detroit Tigers AL (1959–1960)
Cleveland Indians AL (1960)
St. Louis Cardinals NL (1960)
Los Angeles Angels AL (1961)

Dick Brodowski

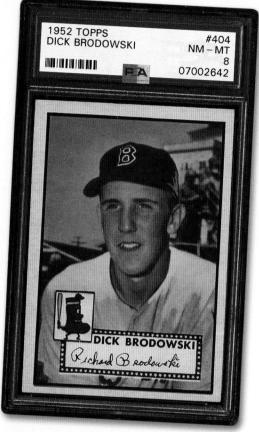

A 19 year-old rookie with the Red Sox in 1952, Dick Brodowski went 5–5 in 20 appearances with a 4.40 ERA. He missed the next two seasons serving in the US Army at Fort Dix in New Jersey. Brodowski played ball while in the military and participated in the 1954 All-Army Championship in Colorado Springs. He returned to the Red Sox in 1955 and went 1–0. Traded to Washington during that offseason, Brodowski did not win a game for the Senators over the next two seasons. His big-league career came to an end with Cleveland in 1959. Plagued by wildness throughout his MLB career, Brodowski finished with 124 walks compared to just 85 strikeouts. He once won 21 games in the minors and he played winter ball in both Puerto Rico and Cuba. In 2019, Brodowski passed away in his adopted home of Massachusetts at age 86.

Career Stats

Record:	9–11
ERA:	4.76
IP:	215.2
Ks:	85
Threw:	RH

Teams

Boston Red Sox AL (1952, 1955)
Washington Senators AL (1956–1957)
Cleveland Indians AL (1958–1959)

Tommy Brown

1952 TOPPS #281
TOMMY BROWN MINT 9
17115113

Brooklyn native Tommy Brown joined his hometown Dodgers at the age of 16 in 1944, becoming the youngest MLB position player ever to play in a game, and second-youngest behind 15-year-old Reds pitcher, Joe Nuxhall. While he batted just .164 in 46 games, Brown returned to the big club and raised his average to .245 in 1945. He served in the US Army in 1946 and then returned to Brooklyn as a part-time infielder and outfielder. A member of the 1947 and 1949 Dodgers NL pennant winners, Brown batted .303 in 1949. After brief stints with the Phillies and Cubs, where he hit .320 in 1952, Brown's MLB career ended in 1953 at just 25 years old. He played minor-league ball through 1959 and settled in Nashville where he worked for the Ford Glass Plant for 35 years. At the time of this writing, he is 92 years old.

Career Stats

AB:	1,280	HR:	31
R:	151	RBI:	159
H:	309	OPS:	.647
BA:	.241		

Teams

Brooklyn Dodgers NL (1944–1945, 1947–1951)
Philadelphia Phillies NL (1951–1952)
Chicago Cubs NL (1952–1953)

Johnny Bucha

Johnny Bucha, an All-Star catcher in the minors, was only in the majors for a short period of time. With a total of 195 at-bats, 40 hits, and one home run, there is not a strong body of Major League work to discuss. An outstanding athlete in high school, Bucha lettered in basketball, football, baseball, and track. During his 16-year minor-league career, he had three stints in the majors, playing briefly for the Cardinals in 1948 and 1950 and then for the Tigers, where he caught 56 games in 1953. After closing his minor-league career in 1960, Bucha was an iron worker and a farmer in his native Pennsylvania. Although he was not in the majors for very long, Bucha is still one of the few that made it to the top. He passed away in 1996 at the age of 71.

1952 TOPPS
JOHNNY BUCHA
#19
NM–MT
8
03064835

Career Stats

AB:	195	HR:	1
R:	18	RBI:	15
H:	40	OPS:	.567
BA:	.205		

Teams

St. Louis Cardinals NL (1948, 1950)
Detroit Tigers AL (1953)

Jim Busby

At 6-foot-1, Jim Busby was a tall Texan who spent way too much time in the saddle. Over his 13-year career, the centerfielder played for six different teams. Busby was an All-Star with the White Sox in his second season of 1951. That was the high-water mark for his career, although he did lead the American League in games played with the Senators in 1954. Along the way, Busby was traded for notable baseball luminaries and future managers Larry Doby and Dick Williams. Busby also holds the distinction of being an original Houston Major Leaguer, joining the expansion Colt .45s in 1962 before wrapping up his playing career. He then worked for the Colts, Braves, White Sox, and Mariners as third-base coach through the 1978 season before riding off into the sunset for good. Busby died in 1996 at age 69.

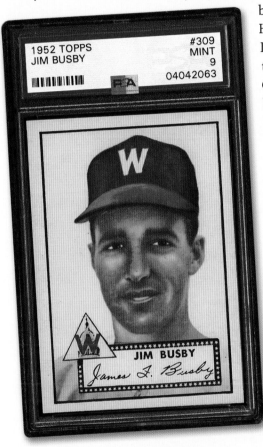

Career Stats

AB:	4,250	HR:	48
R:	541	RBI:	438
H:	1,113	OPS:	.665
BA:	.262		

Teams

Chicago White Sox AL (1950–1952, 1955)
Washington Senators AL (1952–1955)
Cleveland Indians AL (1956–1957)
Baltimore Orioles AL (1957–1958, 1960–1961)
Boston Red Sox AL (1959–1960)
Houston Colt .45s NL (1962)

Bud Byerly

A dependable spot starter and reliever with 237 MLB appearances, Eldred "Bud" Byerly's lifetime 22–22 record doesn't tell the whole story. The fact that he played for 11 years does. The Missouri native signed with the Cardinals in 1940 and debuted in 1943. In the minors for part of the 1944 season, Byerly also helped the big club. He went 2–2 with a 3.40 ERA in nine appearances for the 1944 world champion Cardinals and earned his ring as closer in Game Three of the fall classic. Shuffled between the majors and minors throughout a pro career that spanned from 1940 through 1961, Byerly contributed to all of his teams, jumping in whenever needed. The third-oldest in the league when he left the majors in 1960 at age 40, Byerly worked in construction and lived in St. Louis until his death in 2012 at age 92.

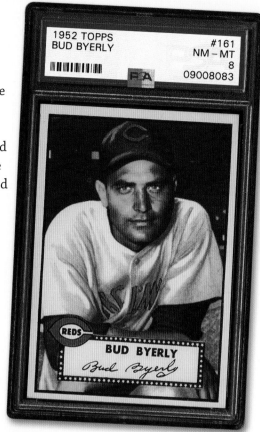

Career Stats

Record:	22–22
ERA:	3.70
IP:	491.2
Ks:	209
Threw:	RH

Teams

St. Louis Cardinals NL (1943–1945)
Cincinnati Reds NL (1950–1952)
Washington Senators AL (1956–1958)
Boston Red Sox AL (1958)
San Francisco Giants NL (1959–1960)

Bob Cain

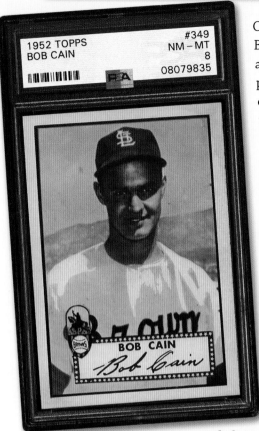

On August 19, 1951, Bob Cain, an otherwise anonymous sub-.500 pitcher, became part of one of the most bizarre moments in baseball history. In the second game of a twin bill against the St. Louis Browns, Cain was on the hill for the Tigers in the bottom of the first inning. Stepping to the plate for St. Louis was Eddie Gaedel, all 3-foot-7 and 65 pounds of him, wearing uniform number "1/8." Baffled by Gaedel's microscopic strike zone, Cain proceeded to walk him on four pitches. The diminutive Gaedel was signed by Browns owner Bill Veeck, who also had him jump out of a cake on the field before the game. Ironically, Cain joined the Browns the next season and won 12 games, but he is remembered for this brief moment in baseball lore. After baseball, Cain worked in sales. He passed away in 1997 at age 72.

Career Stats

Record:	37–44
ERA:	4.50
IP:	628.0
Ks:	249
Threw:	LH

Teams

Chicago White Sox AL (1949–1951)
Detroit Tigers AL (1951)
St. Louis Browns AL (1952–1953)

Frank Campos

Cuban-born Francisco Jose Campos made it to the majors in 1951 with the Washington Senators. Known as "Cisco" in the Cuban and Mexican Leagues, Campos appeared in eight games, registering 11 hits in 26 at-bats for a .423 batting average. Campos played every outfield position in his brief three-year MLB career. He followed up that starry-eyed debut with a more pedestrian season in 1952. Campos played in 53 games for the Senators and batted .259 with six doubles and eight RBI. The Senators finished no higher than fifth place during Campos' three seasons under manager Bucky Harris and GM Calvin Griffith. In 1953, he appeared in just ten games batting a paltry .111 for the club. Hardly a Major League star, Campos did have a productive career playing in Cuba, Mexico, and in the minors. He settled in Miami, where he passed away in 2006 at age 81.

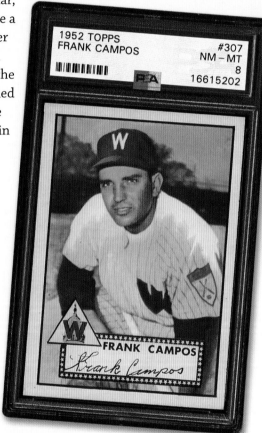

Career Stats

AB:	147	HR:	0
R:	13	RBI:	13
H:	41	OPS:	.665
BA:	.279		

Teams

Washington Senators AL (1951–1953)

Pete Castiglione

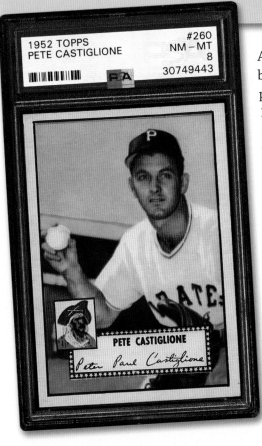

A versatile infielder, Pete Castiglione broke in with the Pirates in 1947. He played in 118 games for the Bucs in 1949, batting .268 with 20 doubles and 43 RBI. The dependable platoon player struggled for playing time, but he did get into 132 games in 1951, hitting .261 with 42 RBI. Traded to the Cardinals in 1953, Castiglione played his final MLB game in April 1954 and continued on in the minors through 1958. While he never became a baseball hero, Castiglione certainly fit that moniker before his MLB days. In 1943, he joined the US Navy and served as chief radioman on the USS *Crouter* and the USS *Ponaganset*. Castiglione saw action at several WWII sites, including the Philippines and Okinawa. After baseball, he worked as a mail carrier in Pompano, Florida, where he coached and umpired locally. Castiglione died in 2010 at age 89.

Career Stats

AB:	1,670	HR:	24
R:	205	RBI:	150
H:	426	OPS:	.648
BA:	.255		

Teams

Pittsburgh Pirates NL (1947–1953)
St. Louis Cardinals NL (1953–1954)

Bob Chakales

The prototypical journeyman pitcher, Bob Chakales was a starter, middle reliever, and closer for five different teams in seven MLB seasons. The promising righty with a good bat started with Cleveland in 1951 but found it difficult to break into a rotation that included stars like Feller, Wynn, Garcia, and Lemon. An early contributor to the 1954 Indians' 111-win season, Chakales missed the AL pennant win and Series loss to the Giants because he was traded to the Orioles in June straight-up for Vic Wertz. Chakales retired in 1957 with a 15–25 record, 4.54 ERA, 187 strikeouts, and a career .271 batting average. After baseball, the US Army veteran launched a successful golf course construction company, built more than 200 golf courses, and served as president of the Golf Course Builders Association of America. Chakales passed away in 2010 at age 82 in Richmond, Virginia.

Career Stats

Record:	15–25
ERA:	4.54
IP:	420.1
Ks:	187
Threw:	RH

Teams

Cleveland Indians AL (1951–1954)
Baltimore Orioles AL (1954)
Chicago White Sox AL (1955)
Washington Senators AL (1955–1957)
Boston Red Sox AL (1957)

Cliff Chambers

1952 TOPPS #68
CLIFF CHAMBERS
BLACK BACK
NM – MT 8
09044493

The highlight of Cliff Chambers' big-league career took place on May 6, 1951. He pitched a no-hitter for the Pirates vs. the Boston Braves, the first Pirates no-no in 44 years. The hard-throwing lefty debuted with the Cubs in 1948 after posting a 24–9 season in the Pacific Coast League. A marginal MLB pitcher, with a sub-.500 lifetime record, Chambers' best year was 1949 when he compiled a 13–7 record with 3.96 ERA for the Bucs. The following year he lost 15 games. His no-hitter was one of three wins in 1951 before he was traded to St. Louis, where he had an 11–6 record for the Cards over the balance of the season. A broken wrist in 1952 essentially ended his fairly vanilla Major League career. The Washington State University grad later became a certified financial planner in Idaho. He passed away in 2012 at 90 years old.

Career Stats

Record:	48–53
ERA:	4.29
IP:	897.1
Ks:	374
Threw:	LH

Teams

Chicago Cubs NL (1948)
Pittsburgh Pirates NL (1949–1951)
St. Louis Cardinals NL (1951–1953)

Bob Chipman

Brooklyn native Bob Chipman won 51 games over a 12-year MLB career. His best year was 1944, when he won 12 games, splitting time between the Dodgers and Cubs. Chipman was a member of the 1945 Chicago Cubs pennant-winning team that lost the World Series to the Tigers. A lefty starter and reliever, Chipman played on the Dodgers' 1941 pennant-winning team, but was ineligible for the World Series. He indirectly helped Brooklyn to the 1947 National League flag when he was traded to the Cubs for Eddie Stanky in 1944, because Stanky played a key role in Brooklyn's 1947 World Series run. Nicknamed Mr. Chips at Northport High School in New York, Chipman won 17 games twice in the minors. He was inducted into the Suffolk County, New York, Sports Hall of Fame and, sadly, succumbed to cancer at the young age of 55 in 1973.

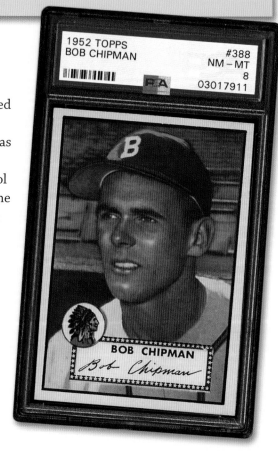

1952 TOPPS #388
BOB CHIPMAN
NM – MT 8
03017911

Career Stats

Record:	51–46
ERA:	3.72
IP:	880.2
Ks:	322
Threw:	LH

Teams

Brooklyn Dodgers NL (1941–1944)
Chicago Cubs NL (1944–1949)
Boston Braves NL (1950–1952)

Bubba Church

Born and bred in Alabama, Bubba Church made his name up north with the Philadelphia Phillies. In 1951, he was the number two starter behind 21-game winner and eventual Hall of Famer Robin Roberts. That season, Church gave up almost as many hits as he had innings pitched, but he worked out of jams to the tune of a 15–11 record. In his rookie season, Church nearly became a baseball casualty. During the Phillies' September run for the 1950 NL pennant, he was hit in the face by a line drive off the powerful bat of Cincinnati's Ted Kluszewski. Church recovered but played sparingly for the rest of the season and did not pitch in the Series. His MLB career ended in 1955, but in 1957, Church pitched for the minor-league Miami Marlins alongside the great Satchel Paige. Bubba Church died in 2001 at age 77.

Career Stats

Record:	36–37
ERA:	4.10
IP:	713.1
Ks:	274
Threw:	RH

Teams

Philadelphia Phillies NL (1950–1952)
Cincinnati Reds NL (1952–1953)
Chicago Cubs NL (1953–1955)

Allie Clark

Despite his promising start when rookie Allie Clark batted .373 for the Yankees in 1947, New York traded him to Cleveland in the offseason. Clark went on to enjoy a seven-year career in the majors playing for the Yankees, Indians, Athletics, and White Sox. He hit .310 in 81 games with 38 RBI in 1948, but his numbers dipped drastically over the next two seasons. The highlight of Clark's career occurred in 1947 with the Yanks. In Game Seven of the World Series vs. Brooklyn, Clark pinch-hit for Yogi Berra in the sixth inning with New York leading 3–2. He came through with a base hit scoring Phil Rizzuto, and the Yankees eventually won the game 5–2. Clark would earn another World Series ring with Cleveland the following season. An ironworker after baseball, Clark died in his native New Jersey in 2012 at age 88.

Career Stats

AB:	1,021	HR:	32
R:	131	RBI:	149
H:	267	OPS:	.722
BA:	.262		

Teams

New York Yankees AL (1947)
Cleveland Indians AL (1948–1951)
Philadelphia Athletics AL (1951–1953)
Chicago White Sox AL (1953)

Gil Coan

On April 21, 1951, Mickey Mantle hit his first career double, but a player on the opposing team, the Washington Senators, tied a Major League record with two triples in the same inning. That player was Gil Coan. The Yankees won the game 8–7, but Coan went on to hit .303 that season for the seventh-place Senators. Coan was born in North Carolina and attended Brevard College. His 1951 season was a follow-up to an impressive 1950 campaign when he batted an identical .303. The speedy leftfielder was traded to the Orioles straight up for Roy Sievers in 1954. Sievers became an All-Star in Washington, while Coan's career ended in 1956 after brief stints with the White Sox and Giants. After his MLB days, Coan owned and operated an insurance agency in Brevard, North Carolina. He passed away in 2020 at the age of 97.

Career Stats

AB:	2,877	HR:	39
R:	384	RBI:	278
H:	731	OPS:	.675
BA:	.254		

Teams

Washington Senators AL (1946–1953)
Baltimore Orioles AL (1954–1955)
Chicago White Sox AL (1955)
New York Giants NL (1955–1956)

Ray Coleman

A great teammate and all around good guy, outfielder Ray Coleman played for three different teams and had three different stints with the St. Louis Browns. A product of the Browns farm system, Coleman's development was interrupted by the US Navy. He served on ships that protected ammunition and supply transports in the Mediterranean and the Pacific during World War II. Coleman returned to the minors until his call-up to the Browns in 1947. His best year was 1951, when he batted .280 with 76 RBI and eight home runs in a season split between the Brownies and the White Sox. When his MLB career wound down, Coleman played in the minors several seasons and retired in 1956. After baseball, he lived and worked in Kentucky, later returned to his native California, and was involved with the St. Louis Browns Historical Society. Coleman passed away in 2010 at age 88.

Career Stats

AB:	1,729	HR:	20
R:	208	RBI:	199
H:	446	OPS:	.692
BA:	.258		

Teams

St. Louis Browns AL (1947–1948, 1950–1951, 1952)
Philadelphia Athletics AL (1948)
Chicago White Sox AL (1951–1952)

Joe Collins

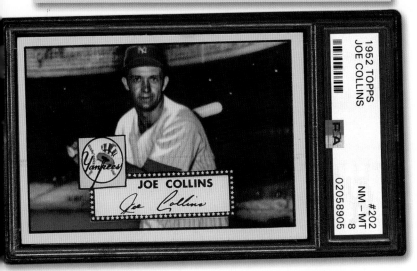

A good player who was in the right place at the right time, Joe Collins played on five Yankees World Series championship teams. The regular first baseman for the Yankees from 1952 through 1954, Collins platooned with Moose Skowran later in his career. A good clutch hitter, Collins' best offensive season was 1952, when he batted .280 with 18 home runs and 120 hits. Excellent defensively, Collins compiled a career .990 fielding percentage at first base. With the Bronx Bombers his entire ten-year career, Collins played on some of the greatest Yankees teams of all time with Joe DiMaggio, Mickey Mantle, and other greats as teammates. Collins served in the US Naval Air Corps before joining the Yankees. After his MLB career he was a businessman and was also involved in community service in Newark, New Jersey. He died in 1989 at 66 years old.

Career Stats

AB:	2,329	HR:	86
R:	404	RBI:	329
H:	596	OPS:	.771
BA:	.256		

Teams
New York Yankees AL (1948–1957)

Merl Combs

Merrill "Merl" Combs was your typical utility infielder who was kept around primarily for his glove and certainly not his bat. With his .202 lifetime batting average and two career home runs in the majors, he clearly hit for neither average nor power. Playing most of his short career with the Boston Red Sox, Combs was usually a late-inning insert for defensive purposes. Actually, because of his glove, he probably could have started for some other MLB teams. Following his relatively short five-year career, he became a sales representative for Pepsi-Cola. He also worked as a scout for the Cincinnati Reds, New York Mets, and Philadelphia Phillies before moving on to work as first-base coach and scout for the Texas Rangers. He finished up as California scout for the Cleveland Indians. Not a bad post-playing career. Combs passed away at the age of 61 in 1981.

Career Stats

AB:	361	HR:	2
R:	45	RBI:	25
H:	73	OPS:	.555
BA:	.202		

Teams
Boston Red Sox AL (1947, 1949–1950)
Washington Senators AL (1950)
Cleveland Indians AL (1951–1952)

Bobby Del Greco

1952 TOPPS #353
BOB DEL GRECO MINT 9
17117808

Pittsburgh native Bobby Del Greco broke in with the Pirates at age 19 in 1952. Discovered by Pie Traynor in 1949, Del Greco was one of the first and most exciting products of Pittsburgh's innovative farm system established by GM Branch Rickey. Del Greco impressed early, going 3-for-4 in his MLB debut vs. the Cardinals and repeating that feat two days later in his first home game for the Bucs. The young centerfielder smashed his first Major League home run in June at Forbes Field, but went back to the minors until 1956. Del Greco played on the 1958 world champion Yankees, and he was hit by a pitch a league-leading 13 times as an Athletic in 1962. He struck out against future Hall of Famer Warren Spahn in his final MLB at-bat in 1965. Bobby Del Greco was 86 years old when he passed away in 2019.

Career Stats

AB:	1,982	HR:	42
R:	271	RBI:	169
H:	454	OPS:	.682
BA:	.229		

Teams

Pittsburgh Pirates NL (1952, 1956)
St. Louis Cardinals NL (1956)
Chicago Cubs NL (1957)
New York Yankees AL (1957–1958)
Philadelphia Phillies NL (1960–1961, 1965)
Kansas City Athletics AL (1961–1963)

Ike Delock

Ivan "Ike" Delock was a versatile starter and reliever for the Boston Red Sox for most of his career. In his best stretch, from 1956 through 1959, he won 47 games and saved 22 more. Delock first learned to pitch in the US Marine Corps from 1946 to 1948, and he brought that same tough and battling demeanor to the majors. In 1952, his rookie year, Delock got the victory when Ted Williams, in his last game before being called to Korean War service, smashed a game-winning home run against Detroit. Delock was released by Boston in 1963 and finished his career that season with the Orioles. He was head baseball coach for Brandeis University in 1969 and 1970 and later worked in sales for Northwest Airlines. Delock retired to Naples, Florida, in 1988 and at the time of this writing, he is 90 years old.

1952 TOPPS #329
IVAN DELOCK NM – MT 8
09022433

Teams

Boston Red Sox AL (1952–1953, 1955–1963)
Baltimore Orioles AL (1963)

Career Stats

Record:	84–75
ERA:	4.03
IP:	1,238.0
Ks:	672
Threw:	RH

Jim Delsing

1952 TOPPS   #271
JIM DELSING   MINT   9
09025506

JIM DELSING
Jim Delsing

Well-respected by teammates and opponents alike, Jim Delsing spent a decade in the big leagues playing for five teams. A .255 lifetime hitter, he was a backup outfielder for much of his career with the Tigers, Browns, Yankees, White Sox, and A's. The Wisconsin native was part of the 1949 Yankees World Series champions club, but as a late-season call-up he was ineligible to play in the Series. Perhaps Delsing's greatest claim to fame involved Eddie Gaedel, the 3-foot-7 player signed by Browns owner Bill Veeck in 1951. Gaedel had one at-bat and walked. It was Delsing who came in to pinch-run. A carpenter during baseball offseasons, Delsing was an advertising salesman and active in charity work in retirement. A dedicated family man who loved having his wife and kids join him on the road, Jim Delsing passed away in 2006 at age 80.

Career Stats

AB:	2,461	HR:	40
R:	322	RBI:	286
H:	627	OPS:	.705
BA:	.255		

Teams

Chicago White Sox AL (1948, 1956)
New York Yankees AL (1949–1950)
St. Louis Browns AL (1950–1952)
Detroit Tigers AL (1952–1956)
Kansas City Athletics AL (1960)

Joe DeMaestri

1952 TOPPS   #286
JOE DeMAESTRI   MINT   9
01602129

JOE DE MAESTRI
Joseph P De Maestri

A good defensive infielder, Joe DeMaestri was originally signed by the Red Sox, but he broke in with the White Sox in 1951. He was traded to the Browns for the 1952 season and then spent seven years with the Athletics in Philadelphia and Kansas City before finishing up with the Yankees in 1961. DeMaestri posted a career average of just .236, but for one day, however, he was the best hitter in baseball. It was July 8, 1955. Playing for the Athletics, DeMaestri had six singles against the Tigers. An All-Star shortstop in 1957, DeMaestri led the league in fielding percentage that year and again in 1958. He played for New York in the 1960 World Series and was a member of the 1961 Yankees World Series champion team. After baseball, DeMaestri owned a beer distributorship for many years. He died in 2016 at age 87.

Career Stats

AB:	3,441	HR:	49
R:	322	RBI:	281
H:	813	OPS:	.599
BA:	.236		

Teams

Chicago White Sox AL (1951)
St. Louis Browns AL (1952)
Philadelphia/Kansas City Athletics AL (1953–1959)
New York Yankees AL (1960–1961)

Con Dempsey

A promising sidearm pitcher in the Pacific Coast League, Con Dempsey was the league strikeout leader in both 1948 and 1949. Sadly, he could not replicate this success in the majors, going just 0–2 lifetime with a 9.00 ERA. The mistake was made when the Pittsburgh Pirates converted Dempsey from a sidewinder to an overhand pitcher. GM Branch Rickey made some brilliant moves over his illustrious career, but this was not one of them. Prior to playing professional ball, Dempsey starred in baseball and basketball at the University of San Francisco and served in WWII. After his brief Major League stint, Dempsey earned his master's degree at USF and was a respected teacher and coach in the San Francisco public school system for over 30 years. The first baseball player elected into the USF Hall of Fame, Dempsey died at the age of 83 in 2006.

Career Stats

Record:	0–2
ERA:	9.00
IP:	7.0
Ks:	3
Threw:	RH

Teams

Pittsburgh Pirates NL (1951)

Sam Dente

A versatile infielder, Sam Dente was a platoon man for most of his career. Signed by the Red Sox in 1941, Dente's minor-league seasoning was interrupted by two years in the US Army where the antiaircraft gunner lost the hearing in his left ear. He came up to Boston in 1947 and moved on to Washington where, as starting shortstop, he batted .273 in 1949 with 53 RBI. In 1954, Dente was a part of the 111-win Cleveland AL pennant-winning squad that lost the World Series to the Giants. He went hitless in three fall classic at-bats. Dente retired in 1955 after an operation to correct his hearing problem caused vertigo. A fiery competitor, Dente mellowed in retirement and was an instructor for numerous baseball clinics. He died in 2002 at age 79, but his baseball legacy lived on in grandson and 2016 Cy Young Award winner Rick Porcello.

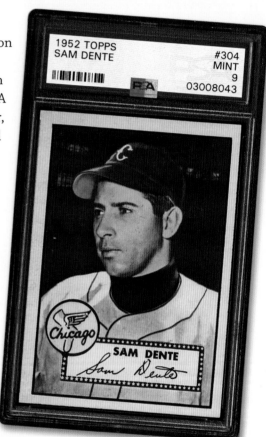

Career Stats

AB:	2,320	HR:	4
R:	205	RBI:	214
H:	585	OPS:	.608
BA:	.252		

Teams

Boston Red Sox AL (1947)
St. Louis Browns AL (1948)
Washington Senators AL (1949–1951)
Chicago White Sox AL (1952–1953)
Cleveland Indians AL (1954–1955)

Murry Dickson

1952 TOPPS #266
MURRY DICKSON
MINT 9
02071287

Thanks to an inventive style and a vast repertoire of pitches, Murry Dickson enjoyed an 18-year Major League career. He broke in with the Cardinals in 1939 and later lost two seasons to US Army combat in Europe during World War II. He returned to have a breakout season in 1946 when he posted a 15–6 record for the World Champion Cards. Twelve years later, Dickson won another title as a 41-year-old hurler for the Yankees. The Missouri native and rabid innings-eater won 20 games in 1951 and lost 21 games in 1952. Amazingly, he was an All-Star in 1953 despite a final record of 10–19. Dickson compiled a career mark of 172–181 and led the National League several times in losses, earned runs, and homers allowed. A union carpenter during and after his time in baseball, Murry Dickson passed away in 1989 at age 73.

Career Stats

Record:	172–181
ERA:	3.66
IP:	3,052.1
Ks:	1,281
Threw:	RH

Teams

St. Louis Cardinals NL (1939–1940, 1942–1943, 1946–1948, 1956–1957)
Pittsburgh Pirates NL (1949–1953)
Philadelphia Phillies NL (1954–1956)
Kansas City Athletics AL (1958, 1959)
New York Yankees AL (1958)

Chuck Diering

Known for his speed in the outfield, Chuck Diering was a solid platoon man who struggled to secure playing time throughout his Major League career. Before his MLB days, Diering served three years in the US Army and became known as an excellent hitter while playing military baseball. The St. Louis native joined his hometown Cardinals in 1947, and in 1949 he played in 131 games and batted a career-high .263 with 21 doubles. Before the 1952 season, the Cards traded Diering to the Giants in exchange for Eddie Stanky. Diering played one season at the Polo Grounds and one in the minors before moving to the Orioles, where he was named team MVP in 1954, their first season in Baltimore. After retiring from the majors in 1956, Diering owned a car dealership in St. Louis and passed away in his hometown at the age of 89 in 2012.

Career Stats

AB:	1,648	HR:	14
R:	217	RBI:	141
H:	411	OPS:	.683
BA:	.249		

Teams

St. Louis Cardinals NL (1947–1951)
New York Giants NL (1952)
Baltimore Orioles AL (1954–1956)

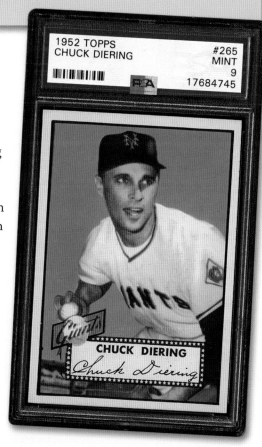

1952 TOPPS #265
CHUCK DIERING
MINT 9
17684745

Fritz Dorish

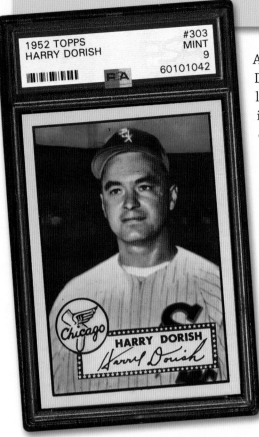

1952 TOPPS #303
HARRY DORISH MINT 9
60101042

A stocky sinker-ball artist, Harry "Fritz" Dorish spent a decade in the majors and led the American League with 11 saves in 1952. When he retired, he held the distinction of being the last AL pitcher to steal home. Dorish broke in with the Red Sox in 1947 and later pitched for the Browns, White Sox, and Orioles. The ultimate swingman, he could start and finish games effectively. Dorish followed up his 11-save 1952 season with ten wins, 17 saves, and a 3.40 ERA in 1953. While in the minors, he served three years in the US Army Medical Corps and played military baseball. Dorish finished his career in 1956 with 45 wins, 48 saves, and a 3.83 ERA. He continued in baseball until 1988 with several organizations, working as a Major League scout and pitching coach as well as a minor-league manager and pitching instructor. He died in 2000 at age 79.

Career Stats

Record:	45–43
ERA:	3.83
IP:	834.1
Ks:	332
Threw:	RH

Teams

Boston Red Sox AL (1947–1949, 1956)
St. Louis Browns AL (1950)
Chicago White Sox AL (1951–1955)
Baltimore Orioles AL (1955–1956)

Karl Drews

Karl Drews' playing career was an exercise in highs and lows. In 1947, just his second season in the majors, he won a World Series with the Yankees. The next season, Drews was sold to the St. Louis Browns who finished sixth in 1948 and seventh in 1949. More highs and lows came for Drews with the 1952 Phillies. He won a career-high 14 games and lost a career-high 15 games. At 6-foot-4, Drews was blessed with an intimidating presence and fastball. Alas, his penchant for giving up the long ball precluded him from pitching stardom. Before and after his MLB career, Drews compiled a 146–113 record in the minors over 14 years and retired in 1960. Sadly, Drews' highs and lows continued after baseball. Married with four children and a successful career in sales, Drews was tragically killed by a drunk driver at the young age of 43 in 1963.

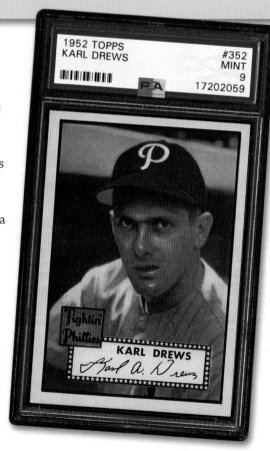

1952 TOPPS #352
KARL DREWS MINT 9
17202059

Career Stats

Record:	44–53
ERA:	4.76
IP:	826.2
Ks:	322
Threw:	RH

Teams

New York Yankees AL (1946–1948)
St. Louis Browns AL (1948–1949)
Philadelphia Phillies NL (1951–1954)
Cincinnati Redlegs NL (1954)

Monk Dubiel

Signed by the Yankees in 1941, Walter "Monk" Dubiel came up in 1944 to help cover for their depleted wartime pitching staff. The Hartford, Connecticut, native went 13–13 in 1944 and 10–9 in 1945 for the Yanks, but went back to the minors when the Yankees pitching aces returned from the war. Dubiel got another MLB shot with the 1948 Phillies and went 8–10 with a 3.89 ERA. Although he struggled with back and hip injuries, Dubiel continued on to play four seasons with the Cubs and finished his MLB career with a 45–53 record and a 3.87 lifetime ERA. Dubiel had the ability to log innings on the mound, pitching a total of 879.1 innings in his relatively brief Major League career. In retirement, Dubiel worked for Rockwell Manufacturing Co. and the Hartford Post Office. He passed away in 1969 at the age of 51.

Career Stats

Record:	45–53
ERA:	3.87
IP:	879.1
Ks:	289
Threw:	RH

Teams

New York Yankees AL (1944–1945)

Philadelphia Phillies NL (1948)

Chicago Cubs NL (1949–1952)

Erv Dusak

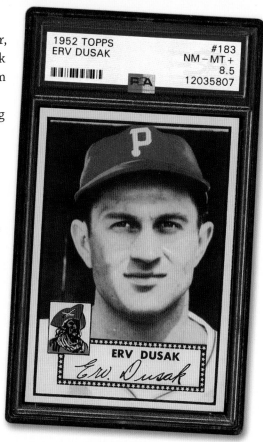

A utility infielder, outfielder, and pitcher, Erv "Four Sack" Dusak got his nickname from a poem a fan wrote about a game-winning home run he hit in the minors. After a couple of brief looks with the Cardinals, Dusak served three years in the US Army. He returned in 1946, contributed to the Cardinals pennant run, and batted .250 in four at-bats in their World Series victory vs. the Red Sox. In 1947, Dusak batted .284 with 50 walks in 328 at-bats but he struggled at the plate the next year. He spent 1949 in the minors, working to convert to a pitcher, and returned to St. Louis in 1950 as a spot starter and reliever, without success. With Pittsburgh his last two seasons, he returned to the outfield. After baseball, Dusak was an insurance agent and worked in a bowling alley. He died in 1994 at the age of 74.

Career Stats

AB:	1,035	HR:	24
R:	168	RBI:	106
H:	251	OPS:	.688
BA:	.243		

Teams

St. Louis Cardinals NL (1941–1942, 1946–1951)

Pittsburgh Pirates NL (1951–1952)

Bruce Edwards

A good defensive catcher, Bruce "Bull" Edwards wore Dodger Blue for the first six years of his career. Signed in 1941, he toiled in the minors and in the military before arriving in Brooklyn in 1946. As regular backstop for the Dodgers in 1946 and 1947, he was a steadying presence behind the plate. In 1947, he batted a career-high .295, made the All-Star team, and played in all seven games of Brooklyn's World Series loss to the Yankees. After the appearance of future Hall of Famer, Roy Campanella, on the scene in 1948, Edwards became a part-time player. He did appear in the 1949 Series as pinch-hitter and was an All-Star again in 1951. After retiring, Edwards was a player-manager in the minors, and he worked as an inventory-control analyst in the aerospace industry. He died of a heart attack in 1975 at age 51.

Career Stats

AB:	1,675	HR:	39
R:	191	RBI:	241
H:	429	OPS:	.725
BA:	.256		

Teams

Brooklyn Dodgers NL (1946–1951)

Chicago Cubs NL (1951–1952, 1954)

Washington Senators AL (1955)

Cincinnati Redlegs NL (1956)

Hank Edwards

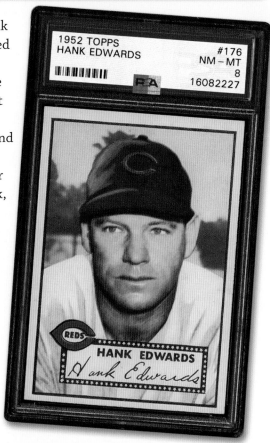

Ohio native Hank Edwards patrolled the outfield for 11 Major League seasons, the first seven of those with the Cleveland Indians. A solid all-around player with a good stick, Edwards had a .280 lifetime batting average. With Cleveland in 1946, he led the American League with 16 triples to go along with his .301 batting average. Known for his hustle and acrobatic plays in the outfield, Edwards dislocated his shoulder in August 1948 while scaling the right field wall to rob the Red Sox Stan Spence of a three-run homer. This was just the latest mishap for the injury-prone Edwards, who had previously suffered a broken ankle and fractured collarbone. A utility player after that season, Edwards moved on to the Cubs where he batted .364 with 110 at-bats in 1950. The tough World War II US Army veteran passed away at the age of 69 in 1988.

Career Stats

AB:	2,191	HR:	51
R:	285	RBI:	276
H:	613	OPS:	.783
BA:	.280		

Teams

Cleveland Indians AL (1941–1943, 1946–1949)

Chicago Cubs NL (1949–1950)

Brooklyn Dodgers NL (1951)

Cincinnati Reds NL (1951–1952)

Chicago White Sox AL (1952)

St. Louis Browns AL (1953)

Eddie Erautt

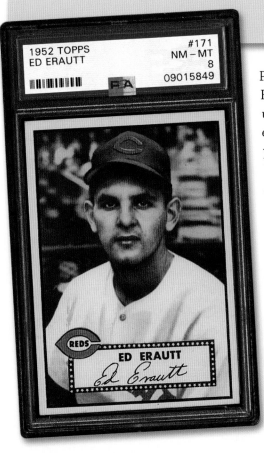

Portland, Oregon, native Eddie Erautt's excellent minor-league stats unfortunately did not translate into an excellent Major League career. After two years in the minors, Erautt served in the US Army infantry during World War II and attracted big-league attention upon his return. In 1946 with the Pacific Coast League's Hollywood Stars, Erautt went 20–14 with a 2.76 ERA and 234 Ks. Promoted to the Cincinnati Reds in 1947, he went 4–9 with a 3.08 ERA. Back in the minors in 1948, he posted a 15–7 record with a 2.97 ERA for the International League's Syracuse club. With the Reds again in 1949 Erautt went 4–11. This pattern continued throughout his pro career. The righty starter and reliever finished with the 1953 Cardinals and posted several notable seasons in the minors before retiring in 1957 with a 113–92 minor-league record. Eddie Erautt passed away in 2013 at the age of 89.

Career Stats

Record:	15–23
ERA:	4.86
IP:	379.2
Ks:	157
Threw:	RH

Teams

Cincinnati Reds NL (1947–1951, 1953)

St. Louis Cardinals NL (1953)

Al Evans

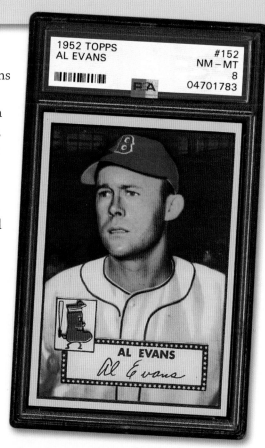

North Carolina native Al Evans started his catching career in the textile leagues. Signed in 1937, he made his debut with the Senators in 1939 at 22 years old. Evans spent November 1942 to May 1944 in the US Navy where the chief petty officer was starting backstop for the Norfolk Naval Air Station baseball team. Primarily a backup catcher in the majors, Evans was good defensively and wasn't a bad hitter, but he had no power. He hit just 13 home runs in his 12-year career spent almost entirely with the Senators. In 1949, Evans led the league with his .992 fielding percentage, while batting .271 in 109 games. He finished with the 1951 Red Sox and continued in the minors through 1955. Evans stayed in the game until 1965, managing in the minors and scouting. He retired to North Carolina where he died in 1979 at the age of 62.

Career Stats

AB:	2,053	HR:	13
R:	188	RBI:	211
H:	514	OPS:	.658
BA:	.250		

Teams

Washington Senators AL (1939–1942, 1944–1950)

Boston Red Sox AL (1951)

Cliff Fannin

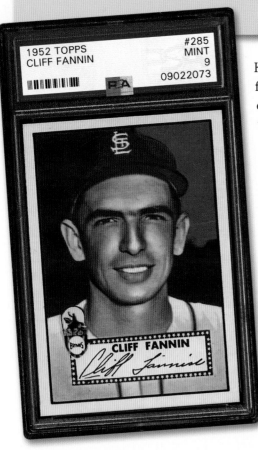

Kentucky native Cliff Fannin pitched for the St. Louis Browns for his entire eight-year career. In his rookie season, the perennially horrible Browns finished with a respectable 81–70 record, good for third place in the American League. For the remainder of his career, Fannin's team would be in or near the cellar. A starter and reliever, Fannin pitched a complete game shutout of the White Sox in his first MLB start on July 5, 1946. He posted a 3.01 ERA in 1946 and 3.58 ERA in 1947. The long and lean right-hander started 29 games in 1948 and posted a 10–14 record, walking more batters than he fanned. Fannin lost another 14 games in 1949, as the Browns lost 101 as a team. Fannin's career ended at 28 years old in 1952.

Tragically, he passed away just 14 years later at age 42 in 1966.

Career Stats

Record:	34–51
ERA:	4.85
IP:	733.0
Ks:	352
Threw:	RH

Teams

St. Louis Browns AL (1945–1952)

Dick Fowler

Toronto, Canada, native Dick Fowler played for the Philadelphia Athletics his entire ten-year career, interrupted by service in the 48th Highlanders of the Canadian Army. He returned to the A's in 1945 for the highlight of his career. On September 9, 1945, his first start in three years, Fowler twirled a no-hitter vs. the Browns. It was the first no-no by a Canadian-born pitcher, the first American-League no-hitter since Bob Feller's gem in 1940, and the first no-hitter by an A's pitcher since Joe Bush did it in 1916. With his fastball, curve, and changeup, Fowler won 12 games with a 2.81 ERA in 1947 and won 15 games in both 1948 and 1949. After baseball, Fowler worked and raised his family in Oneonta, New York, and coached Little League. The 1985 Canadian Baseball Hall of Fame inductee was 51 years old when he passed away in 1972.

Career Stats

Record:	66–79
ERA:	4.11
IP:	1,303.0
Ks:	382
Threw:	RH

Teams

Philadelphia Athletics AL (1941–1942, 1945–1952)

Howie Fox

Curveball pitcher Howie Fox was a workhorse for the Cincinnati Reds for seven of his nine Major League seasons. Signed out of the University of Oregon in 1943, Fox moved between the majors and minors throughout his career. His best season was 1950, when he posted an 11–8 record for the sixth-place Reds, but in 1949 he led the league with 19 losses. In his defense, the Reds were pretty weak during that period. He fared better in the minors where he had two 19-win seasons. Fox played ball in the Venezuelan winter league in 1953 and 1954 and for San Antonio in the Texas League in 1955. He opened up a tavern in San Antonio, and that is when things went bad. Tragically, in October 1955, Fox was fatally stabbed while tossing three unruly patrons out of his bar. He was just 34 years old.

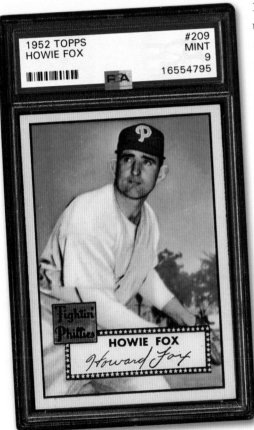

Career Stats

Record:	43–72
ERA:	4.33
IP:	1,108.1
Ks:	342
Threw:	RH

Teams

Cincinnati Reds NL (1944–1946, 1948–1951)
Philadelphia Phillies NL (1952)
Baltimore Orioles AL (1954)

Herman Franks

Backup catcher Herman Franks played six seasons for the Cards, Dodgers, A's, and Giants. A baseball lifer, he found success as a coach, manager, and businessman. Franks' career stats were unimpressive, but his first game as a Dodger in 1940 was outstanding, with four hits, including a home run. He also played on Brooklyn's 1941 pennant-winning team. Franks served in the US Navy from 1942 to 1946. He began his coaching career in 1949 with Leo Durocher's Giants and was at the center of the Giants' purported sign-stealing controversy after Bobby Thomson's 1951 pennant-winning homer. Franks owned the minor-league Salt Lake City Bees and was a financial advisor to Hall of Famers Willie Mays and Willie McCovey. He managed the Giants from 1965 to 1968 and the Cubs from 1977 to 1979, compiling a .537 winning percentage. He died at the age of 95 in 2009.

Career Stats

AB:	403	HR:	3
R:	35	RBI:	43
H:	80	OPS:	.578
BA:	.199		

Teams

St. Louis Cardinals NL (1939)
Brooklyn Dodgers NL (1940–1941)
Philadelphia Athletics AL (1947–1948)
New York Giants NL (1949)

Jim Fridley

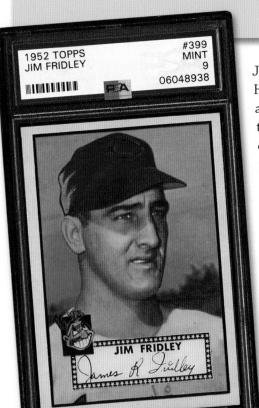

Jim Fridley played for three MLB seasons. He joined the Cleveland Indians in 1952 and hit four homers with 16 RBI. The next time Fridley would step on a big league diamond was in 1954 with Baltimore, playing 85 games for the O's. In 1954, Baltimore traded Fridley to the Yanks to complete a multi-player deal. One of the pitchers they received from the Orioles was future 1956 World Series perfect-game hero Don Larsen. Fridley's last year in the majors was 1958 with Cincinnati. He spent 14 seasons in the minors around his MLB days and retired in 1961. Outside of baseball, Fridley worked for the FBI before serving four years in the US Army in WWII. His Major League career was brief, but he made up for that with his marriage of 53 years to wife Jean. Fridley died in 2003 at the age of 78.

Career Stats

AB:	424	HR:	8
R:	50	RBI:	53
H:	105	OPS:	.665
BA:	.248		

Teams

Cleveland Indians AL (1952)
Baltimore Orioles AL (1954)
Cincinnati Redlegs NL (1958)

Owen Friend

Utility infielder Owen "Red" Friend had a longer career as minor-league manager than as a Major League player. Primarily a second baseman, Friend was strictly a part-timer who was not bad with the glove but had a weak bat. After five minor-league seasons, he debuted with the Browns in October 1949 and batted .375 in a total of eight at-bats. Friend never again hit above .237 in the Bigs, but fared better in his 14 years as a minor-league player. In the majors, he played for five teams in five seasons, interrupted by two years in the US Army Medical Corps during the Korean War. After his playing days, Friend managed in the minors through 1975 for the Cardinals, Senators, Orioles, Royals, and Mets. He coached for the 1969 Kansas City Royals and scouted for the Astros, Orioles, and Royals. He passed away in 2007 at age 80.

Career Stats

AB:	598	HR:	13
R:	69	RBI:	76
H:	136	OPS:	.634
BA:	.227		

Teams

St. Louis Browns AL (1949–1950)
Detroit Tigers AL (1953)
Cleveland Indians AL (1953)
Boston Red Sox AL (1955)
Chicago Cubs AL (1955–1956)

Les Fusselman

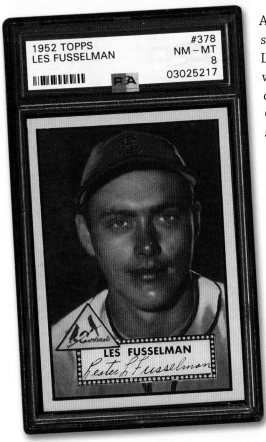

A backup to starter Del Rice, Les Fusselman was a hard-nosed catcher for the Cardinals in 1952 and 1953, playing alongside some of the game's great names including Stan Musial, Enos Slaughter, Red Schoendienst, and Eddie Stanky. In his two MLB seasons, Fusselman batted just .169 with one homer and three RBI. Signed by the Cards in 1942, the Western Illinois University product served in the US Army in World War II and returned to toil in the St. Louis farm system. Known as a terrific handler of pitchers in the minors, Fusselman had some good offensive numbers with the Houston Buffs when they won the Texas League title in 1951. He also batted over .300 in a couple of lower-level minor-league stops. Sadly, Fusselman's life mirrored his brief big-league career. He died in Cleveland at the young age of 49 in 1970.

Career Stats

AB:	71	HR:	1
R:	6	RBI:	3
H:	12	OPS:	.437
BA:	.169		

Teams

St. Louis Cardinals NL (1952–1953)

Ned Garver

A pitcher who should have fared better, Ned Garver had the bad luck to pitch for some God-awful teams. His career 3.73 ERA gives an indication that Garver was not the problem. Amazingly, in 1951, Garver won 20 games on a Brownies team that lost 102 games. He made the All-Star team and was second to Yogi Berra in MVP voting. Known for his control and command of his breaking balls, Garver led the league in complete games in 1950 and 1951. Also a well-regarded hitter, Garver usually batted higher up in the order and was sometimes used as a pinch-hitter. Always a competitor, in the injury-prone latter part of his career, Garver went 14–11 with an 2.81 ERA for the 1954 Tigers. After his retirement, Garver worked in the food service business and was elected mayor of Ney, Ohio. He died in 2017 at age 91.

Career Stats

Record:	129–157
ERA:	3.73
IP:	2,477.1
Ks:	881
Threw:	RH

Teams

St. Louis Browns AL (1948–1952)
Detroit Tigers AL (1952–1956)
Kansas City Athletics AL (1957–1960)
Los Angeles Angels AL (1961)

Dick Gernert

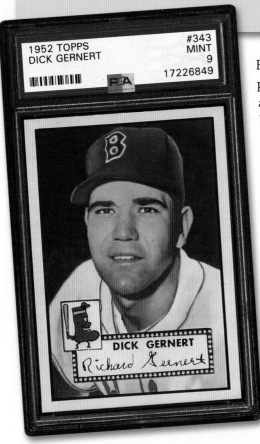

From 1952 to 1959, Dick Gernert was the prototypical Red Sox player. At 6-foot-3 and 209 pounds, the big right-handed batter had lots of power and no speed. In 1952, his rookie year, Gernert struck out 83 times but slammed 19 home runs. Gernert swatted 21 homers in 1953 and 20 in 1958. He batted .291 in 1956, but his career batting average was just .254. Born in Reading, Pennsylvania, known as "Baseballtown," Gernert graduated from Temple University and had cups of coffee with the Cubs, Tigers, Colt .45s, and the 1961 NL pennant-winning Reds. A baseball lifer, Gernert worked as a coach, scout, and executive, eventually retiring in 2000. He was inducted into the Reading Baseball Hall of Fame in 1994 and named "King of Baseballtown" in 2005. Gernert was 89 when he died in 2017.

Career Stats

AB:	2,493	HR:	103
R:	357	RBI:	402
H:	632	OPS:	.776
BA:	.254		

Teams

Boston Red Sox AL (1952–1959)
Chicago Cubs NL (1960)
Detroit Tigers AL (1960–1961)
Cincinnati Reds NL (1961)
Houston Colt .45s NL (1962)

Tookie Gilbert

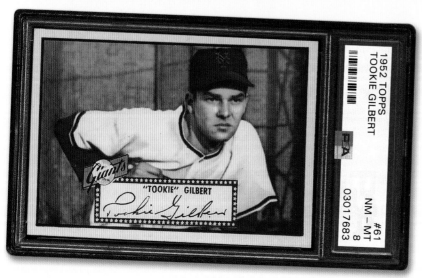

Pegged as a "can't miss" prospect, Tookie Gilbert, unfortunately missed. The power-hitting first baseman had some fabulous years in the high-level minors, batting well over .300 three seasons and slamming more than 20 home runs five seasons. Unfortunately, he could not duplicate this success in the majors. After batting .334 with 33 home runs in 1949 for Nashville in the Southern Association, Gilbert came up to the New York Giants in 1950, but returned to the minors later that season. He got one more shot with the Giants in 1953, with no success. In the majors, Gilbert hit a career seven home runs and batted .203, barely over the Mendoza line. After an unsuccessful comeback attempt in 1959, Gilbert was sheriff of Orleans County, Louisiana. He suffered a massive heart attack in 1967 and died at the age of 38.

Teams

New York Giants NL (1950, 1953)

Career Stats

AB:	482	HR:	7
R:	52	RBI:	48
H:	98	OPS:	.586
BA:	.203		

Joe Ginsberg

A dependable catcher for seven teams over his 13-year Major League career, Joe Ginsberg was a no-nonsense, hardworking "dirt dog" who gave 100 percent. Ginsberg was a good defensive catcher who was noted for handling pitchers and calling good games. Offensively, he was an adequate hitter who could chip in with a key hit. A backup for most of his career, Ginsberg got the most playing time in 1951 and 1952 as starting catcher for the Detroit Tigers. In 1951, he batted .260 and hit eight home runs in 304 at-bats, and in 1952 Ginsberg caught the first of Virgil Trucks' two no-hitters. The World War II US Army veteran retired in 1962 and returned home to Michigan, where he worked in sales for the Jack Daniels distillery, participated in charity golf outings, and maintained ties with the Tigers. He died in 2012 at the age of 86.

Career Stats

AB:	1,716	HR:	20
R:	168	RBI:	182
H:	414	OPS:	.652
BA:	.241		

Teams

Detroit Tigers AL (1948, 1950–1953)
Cleveland Indians AL (1953–1954)
Kansas City Athletics AL (1956)
Baltimore Orioles AL (1956–1960)
Chicago White Sox AL (1960–1961)
Boston Red Sox AL (1961)
New York Mets NL (1962)

Tommy Glaviano

Tommy Glaviano's Major League career got off to a fairly good start but tailed off quickly. The California native and WWII US Coast Guard veteran was 25 years old in 1949 when he debuted with the St. Louis Cardinals. In 1950, as the Cards starting third baseman, Glaviano batted .285 with 11 home runs. However, he is known for his performance in one game. On May 18, 1950, Glaviano hit a fourth-inning home run off Brooklyn Dodgers Joe Hatten, but his three consecutive errors in the ninth inning caused St. Louis to blow an 8–5 lead and lose the game. As a part-timer in 1951, Glaviano batted .183, and after two more weak seasons, he returned to the minors, where he played until 1957. Although Glaviano had a mediocre career, he did have a few Major League moments. Tommy Glaviano passed away in Sacramento, California in 2004 at 80 years old.

Career Stats

AB:	1,008	HR:	24
R:	191	RBI:	108
H:	259	OPS:	.789
BA:	.257		

Teams

St. Louis Cardinals NL (1949–1952)
Philadelphia Phillies NL (1953)

Gordon Goldsberry

After a short stint as a Major League ballplayer, Gordon Goldsberry had a nice run as a scout and front office guy for many years. The UCLA graduate spent five years in the minors before joining the Chicago White Sox in 1949 as backup first baseman. With only 510 at-bats and a .241 BA, Goldsberry's MLB playing years were not memorable, but he honed his baseball IQ, and that paid off. After retiring, Goldsberry worked as a scout for several franchises. While with the Brewers, he signed future Hall of Famer Robin Yount. He was then director of player development and scouting for the Chicago Cubs before working for the Baltimore Orioles as special assistant to the general manager. Well-respected throughout the Major Leagues for mentoring young players, Goldsberry passed away in 1996 at the age of 68 from an apparent heart attack.

Career Stats

AB:	510	HR:	6
R:	78	RBI:	56
H:	123	OPS:	.687
BA:	.241		

Teams

Chicago White Sox AL (1949–1951)
St. Louis Browns AL (1952)

Ted Gray

A lefty pitcher with potential, Detroit native Ted Gray signed with the Tigers out of high school in 1942. After seasoning in the minors and three years as an ace pitcher for the US Navy during WWII, Gray joined Detroit in 1948. He went 10–7 and pitched in the first televised All-Star game in 1950. A back of the rotation guy through 1954, Gray's performance was hampered by chronic blisters. He hit a low point in 1952, losing 17 games. Ironically, although Gray was up with the strikeout leaders for several years, he also led the league in home runs allowed. Traded by Detroit to the White Sox in 1955, Gray also played for the Indians, Yankees, and Orioles that year and retired that season with a career 59–74 record. He returned to Michigan to a career in the automobile industry and died in 2011 at age 86.

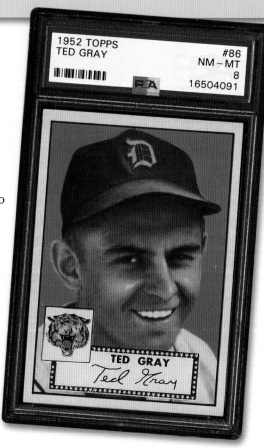

Career Stats

Record:	59–74
ERA:	4.37
IP:	1,134.0
Ks	687
Threw:	LH

Teams

Detroit Tigers AL (1946, 1948–1954)
Chicago White Sox AL (1955)
Cleveland Indians AL (1955)
New York Yankees AL (1955)
Baltimore Orioles AL (1955)

Hal Gregg

Hal Gregg's 1944 pitching line can only be described as dreadful. In that season with Brooklyn, Gregg was 9–16 with a 5.46 ERA. He led the league in walks, earned runs, wild pitches, and hit batsmen. He also surrendered more hits than innings pitched. Even in 1945, when he won 18 games with a 3.47 ERA, Gregg again topped the league with 120 walks. The hard-throwing right-hander with a mean fastball struggled with control throughout his nine-year MLB career. Used primarily as a reliever after 1945, Gregg had some notable moments in 1947. Brooklyn's winning pitcher on April 15, Jackie Robinson's first MLB game, Gregg pitched a complete game shutout on April 22, and he pitched in three games of the 1947 World Series. After retiring, Gregg returned to California to run his family's orange business. He died in 1991 at age 69.

Career Stats

Record: 40–48
ERA: 4.54
IP: 827.0
Ks: 401
Threw: RH

Teams

Brooklyn Dodgers NL (1943–1947)
Pittsburgh Pirates NL (1948–1950)
New York Giants NL (1952)

Steve Gromek

A switch-hitting infielder turned pitcher, Steve Gromek enjoyed a 17-year big league career and won 123 games playing for the Indians and Tigers. In 1945, he was 19–9 with a 2.55 ERA for Cleveland. That season, he registered 21 complete games and walked just 66 batters in 251 innings pitched. A member of Cleveland's 1948 world championship team, Gromek pitched a complete game win in Game Four of the fall classic. That game was the backdrop for a memorable photo of Gromek celebrating the victory with teammate Larry Doby, who hit the game-winning homer. A year earlier, Doby had become the American League's first African American player, and the groundbreaking image of a black man and a white man joyously hugging each other raised social consciousness. Traded to Detroit in 1953, Gromek later managed in the Tigers farm system. He died in 2002 at the age of 82.

Career Stats

Record: 123–108
ERA: 3.41
IP: 2,064.2
Ks: 904
Threw: RH

Teams

Cleveland Indians AL (1941–1953)
Detroit Tigers AL (1953–1957)

Johnny Groth

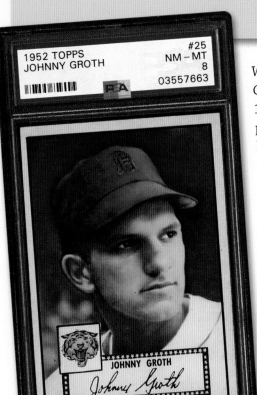

When the Detroit Tigers signed Johnny Groth in 1946, the press touted the 19-year-old as the next DiMaggio. That pressure may well have been a factor in his performance, which never met those lofty expectations. However, the US Navy veteran did carve out a solid career. A .279 lifetime hitter, his best season was in 1950 when he batted .306 with 173 hits. A good defensive outfielder, Groth finished his 15-year MLB career with a .987 lifetime fielding percentage. His two stints with the Tigers were separated by four trades in five years. During this period, while playing for St. Louis, Groth scored the last run in the Browns' team history. After he retired as a player, Groth managed in the minors for a few seasons and scouted for the Atlanta Braves for 27 years. At the time of this writing, Johnny Groth is 93 years old.

Career Stats

AB:	3,808	HR:	60
R:	480	RBI:	486
H:	1,064	OPS:	.746
BA:	.279		

Teams

Detroit Tigers AL (1946–1952, 1957–1960)
St. Louis Browns AL (1953)
Chicago White Sox AL (1954–1955)
Washington Senators AL (1955)
Kansas City Athletics AL (1956–1957)

Randy Gumpert

A 1951 All-Star, Randy Gumpert broke in with the Athletics in 1936. Sent to the minors in 1938, Gumpert served three years in the US Coast Guard and resurfaced in the majors with the 1946 Yankees. The Pennsylvania native went 11–3 with a fine 2.31 ERA, striking out 63 batters, and walking just 32 in just over 132 innings pitched. Gumpert went 4–1 for the 1947 world champion Yankees, but did not play in the Series. In 1949, he went 13–16 for the White Sox with a respectable 3.81 ERA. A starter and reliever, Gumpert finished with the Red Sox and Senators in 1952. He managed in the minors, coached and scouted for the Yankees, and worked for the Major League Scouting Bureau until 1993. A member of the Pennsylvania Sports Hall of Fame and the Major League Scouting Hall of Fame, Gumpert died in 2008 at age 90.

Career Stats

Record:	51–59
ERA:	4.17
IP:	1,052.2
Ks:	352
Threw:	RH

Teams

Philadelphia Athletics AL (1936–1938)
New York Yankees AL (1946–1948)
Chicago White Sox AL (1948–1951)
Boston Red Sox AL (1952)
Washington Senators AL (1952)

Warren Hacker

Illinois native Warren Hacker experienced both the ultimate dream and worst nightmare. He pitched for his hometown Cubbies from 1948 through 1956, surely a Windy City fantasy come true. In 1952, the knuckleball and sinkerball pitcher put together a 15–9 record with a 2.58 ERA. In 1953, however, it was nightmare time. Hacker surrendered a league-leading 35 home runs, lost a league-high 19 games, and allowed the most earned runs in the NL as the sad sack Cubs finished seventh. Hacker lost 15 and 13 games with the Cubs in 1955 and 1956, respectively, before moving to the Redlegs and Phillies. He pitched in the minors through 1966 with one trip back to the Bigs as a White Sox reliever in 1961. Hacker later managed and coached in the minors for several years. He was 77 years old when he died in 2002.

Career Stats

Record:	62–89
ERA:	4.21
IP:	1,283.1
Ks:	557
Threw:	RH

Teams

Chicago Cubs NL (1948–1956)
Cincinnati Redlegs NL (1957)
Philadelphia Phillies NL (1957–1958)
Chicago White Sox AL (1961)

Andy Hansen

A two-sport athlete at Lake Worth High School, Andy "Swede" Hansen was signed by the Giants in 1943. That year, the high school senior pitched Lake Worth to the Florida state tournament before posting a 12–3 record in the Giants farm system. With the big club in 1944 and 1945, he won a combined seven games as a spot starter and reliever. Hansen missed the 1946 season due to a commitment to Uncle Sam, but he returned in 1947 to post four mediocre seasons for the Giants. Acquired by the Philadelphia Phillies in the 1950 Rule 5 draft, Hansen was used primarily as a relief pitcher, and by 1954 he was out of baseball. He returned to Lake Worth and worked for the Postal Service for 31 years. The 1988 inductee to the Palm Beach County Sports Hall of Fame died in 2002 at age 77.

Career Stats

Record:	23–30
ERA:	4.22
IP:	618.2
Ks:	188
Threw:	RH

Teams

New York Giants NL (1944–1945, 1947–1950)
Philadelphia Phillies NL (1951–1953)

Mickey Harris

After starting for the Red Sox in 1941, his first full Major League season, southpaw Mickey Harris played ball for Uncle Sam for the next four years in the Panama Canal Zone. Upon his return in 1946, Harris posted a career-best 17–9 record with a 3.64 ERA, made the All-Star team, and contributed to the Red Sox' 1946 American League pennant win. Harris started Game Two and Game Six in the disappointing World Series loss to the Cardinals. Plagued by arm woes, Harris became a sub .500 pitcher after that one shining season. After the Washington Senators converted him to a reliever, Harris led the league with 43 games finished and 15 saves in 1950. He wrapped up with the Indians in 1952 and later worked in sales and maintenance. Harris died of a sudden heart attack while bowling in 1971 at the age of 54.

Career Stats

Record:	59–71
ERA:	4.18
IP:	1,050.0
Ks:	534
Threw:	LH

Teams

Boston Red Sox AL (1940–1941, 1946–1949)
Washington Senators AL (1949–1952)
Cleveland Indians AL (1952)

Earl Harrist

Knuckleballer Earl Harrist became part of baseball history on July 5, 1947. Harrist was on the hill for the Chicago White Sox when Cleveland's Larry Doby pinch-hit in the seventh inning at Comiskey Park, becoming the first African American to play in the American League. Harrist played five seasons in the Bigs for the Reds, White Sox, Senators, Browns, and Tigers, posting a 12–28 career record with a 4.34 ERA. In 1952 with the Browns, he led the league in hit batsmen. Harrist enjoyed more success in the minors, compiling a 148–135 record in 15 seasons. The World War II US Army Air Force veteran wrapped up his MLB career in 1953. He continued in the minors until 1958 and went on to scout for Cleveland and Houston. Harrist died in his native Louisiana in 1998 at age 79.

Career Stats

Record:	12–28
ERA:	4.34
IP:	383.1
Ks:	162
Threw:	RH

Teams

Cincinnati Reds NL (1945)
Chicago White Sox AL (1947–1948, 1953)
Washington Senators AL (1948)
St. Louis Browns AL (1952)
Detroit Tigers AL (1953)

Clint Hartung

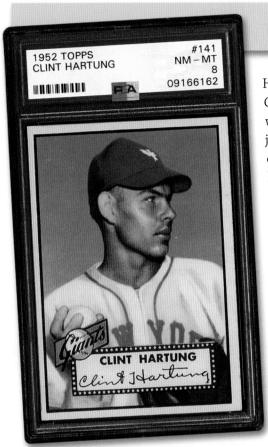

Hyped as the savior of the Giants, Clint Hartung received $35,000 to sign with New York in 1947. Hartung was just back from four years of pitching domination in the military service leagues, and the 6-foot-5, 210-pound Texas native with the blazing fastball seemed like a sure thing. Hartung didn't live up to the hype, never winning more than nine games in a season. After four years, the Giants converted Hartung to an outfielder, without much success. His claim to fame? Hartung was on third base as pinch-runner for Don Mueller when Bobby Thomson hit the "Shot Heard 'Round the World" to win the 1951 NL pennant. By 1952 he was out of the majors, finishing with a career .238 BA. After baseball, he worked for an oil refinery in Sinton, Texas, where he passed away at the age of 87 in 2010.

Career Stats

Record:	29–29
ERA:	5.02
IP:	511.1
Ks:	167
Threw:	RH

Teams

New York Giants NL (1947–1952)

Fred Hatfield

Fred Hatfield was born in Alabama, but made his name up north as an infielder for the Boston Red Sox and Detroit Tigers. In 1951, his second season in the Bigs, Hatfield batted just .172. He bounced back and was hitting .320 for Boston 19 games into the 1952 season when he was dealt to Detroit. Hatfield would keep his bags packed throughout a MLB career in which he played for five teams in nine years. Along the way, he was traded with stars like Johnny Pesky and for luminaries such as Early Wynn. The US Army veteran and Troy State grad became a Hall of Fame coach at Florida State and a successful minor-league manager and scout, but never fulfilled his dream of being a big-league manager. He was 73 years old when he died of cancer in 1998.

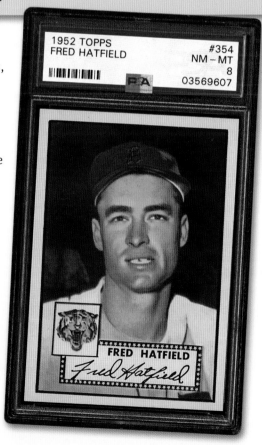

Career Stats

AB:	2,039	HR:	25
R:	260	RBI.	165
H:	493	OPS:	.654
BA:	.242		

Teams

Boston Red Sox AL (1950–1952)
Detroit Tigers AL (1952–1956)
Chicago White Sox AL (1956–1957)
Cleveland Indians AL (1958)
Cincinnati Redlegs NL (1958)

Joe Hatten

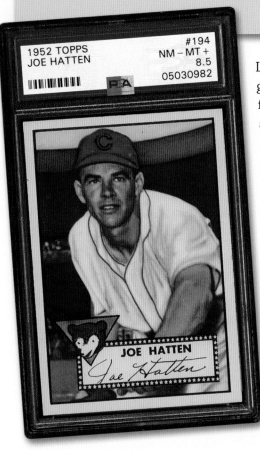

Like a pitching meteor, Joe Hatten showed great promise right out of the gate but flamed out quickly. Over his first four seasons with the Brooklyn Dodgers, Hatten compiled 56 wins, but he had just nine wins over his final three seasons. Hatten's command was not the best. It was not unusual for him to walk a batter or even plunk him. Hatten's claim to fame is his complete game shutout vs. Cincinnati in 1948 when he threw only 51 pitches for the win. However, it was a five-inning game. By 1952, Hatten found himself back in the minors. He played nine more years, mostly in the Pacific Coast League. The highlight of that period was his 17-win season in 1953 for Los Angeles. Hatten went on to work as a mailman for the US Postal Service and died in 1988 at age 72 from cancer.

Career Stats

Record:	65–49
ERA:	3.87
IP:	1,087.0
Ks:	381
Threw:	LH

Teams

Brooklyn Dodgers NL (1946–1951)
Chicago Cubs NL (1951–1952)

Phil Haugstad

A must at the minor-league level with 94 wins, pitcher Phil Haugstad was a bust at the Major League level, with only one win. Pitching for the Brooklyn affiliate AAA level St. Paul Saints, Haugstad won more than 12 games on four different occasions with his high posting a 22–7 record in 1949. The US Army Air Force veteran was called up to the Dodgers in September 1947 and recorded his only MLB career win for the NL pennant winners. He was back with the Saints for most of 1948 and all of the next two seasons. With the big club in 1951 he posted a 0–1 record in 30 innings pitched, with an inflated 6.46 ERA. Haugstad closed out his Major League career with the Reds in 1952 but continued in the minors until 1955. In retirement, Haugstad launched a successful logging business. He died in 1998 at age 74.

Career Stats

Record:	1–1
ERA:	5.59
IP:	56.1
Ks:	28
Threw:	RH

Teams

Brooklyn Dodgers NL (1947, 1948, 1951)
Cincinnati Reds NL (1952)

Jim Hearn

A solid, unheralded pitcher, "Big Jim" Hearn compiled a 109–89 career record playing for the Cardinals, Giants, and Phillies. The Georgia native posted 11 wins and led the NL with his 2.49 ERA in 1950. The following two seasons, he won 17 and 14 games, respectively, for the Giants. The 1951 pennant winners boasted a rotation that included Hearn along with a pair of 23-game winners, Sal Maglie and Larry Jansen. Hearn was at his best when it counted most. He won the first game of the NL playoff series vs. Brooklyn, and Game Three of the 1951 World Series vs. the Yanks. Hearn served three years in the US Army, married a former Miss Atlanta, and, after baseball, started the Jim Hearn Golf Center in Atlanta. He was inducted into the Georgia Sports Hall of Fame in 1983. Hearn died from Hodgkin's lymphoma in 1998 at age 77.

Career Stats

Record:	109–89
ERA:	3.81
IP:	1,703.2
Ks:	669
Threw:	RH

Teams

St. Louis Cardinals NL (1947–1950)
New York Giants NL (1950–1956)
Philadelphia Phillies NL (1957–1959)

Ken Heintzelman

Fireballing left-hander Ken "Cannonball" Heintzelman pitched through 13 MLB seasons with the Pirates and Phillies. His longevity is somewhat of a mystery considering he regularly surrendered more hits than innings pitched, although he did compile a respectable career 3.93 ERA. Heintzelman missed three seasons to US Army service in various combat roles but ended his time in Europe playing and coaching baseball. In 1949, at age 33, Heintzelman won 17 games for the Phils with a 3.02 ERA. The next year, as a member of Philadelphia's Whiz Kids, Heintzelman started Game Three of the World Series. Although Philly lost the game, Heintzelman surrendered just one earned run in nearly eight innings of work. His MLB career ended in 1952, but Heintzelman's baseball legacy lived on in his son, Tom, who played for the Cardinals and Giants in the 1970s. Heintzelman died in 2000 at the age of 84.

Career Stats

Record:	77–98
ERA:	3.93
IP:	1,501.2
Ks:	564
Threw:	LH

Teams

Pittsburgh Pirates NL (1937–1942, 1946–1947)
Philadelphia Phillies NL (1947–1952)

Solly Hemus

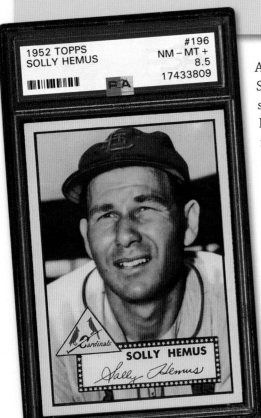

A decent shortstop and second baseman, Solly Hemus started for the Cardinals several seasons. The World War II US Navy veteran led the league with 105 runs in 1952. Later in his 11-year career, he was a utility infielder for the Phillies and the Cards. In 1959, Hemus was tabbed to be the St. Louis manager, and over three seasons he led the Cardinals to a 190–192 record. He then coached for the Mets and the Indians until 1965. Known for his fiery temper as a player, coach, and manager, Hemus was tossed out of games at least 30 times. Hemus claimed to use insults to motivate his players, but future Hall of Famer Bob Gibson maintained that Hemus was racist. This impeded his relationship with both Gibson and Curt Flood.

After baseball, Hemus found success as an oil wildcatter in Houston, Texas. He died in 2017 at age 94.

Career Stats

AB:	2,694	HR:	51
R:	459	RBI:	263
H:	736	OPS:	.801
BA:	.273		

Teams

St. Louis Cardinals NL (1949–1956, 1959)
Philadelphia Phillies NL (1956–1958)

Gene Hermanski

Although essentially a platoon player, Gene Hermanski did play in one of MLB's most historic games. He was starting left fielder for the Brooklyn Dodgers on April 15, 1947, the day his teammate Jackie Robinson broke the color barrier. Hermanski got a hit in that historic game, which the Dodgers won 5–3. A decent outfielder and good hitter, he started all seven games for the Dodgers in the 1947 World Series against the Yankees. Incredibly, on August 5, 1948, at Ebbets Field, Hermanski went yard three times. The next year Hermanski batted a gaudy .308 against the pinstripes in the 1949 World Series. After trades to the Cubs and the Pirates, Hermanski wrapped up his nine-season career in the majors. He played briefly in the minors before starting a career in heavy construction-equipment sales. Hermanski retired to Florida where he died at the age of 90 in 2010.

Career Stats

AB:	1,960	HR:	46
R:	276	RBI:	259
H:	533	OPS:	.776
BA:	.272		

Teams

Brooklyn Dodgers NL (1943, 1946–1951)
Chicago Cubs NL (1951–1953)
Pittsburgh Pirates NL (1953)

Frank Hiller

An injury-plagued pitcher in the majors, Frank Hiller was a highly touted prospect who posted a 22–2 record for Lafayette College. He signed with the Yankees in 1943, delivered three consecutive double-digit wins seasons for the Newark Bears, but injured his elbow. Soon after his Yankees debut in 1946, Hiller had an elbow operation, and he ended up in the minors for most of his time with the Yanks. Dispatched to the Chicago Cubs in 1950, Hiller responded with a 12–5 record and 3.53 ERA, but his woes continued over the next few seasons with a back injury, wrenched knee, and broken nose. Hiller wrapped it up the in the minors in 1954, posting an 11–8 record with a 2.92 ERA in the Pacific Coast League during his final season. He worked in the life insurance business and passed away in 1987 at the age of 66.

Career Stats
Record:	30–32
ERA:	4.42
IP:	533.2
Ks:	197
Threw:	RH

Teams
New York Yankees AL (1946, 1948–1949)
Chicago Cubs NL (1950–1951)
Cincinnati Reds NL (1952)
New York Giants NL (1953)

Billy Hoeft

A hot prospect, Billy Hoeft broke in with the Detroit Tigers at the age of 20 in 1952. He won 16 games for the Tigers, led the league with seven shutouts, and was an All-Star in 1955. Hoeft followed up that season with a 20–14 record in 1956. He would never again approach those numbers, but Hoeft did pitch for 15 seasons with six clubs. In 1959, Hoeft barely had a chance to unpack, playing for the Tigers, Red Sox, and Orioles. He spent parts of four seasons in Baltimore before moving on to the Giants, Braves, and Cubs. The lefty once won 34 straight games as a high school hurler, including three no-hitters, but arm soreness derailed his road to MLB immortality. After baseball, Hoeft worked in sales and enjoyed spending time with his family. He passed away in 2010 at the age of 77.

Career Stats
Record:	97–101
ERA:	3.94
IP:	1,847.1
Ks:	1,140
Threw:	LH

Teams
Detroit Tigers AL (1952–1959)
Boston Red Sox AL (1959)
Baltimore Orioles AL (1959–1962)
San Francisco Giants NL (1963, 1966)
Milwaukee Braves NL (1964)
Chicago Cubs NL (1965–1966)

Bobby Hofman

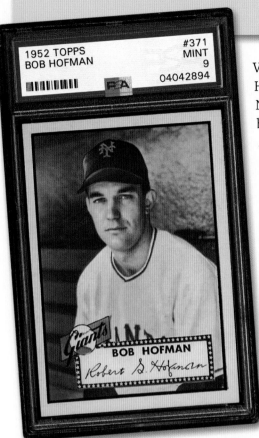

1952 TOPPS
BOB HOFMAN

#371
MINT
9
04042894

Versatile infielder and catcher, Bobby Hofman played seven seasons for the New York Giants. A platoon player, his best season was in 1952 when he batted .286 in 32 games. Born in St. Louis, Hofman played Legion ball with fellow Missourian, Yogi Berra. In 1944, he enlisted in the US Army, served for two years, and fought at the Battle of the Bulge. Hofman was a solid minor-league player and a specialist at catching the knuckleball. After his playing days, he managed in the minors, and coached and scouted for the Athletics, including their 1974 world championship team. Hoffman was also director of scouting and player development for the Yankees, making him one of those rare breeds who survived working for both Charlie Finley and George Steinbrenner. Hofman passed away in 1994 at the age of 68, ending a life in baseball that spanned over four decades.

Career Stats

AB:	670	HR:	32
R:	81	RBI:	101
H:	166	OPS:	.764
BA:	.248		

Teams

New York Giants NL (1949, 1952–1957)

Bobby Hogue

As relief pitchers go, Bobby Hogue was not bad. A rookie reliever for the Boston Braves in 1948, Hogue compiled an 8–2 record, helping the Braves to the National League pennant. Although Johnny Sain and Warren Spahn were the pitching catalysts for the Braves that year, Hogue's relief pitching was still key. A slider and knuckler specialist, Hogue kept hitters off balance by mixing up his pitches. Eventually winding up with the Yankees, Hogue again was a contributor. In the 1951 World Series, he appeared in two games and pitched very well. Bobby Hogue did not have a very long career, appearing in only 172 games with three different teams, but he was a contributor, nonetheless. A Miami, Florida, native, Hogue went on to work for the *Miami Herald* and enjoyed fishing the Florida Keys. He lost his battle with cancer in 1987 at the age of 66.

1952 TOPPS
BOBBY HOGUE

#9
NM – MT
8
05031199

Career Stats

Record:	18–16
ERA:	3.97
IP:	326.2
Ks:	108
Threw:	RH

Teams

Boston Braves NL (1948–1951)
St. Louis Browns AL (1951, 1952)
New York Yankees AL (1951–1952)

Ken Holcombe

1952 TOPPS #95
KEN HOLCOMBE MINT 9
15688716 PSA

A pitcher with potential, 26-year-old Ken Holcombe had a solid rookie season in 1945. He put up sparkling numbers for the Yankees, pitching a total of 55 innings with a 3–3 record and an excellent 1.79 ERA. Unfortunately, Holcombe developed bursitis and was plagued with arm woes for the rest of his career. He went from the Yanks, to the Reds, to the White Sox, to the Browns, before ending his career with the Red Sox. His best year was 1951 when, as a starter for the Chicago White Sox, he won 11 games with a nice 3.78 ERA. Around his Major League stints, Holcombe toiled in the minors for 14 years, compiling a 133–112 record before retiring in 1954. After baseball, he returned home to North Carolina and worked as a textile manufacturing supervisor. He passed away in 2010 at the age of 91.

Career Stats

Record: 18–32
ERA: 3.98
IP: 375.0
Ks: 118
Threw: RH

Teams

New York Yankees AL (1945)
Cincinnati Reds NL (1948)
Chicago White Sox AL (1950–1952)
St. Louis Browns AL (1952)
Boston Red Sox AL (1953)

Bob Hooper

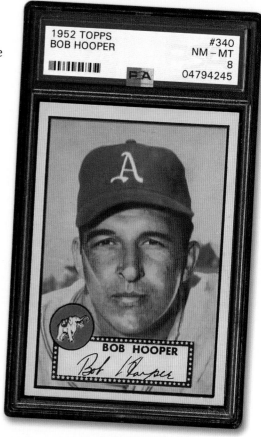

1952 TOPPS #340
BOB HOOPER NM – MT 8
04794245 PSA

Canadian-born and New Jersey-bred Bob Hooper broke into the big leagues in 1950, winning a total of 27 games in his first two seasons with the Athletics. Hooper's obvious talent was hampered by a lack of control, which led to baserunners and a career ERA of 4.80 with nearly 100 more walks than strikeouts. A US Army Air Force veteran, Hooper struggled with arm woes. His numbers dipped sharply after 1951, and after brief stops in Cleveland and Cincinnati, he was out of MLB baseball by 1955. Hooper returned to the minors and retired in 1958 with a 74–56 record compiled over ten minor-league seasons. In retirement, he briefly managed in the minors, earned a degree in education, and taught physical education at the high-school level until 1979. Hooper died of a heart attack in 1980 at age 57.

Career Stats

Record: 40–41
ERA: 4.80
IP: 620.2
Ks: 196
Threw: RH

Teams

Philadelphia Athletics AL (1950–1952)
Cleveland Indians AL (1953–1954)
Cincinnati Redlegs NL (1955)

Frank House

According to news reports, Alabama native Frank House, a multi-sport star in high school, so impressed the Tigers that they gave him a huge $75,000 bonus plus two cars when they signed him right out of high school. The 6-foot-1 and 190-pound backstop nicknamed "Pig" debuted with Detroit in 1950 and served in the military during the Korean War. Upon his return, House was the Tigers starting catcher for four seasons. A solid backstop known for his handling of pitchers and his strong arm, House was not bad with the bat either. His best year offensively was 1955 when he batted .259 with 15 home runs for the Tigers. After his playing days, House served in the Alabama Legislature and helped establish the Alabama Sports Hall of Fame in 1967. A 1975 Alabama Sports Hall of Fame inductee, House passed away in 2005 at the age of 75.

Career Stats

AB:	1,994	HR:	47
R:	201	RBI:	235
H:	494	OPS:	.663
BA:	.248		

Teams

Detroit Tigers AL (1950–1951, 1954–1957, 1961)
Kansas City Athletics AL (1958–1959)
Cincinnati Reds NL (1960)

Art Houtteman

Art Houtteman played 12 seasons in the majors with the Tigers, Indians, and Orioles. He had two solid years with Detroit. In 1949, he went 15–10 with a 3.71 ERA. An All-Star the next season, Houtteman logged a 19–12 record with a 3.54 ERA and a league-leading four shutouts. In 1952, he lost a league-high 20 games, but he rebounded in 1954, going 15–7 with a 3.35 ERA for the AL pennant-winning Indians. Nicknamed "Hard Luck" Houtteman, the Detroit native certainly lived up to the moniker. He once lost a no-hitter with two outs in the ninth inning. During spring training in 1949, Houtteman fractured his skull in a car accident. Three years later, another vehicle accident tragically took the life of his seven-month-old daughter. After baseball, Houtteman owned show horses, worked in television, and worked in steel industry sales. He died in 2003 at age 75.

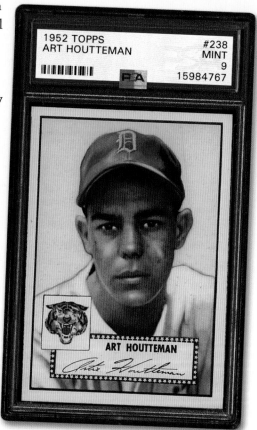

Career Stats

Record:	87–91
ERA:	4.14
IP:	1,555.0
Ks:	639
Threw:	RH

Teams

Detroit Tigers AL (1945–1953)
Cleveland Indians AL (1953–1957)
Baltimore Orioles AL (1957)

Dixie Howell

A pretty good defensive catcher, 27-year-old Homer "Dixie" Howell batted a career-best .276 with the Pittsburgh Pirates in 1947, his rookie season. Before that, Howell bounced around the minors for seven years and served two years in the US Army. In 1946, he played with Jackie Robinson on the Montreal Royals in the International League, the first integrated professional baseball team since the 1880s. The Louisville, Kentucky, native was one of the few southern players who welcomed Robinson. After four seasons in Cincinnati, Howell landed with the Dodgers in 1953 and was Robinson's teammate once again. As backup to Roy Campanella on the 1955 and 1956 Dodgers' pennant-winning squads, Howell got a ring in 1955 but did not play in the Series. Howell later played and managed in the minors, scouted for the Braves, and worked in insurance. He passed away in 1990 at the age of 70.

Teams

Pittsburgh Pirates NL (1947)
Cincinnati Reds NL (1949–1952)
Brooklyn Dodgers NL (1953, 1955–1956)

Career Stats

AB:	910	HR:	12
R:	98	RBI:	93
H:	224	OPS:	.651
BA:	.246		

Bill Howerton

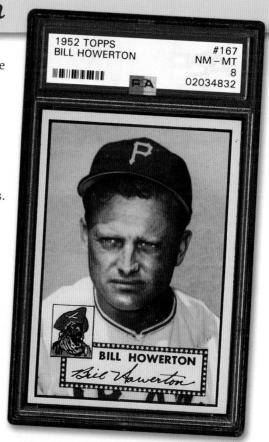

A utility outfielder, Bill "Hopalong" Howerton toiled six years in the minors before getting a late season call-up to St. Louis after batting .329 with 21 home runs for the Columbus Red Birds in 1949. The 28-year-old Howerton responded by batting .281 with 59 RBI and ten home runs in his rookie season. The next year, he batted .271 with 41 RBI and 12 homers in a season split between St. Louis and Pittsburgh. By the way, "Hopalong" earned his nickname because he favored his left leg due to a childhood horseback riding injury. Although he showed star potential in the minors, Bill was only an adequate reserve outfielder in the majors. However, his baseball legacy lived on in his son Bill Jr., who was head baseball coach at the University of Scranton for many years. Howerton passed away in 2001 at 80 years old.

Career Stats

AB:	650	HR:	22
R:	95	RBI:	106
H:	178	OPS:	.836
BA:	.274		

Teams

St. Louis Cardinals NL (1949–1951)
Pittsburgh Pirates NL (1951–1952)
New York Giants NL (1952)

Sid Hudson

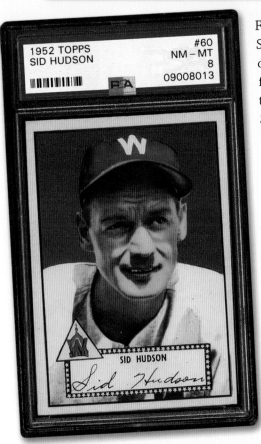

For most of his career, Sid Hudson was a front of the rotation guy for a back of the pack team, the Washington Senators. The right-hander debuted in 1940 with a 17-win season. Although Hudson was an All-Star with 13 wins in 1941 and ten wins in 1942, he had a sub .500 record those two seasons. A hard-luck pitcher, Hudson would likely have fared better if he played for better teams. After losing three seasons to service in the US Army Air Force, Hudson returned to the Senators in 1946. He continued on without much success and even led the league with 17 losses in 1949. Hudson finished up with the Red Sox and retired in 1954. He scouted for the Sox, and coached for the Senators, Rangers, and Baylor University, retiring in 1992. Hudson died in 2008 at the age of 93 in Waco, Texas.

Career Stats

Record:	104–152
ERA:	4.28
IP:	2,181.0
Ks:	734
Threw:	RH

Teams

Washington Senators AL (1940–1942, 1946–1952)
Boston Red Sox AL (1952–1954)

Randy Jackson

Baseball history is littered with firsts, but how about the lasts? Randy "Handsome Ransom" Jackson will go down in history as the last Brooklyn Dodger to ever hit a home run. In the next to last game of the 1957 season, Jackson blasted just his second homer of the season, helping the Dodgers to an 8–4 win at Philadelphia. The next day, Brooklyn lost to the Phillies in their final game as the Brooklyn Dodgers. Jackson played in Los Angeles the next season before being sold to the Indians in August. His best years were with the Cubbies, where he was a two-time All-Star as a third sacker. A scratch golfer, the southern-bred Jackson played at Augusta and was a punter and halfback for Texas Christian University. His memoir, *Handsome Ransom Jackson: Accidental Big Leaguer*, was published in 2016. Jackson died in 2019 at age 93.

Career Stats

AB:	3,203	HR:	103
R:	412	RBI:	415
H:	835	OPS:	.741
BA:	.261		

Teams

Chicago Cubs NL (1950–1955, 1959)
Brooklyn/Los Angeles Dodgers NL (1956–1958)
Cleveland Indians AL (1958–1959)

Hal Jeffcoat

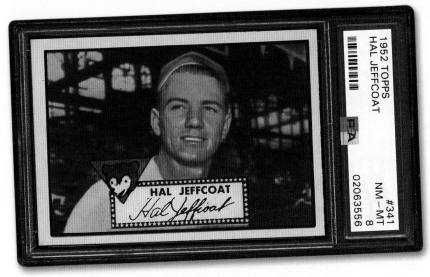

A solid big leaguer for 12 seasons with the Cubs, Reds, and Cardinals, Hal Jeffcoat was an outfielder by trade who transitioned to pitcher. The career .248 hitter, valued for his speed and his arm in the outfield, started throwing batting practice in 1951 and pitched his first game with the Cubs in 1954. With his fastball, curveball, and screwball, the righty compiled a 39-37 career record with a 4.22 ERA and 239 Ks in 697.0 innings pitched over six seasons. Primarily a reliever, Jeffcoat infamously hit Don Zimmer in the face in 1956, changing the course of the future manager's big league career. As a Cubbie, he roomed with Chuck Connors, future star of *The Rifleman*. Jeffcoat's older brother George pitched for the Dodgers and Braves. The former US Army Engineers Airborne Division paratrooper with a Purple Heart died in 2007 at age 82.

Career Stats

AB:	1,963	HR:	26
R:	249	RBI:	188
H:	487	OPS:	.645
BA:	.248		

Teams
Chicago Cubs NL (1948–1955)
Cincinnati Redlegs/Reds NL (1956–1959)
St. Louis Cardinals NL (1959)

Billy Johnson

Mentored by Yankees manager Joe McCarthy, Billy "Bull" Johnson came out of the chute in 1943 batting .280 with 166 hits, and he batted .300 in the Yanks' World Series win over the Cardinals. Not a bad rookie season. A solid third baseman, Johnson played for the Yankees until 1951, but he missed the 1944 and 1945 seasons while serving in World War II. He was a member of three more world championship teams (1947, 1949, 1950) and was an All-Star in 1947. Johnson arguably had his best year in 1948, when he batted .294 and slammed 12 homers. In 1951, Johnson was traded to the St. Louis Cardinals where he anchored the hot corner for a few seasons before retiring in 1953. After baseball, Johnson worked as a shipping supervisor in Augusta, Georgia, for 30 years. He passed away in 2006 at the age of 87.

Career Stats

AB:	3,253	HR:	61
R:	419	RBI:	487
H:	882	OPS:	.737
BA:	.271		

Teams
New York Yankees AL (1943, 1946–1951)
St. Louis Cardinals NL (1951–1953)

Don Johnson

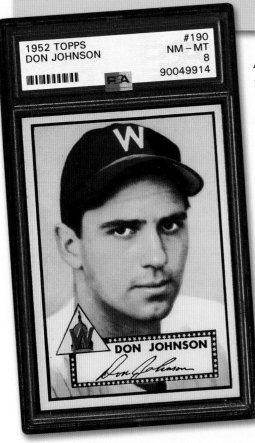

1952 TOPPS
DON JOHNSON
#190
NM – MT
8
90049914

A spot starter and reliever, Don Johnson was a 20-year-old Army veteran when he made it to the majors and went 4–3 for the 1947 world champion Yankees. Johnson jumped from team to team and battled the bottle during his playing days. His best MLB season was 1954, when he posted an 8–7 record with three shutouts, seven saves, and a 3.13 ERA for the White Sox. Before, after, and between his MLB seasons, Johnson pitched in the minors, most successfully with Toronto in the International League. There he had two 15-win seasons and was named Pitcher of the Year in 1957 when he posted a 17–7 record with a 2.96 ERA. After baseball, Johnson returned home to Portland, Oregon. A longtime cabdriver, he survived a holdup attempt on the job when he was shot in the head and neck. He died in 2015 at age 88.

Career Stats

Record:	27–38
ERA:	4.78
IP:	631.0
Ks:	262
Threw:	RH

Teams

New York Yankees AL (1947, 1950)
St. Louis Browns AL (1950–1951)
Washington Senators AL (1951–1952)
Chicago White Sox AL (1954)
Baltimore Orioles AL (1955)
San Francisco Giants NL (1958)

Nippy Jones

With the Cardinals most of his career, first baseman Vernal "Nippy" Jones is best known for one at-bat with the Braves. In 1949, Jones batted a career-best .300 in 380 at-bats for St. Louis. He played on two World Series champion teams: the 1946 Cardinals and the 1957 Milwaukee Braves. In the bottom of the tenth inning of Game Four of the 1957 Series, with the Yankees ahead 5–4, Jones was hit on the foot by a pitch. The umpire called it a ball, but Jones protested. The umpire inspected the ball, found shoe polish on it, and Jones was awarded the base. The Braves surged to win the game and tie the Series. The "shoe-polish incident" is considered the turning point in that fall classic. After baseball, Jones worked in public relations and as a professional fishing guide. He died in 1995 at the age of 70.

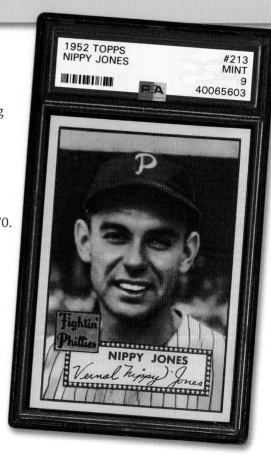

1952 TOPPS
NIPPY JONES
#213
MINT
9
40065603

Career Stats

AB:	1,381	HR:	25
R:	146	RBI:	209
H:	369	OPS:	.687
BA:	.267		

Teams

St. Louis Cardinals NL (1946–1951)
Philadelphia Phillies NL (1952)
Milwaukee Braves NL (1957)

Sheldon Jones

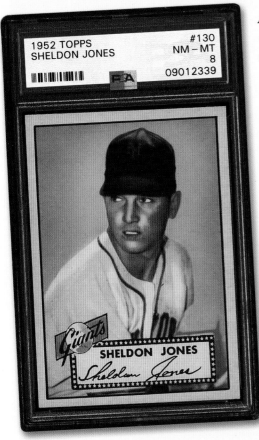

A fairly dependable starter and reliever, Sheldon "Available" Jones enjoyed a few decent years with the New York Giants. His unique nickname came about because of his durability and willingness to step on the mound whenever he was needed. In 1948 and 1949, he had successful seasons as both a starter and reliever going 16–8 and 15–12, respectively, for the Giants. After that, he was used primarily as a reliever with mediocre success. Jones pitched effectively for the Giants in the 1951 World Series, pitching a total of 4.1 innings in two games with a combined 2.08 ERA. Before MLB, Jones spent two years in the minors and three years in the military, where he perfected his fastball and curveball while pitching for Uncle Sam in Florida and Panama. After baseball, Jones worked for General Electric in Dallas, Texas. He passed away in 1991 at age 69.

Career Stats

Record:	54–57
ERA:	3.96
IP:	920.0
Ks:	413
Threw:	RH

Teams

New York Giants NL (1946–1951)
Boston Braves NL (1952)
Chicago Cubs NL (1953)

Eddie Joost

An outstanding defensive shortstop who had a long 17-year MLB career, Eddie Joost never hit for average, compiling a lifetime .239 BA. In 1947, he also led the American League in strikeouts, fanning 110 times. Joost had some pop in his bat, however, slamming 134 career home runs. Dubbed the "A's spark-plug shortstop" by the press, Joost's hitting improved after he began to wear eyeglasses. Although he was a two-time All-Star, primarily because of his glove, Joost was not considered an elite player. Between 1949 and 1951, the Athletics infield with Joost at shortstop turned more than 200 double plays for three consecutive seasons. As player-manager for the A's in 1954, Joost finished with a dismal 51–103 record. He retired from baseball after managing in the minors for a few seasons. The Philadelphia Wall of Fame inductee passed away in 2011 at the age of 94.

Career Stats

AB:	5,606	HR:	134
R:	874	RBI:	601
H:	1,339	OPS:	.727
BA:	.239		

Teams

Cincinnati Reds NL (1936–1937, 1939–1942)
Boston Braves NL (1943, 1945)
Philadelphia Athletics AL (1947–1954)
Boston Red Sox AL (1955)

Howie Judson

Illinois native Howie Judson signed with his "hometown" White Sox in 1946, upon his discharge from the US Navy. A product of the University of Illinois at Urbana-Champaign, where he played basketball and baseball, Judson played his career with a secret. He was losing sight in his left eye due to recurring infections from an old high school injury. The spot starter and reliever struggled in the Major Leagues, playing mostly for sub .500 teams. His best year was with the 1951 White Sox when he posted a 5–6 record and 3.77 ERA in just over 121 innings pitched. Judson had more success in the minors where he finished up in 1959 with a 70–61 record compiled in eight minor-league seasons. After his pro career, Judson ran the shipping department at the Stulper Company in Wisconsin and retired to Florida. At the time of this writing, he is 94 years old.

Career Stats

Record:	17–37
ERA:	4.29
IP:	615.0
Ks:	204
Threw:	RH

Teams

Chicago White Sox AL (1948–1952)
Cincinnati Reds/Redlegs NL (1953–1954)

Alex Kellner

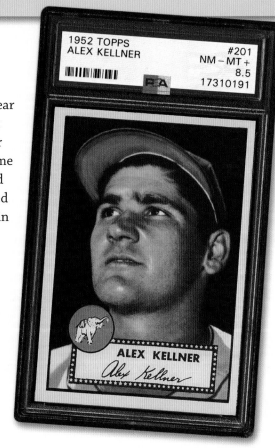

In 1949, rookie southpaw Alex Kellner became the first Athletics pitcher to win 20 games since Lefty Grove did it in 1933. That season playing for Connie Mack's Philadelphia Athletics was his best. He posted a 20–12 record with a 3.75 ERA, made the American League All-Star team, and finished second in Rookie of the Year voting. The next year, the Tucson, Arizona, native lost 20 games. An integral part of some very weak Athletics teams during his 11 years with the franchise, Kellner was regularly in the rotation. He was Opening Day pitcher for the team's first home game after moving to Kansas City in 1955. After brief stints with the Redlegs and the Cardinals, Kellner retired in 1959. Also a good-hitting pitcher, Kellner finished with a .215 average and four home runs. The World War II US Navy veteran died in 1996 at the age of 71.

Career Stats

Record:	101–112
ERA:	4.41
IP:	1,849.1
Ks:	816
Threw:	LH

Teams

Philadelphia/Kansas City Athletics AL (1948–1958)
Cincinnati Redlegs NL (1958)
St. Louis Cardinals NL (1959)

Bob Kelly

Bob Kelly attended Western Michigan, Case Western Reserve, and Purdue universities. The 6-foot, 180-pound, right-handed pitcher broke into the big leagues in 1951 with the Chicago Cubs and also toiled for the Cincinnati Reds and Cleveland Indians. With a 12–18 career record and 4.50 ERA, Kelly was essentially an average pitcher on some so-so teams. Kelly experienced his best MLB season as a rookie when he won seven games as a spot starter and reliever for the Cubbies. Throughout his four MLB seasons, he pitched in the minors and compiled an 87–80 record over eight minor-league seasons. After a four-year hiatus in the minors, the Cleveland native returned to MLB in 1958, at age 30, and had the opportunity to play for his hometown team before his career ended that season. At the time of this writing, Bob Kelly is 92 years old.

Career Stats

Record:	12–18
ERA:	4.50
IP:	362.0
Ks:	146
Threw:	RH

Teams

Chicago Cubs NL (1951–1953)
Cincinnati Reds NL (1953, 1958)
Cleveland Indians AL (1958)

Bill Kennedy

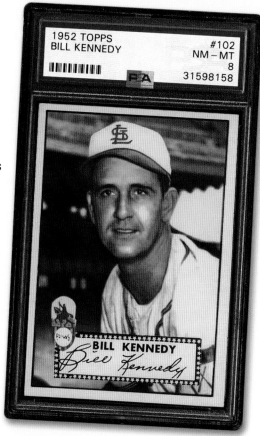

Southpaw Bill "Lefty" Kennedy never really cut it in the majors, but the minors were a different story. He caught the eyes of Major League scouts by striking out 456 batters in 280 innings and going 28–3 with a 1.03 ERA in 1946. Although he played for the "D" level Rocky Mount Rocks, it was still quite an accomplishment. Unfortunately, that was the highlight of his career. In eight MLB seasons, Kennedy played for five different teams without much success. In 1952, his 47 appearances led the American League, and he had a nice 2.80 ERA. Kennedy never had better than a .500 record in the majors, and he finished in 1957 with a career 15–28 record. In contrast, he posted a career 149–82 record in 15 minor-league seasons. The WWII veteran was a bartender in Seattle, Washington, before succumbing to lung cancer in 1983 at age 62.

Career Stats

Record:	15–28
ERA:	4.73
IP:	464.2
Ks:	256
Threw:	LH

Teams

Cleveland Indians AL (1948)
St. Louis Browns AL (1948–1951)
Chicago White Sox AL (1952)
Boston Red Sox AL (1953)
Cincinnati Redlegs NL (1956–1957)

Monty Kennedy

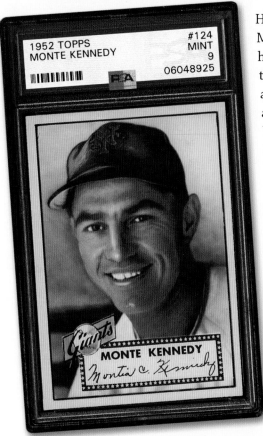

Hard-throwing lefty Monty Kennedy played his entire career for the New York Giants as both a spot starter and reliever. Because World War II cut short his minor-league development time, Kennedy developed his skills while in the military. Throughout his career, Kennedy's biggest problem was his lack of command on the mound. As a rookie with the Giants in 1946, Kennedy led the National League with 116 bases on balls. His best season was 1949, when he posted a 12–14 record with a 3.43 ERA. Kennedy appeared in Game Four and Game Five of the 1951 World Series, pitching a total of three innings in relief. After eight years in the majors, he worked as a police officer and detective in Virginia for 20 years, staying close to the game by playing on the police baseball team. Kennedy died in 1997 at the age of 74.

Career Stats

Record:	42–55
ERA:	3.84
IP:	961.0
Ks:	411
Threw:	LH

Teams
New York Giants NL (1946–1953)

Leo Kiely

A mid-season call-up to the Red Sox, Leo Kiely compiled a 7–7 record in 1951 before losing two years to military service in Korea. While overseas, he became the first Major Leaguer to play in the Japanese Pacific League, posting a 6–0 record with a 1.80 ERA for the Mainichi Orions in 1953. Upon his return to Boston, Kiely had a few so-so seasons and was sent down to the minors for seasoning in 1957. That year, his exceptional 21–6 record as relief pitcher for the Pacific Coast League's San Francisco Seals earned him a trip back to Boston. Kiely became a dependable middle-relief guy for the Sox, but was eventually traded to the Kansas City A's where he performed well until bone chips in his elbow caused his retirement in 1960. A heavy smoker, Leo Kiely was 54 years old when he died from cancer in 1984.

Career Stats

Record:	26–27
ERA:	3.37
IP:	523.0
Ks:	212
Threw:	LH

Teams
Boston Red Sox AL (1951, 1954–1956, 1958–1959)
Kansas City Athletics AL (1960)

Johnny Klippstein

If you looked up the word "workhorse," Johnny Klippstein's picture would be right there. Both a starter and reliever during his 18-year major-league career, Klippstein came up to the Cubs in 1950 at 22 years old and pitched until he was 39. He had some solid seasons for the Cubs and the Reds during the first part of his career. During the second half of his Major League stint, Klippstein successfully morphed into a middle reliever and closer. With Cleveland in 1960, he led the league with 14 saves. Klippstein played in two World Series, winning a ring with the Los Angeles Dodgers in 1959. He was on the Twins AL pennant team that lost to the Dodgers in 1965. He retired in 1967 with 101 career wins and 65 saves. An ardent Cubs fan, Klippstein lived in the Chicago area, where he died in 2003 at age 75.

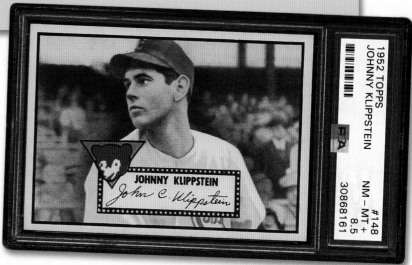

Career Stats

Record:	101–118
ERA:	4.24
IP:	1,967.2
Ks:	1,158
Threw:	RH

Teams

Chicago Cubs NL (1950–1954)
Cincinnati Redlegs/Reds NL (1955–1958, 1962)
Los Angeles Dodgers NL (1958–1959)
Cleveland Indians AL (1960)
Washington Senators AL (1961)
Philadelphia Phillies NL (1963–1964)
Minnesota Twins AL (1964–1966)
Detroit Tigers AL (1967)

Clyde Kluttz

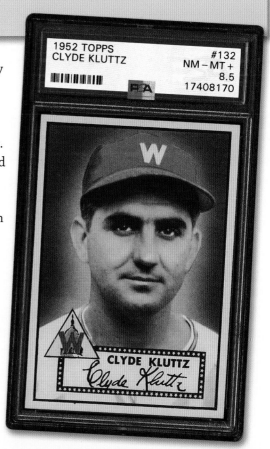

A platoon catcher for six teams in nine seasons, Clyde Kluttz was a good bench guy who could jump into the lineup and do a nice job. On May 1, 1946, he made the news for being on three different teams in one afternoon. The Giants traded him to the Phillies around noon and two hours later he was swapped to the Cardinals. The Cards won the World Series that year, but Kluttz did not play in the fall classic. His primary contribution to the game came after his playing days. Klutz discovered future Hall of Famer Catfish Hunter while scouting for the Kansas City Athletics, and, while working as Yankees director of scouting, Kluttz signed Hunter as a free agent. He worked as director of player development for the Baltimore Orioles from 1976 until his death from heart problems at the age of 61 in 1979.

Career Stats

AB:	1,903	HR:	19
R:	172	RBI:	212
H:	510	OPS:	.671
BA:	.268		

Teams

Boston Braves NL (1942–1945)
New York Giants NL (1945–1946)
St. Louis Cardinals NL (1946)
Pittsburgh Pirates NL (1947–1948)
St. Louis Browns AL (1951)
Washington Senators AL (1951–1952)

Don Kolloway

1952 TOPPS #104
DON KOLLOWAY NM – MT 8
08019948

A steady ballplayer, infielder Don Kolloway had some consistent seasons with both the Chicago White Sox and the Detroit Tigers. The Illinois native joined the White Sox in 1940 and soon became the starting second baseman. In 1941, he hit two home runs, and stole second base, third base, and home all in the same game. Not a bad day. Kolloway led the American League with 40 doubles in 1942 while swiping 16 bases. After missing two seasons to US Army service in World War II, he returned in 1946 to start at second base for the White Sox until his trade to the Tigers in 1949. That year with Detroit, Kolloway enjoyed his most productive season, batting .294 with 142 hits. After his retirement from baseball, Kolloway owned a tavern in Blue Island, Illinois, for many years. He passed away in 1994 at the age of 75.

Career Stats

AB:	3,993	HR:	29
R:	466	RBI:	393
H:	1,081	OPS:	.658
BA:	.271		

Teams

Chicago White Sox AL (1940–1943, 1946–1949)
Detroit Tigers AL (1949–1952)
Philadelphia Athletics AL (1953)

Clem Koshorek

Originally signed by the Tigers in 1946, Clem Koshorek broke into the majors six years later with the Pirates. In 1952, he played in 98 games as a versatile infielder, batting .261 with 17 doubles and 15 RBI. General manager Branch Rickey's 1952 Bucs were one of the worst teams in baseball history, posting a 42–112 record despite having the likes of Ralph Kiner and Gus Bell in the lineup. In 1953, they were not much better, losing 104 games. Similarly, Koshorek's promising rookie season would not lead to staying power as his Major League career ended in 1953. Koshorek retired after bouncing around the minors through the 1959 season. He and his wife Marilyn, a nurse, had two sons and a daughter and settled in Clem's native Royal Oak, Michigan, where he died at the age of 66 in 1991.

1952 TOPPS #380
CLEM KOSHOREK NM – MT 8
11550461

Career Stats

AB:	323	HR:	0
R:	27	RBI:	15
H:	84	OPS:	.319
BA:	.260		

Teams

Pittsburgh Pirates NL (1952–1953)

Dave Koslo

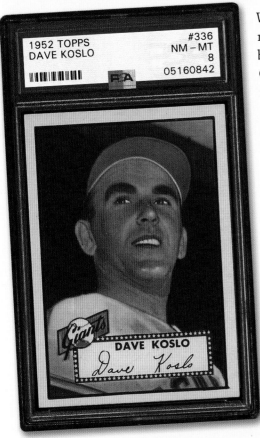

When Wisconsin native Dave Koslo broke in with the Giants in 1941, many believed he had the stuff to succeed Hall of Famer Carl Hubbell. That did not happen, but Koslo did become a Giants mound mainstay and was the winning pitcher in Game One of the 1951 World Series. After three years serving in the military, Koslo's return to baseball in 1946 was less than heroic. He lost a league-high 19 games and led the NL in hits and earned runs allowed. Koslo's vast pitching repertoire included a knuckleball. He won 92 MLB games, but lost 107 despite a 3.68 career ERA. Soon after he left baseball, Koslo suffered a stroke at age 36. He fully recovered but died of a heart attack in 1975 at the young age of 55. The baseball field in his hometown of Menasha, Wisconsin, bears his name.

Career Stats

Record:	92–107
ERA:	3.68
IP:	1,591.1
Ks:	606
Threw:	LH

Teams

New York Giants NL (1941–1942, 1946–1953)
Baltimore Orioles AL (1954)
Milwaukee Braves NL (1954–1955)

Jim Konstanty

Jim Konstanty was a decent relief pitcher who had one banner season. As part of the 1950 Philadelphia Phillies "Whiz Kids" NL pennant-winning team, Konstanty posted a 16–7 record with a 2.66 ERA. The 1950 All-Star led the league with 22 saves, 62 games finished, and 74 appearances. Voted National League MVP, he was the first relief pitcher to be so honored. After that magical 1950 season, Konstanty was reliable but not an elite pitcher, although he did contribute to the 1955 Yankees AL pennant winners. A physical education teacher before baseball, Konstanty made his MLB debut in 1944 at 27 years old and served in the US Navy in 1945. In retirement he owned and operated a sporting goods store, coached in the minors, and was the Athletic Director at Hartwick College in Oneonta, New York. He died in 1976 at the age of 59.

Career Stats

Record:	66–48
ERA:	3.46
IP:	945.2
Ks:	268
Threw:	RH

Teams

Cincinnati Reds NL (1944)
Boston Braves NL (1946)
Philadelphia Phillies NL (1948–1954)
New York Yankees AL (1954–1956)
St. Louis Cardinals NL (1956)

Lou Kretlow

1952 TOPPS   #42
LOU KRETLOW
NM – MT 8
04042004

Probably a better golfer than he was a baseball player, Lou Kretlow played for four different teams, none too successfully. The Oklahoma native and US Army Air Force veteran was a hot prospect. He received a $35,000 signing bonus from the Detroit Tigers in 1946. The journeyman pitcher was both a starter and a reliever who ended his ten-year MLB career with a sub .500 record and a hefty 4.87 ERA. His best season was probably 1952 for the White Sox, where he was 4–4 with a 2.96 ERA. That year he pitched two shutouts in late July, a 3–0 win vs. the Red Sox and a 7–0 victory vs. the Yankees. After baseball, Kretlow owned an oil company and became a golf pro. His golfing claim to fame? He hit a record-setting 427-yard hole-in-one in 1961. Lou Kretlow died in 2007 at the age of 86.

Career Stats

Record:	27–47
ERA:	4.87
IP:	785.1
Ks	450
Threw:	RH

Teams

Detroit Tigers AL (1946, 1948–1949)
St. Louis Browns/Baltimore Orioles AL (1950, 1953–1955)
Chicago White Sox AL (1950–1953)
Kansas City Athletics AL (1956)

Dick Kryhoski

Coming out of the minor leagues with some excellent stats, Dick Kryhoski was called up to the Yankees in 1949 and became a member of a world championship team in his rookie year. He was signed in 1943 but spent time in the Pacific serving Uncle Sam on the USS *Ticonderoga* before playing in the Yankees farm system. The 6-foot-2 and 182-pound New Jersey native was traded after his rookie year and for the next six seasons was a dependable first sacker for three different teams. His best season was 1951 when he batted .287 and hit 12 home runs for the Tigers. He followed that in 1953 when he batted .278 with 16 home runs for the St. Louis Browns. Kryhoski was outstanding defensively with a .990 fielding average. After baseball, he worked in engineering equipment sales and passed away from cancer in 2007 at the age of 82.

1952 TOPPS   #149
DICK KRYHOSKI
NM – MT 8
50016572

Career Stats

AB:	1,794	HR:	45
R:	203	RBI:	235
H:	475	OPS:	.717
BA:	.265		

Teams

New York Yankees AL (1949)
Detroit Tigers AL (1950–1951)
St. Louis Browns/Baltimore Orioles AL (1952–1954)
Kansas City Athletics AL (1955)

Johnny Kucab

One thing you can say for Johnny Kucab, he was numerically consistent. In 1950, he walked eight batters and struck out eight. The next season, he K'd 23 batters and walked 23. His MLB career record was 5–5, and his career ERA was 4.44. Drafted by Cincinnati in 1940, Kucab played in the minors until WWII. He served four years in both Europe and the Pacific, and upon his return Kucab was released by the Reds in 1946. The 30-year-old rookie debuted for the Athletics in mid-September 1950, and on October 1, Connie Mack's last game as manager, he pitched a complete-game 5–3 victory. Kucab was a reliever for the A's for two seasons and returned to the minors, retiring in 1958 with a 128–87 minor-league record compiled over 13 seasons. He was 57 years old when he died of a heart attack in 1977.

Career Stats

Record:	5–5
ERA:	4.44
IP:	152.0
Ks:	48
Threw:	RH

Teams

Philadelphia Athletics AL (1950–1952)

Bob Kuzava

After brief call-ups with the Indians in 1946 and 1947, southpaw, Bob "Sarge" Kuzava went 10–6 for the White Sox in 1949, placing fourth in Rookie of the Year voting. His glory years were as a spot starter and reliever for the 1951, 1952, and 1953 world champion Yankees. Kuzava is credited with saves in the deciding games of both the 1951 and 1952 Series. He posted a 23–20 record with a 3.39 ERA, 13 saves, and four shutouts during his time in New York. The Yanks won the 1953 Series but traded Kuzava to Baltimore the next year. After stops with three more teams, Kuzava retired in 1957 with a career 49–44 record and a 4.05 ERA. He scouted for MLB before returning home to Michigan and a career in the beer industry. The US Army sergeant and WWII veteran died in 2017 at age 93.

Career Stats

Record:	49–44
ERA:	4.05
IP:	862.0
Ks:	446
Threw:	LH

Teams

Cleveland Indians AL (1946–1947)
Chicago White Sox AL (1949–1950)
Washington Senators AL (1950–1951)
New York Yankees AL (1951–1954)
Baltimore Orioles AL (1954–1955)
Philadelphia Phillies NL (1955)
Pittsburgh Pirates NL (1957)
St. Louis Cardinals NL (1957)

Paul LaPalme

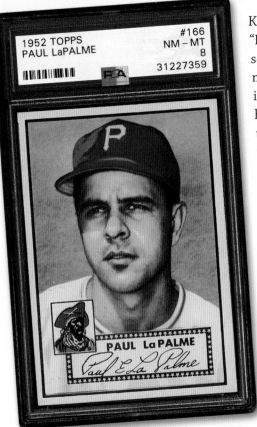

1952 TOPPS #166
PAUL LaPALME NM–MT
8
31227359

PAUL LaPALME

Knuckleballer Paul "Lefty" LaPalme spent seven years in the minors and three years in the US Army before he finally made it to the majors in 1951 with the Pittsburgh Pirates. The 27-year-old rookie started with a bang. On June 5, 1951, his first Major League start, he pitched an 8–0 shutout against the Boston Braves. Unfortunately, the Pirates were at the bottom of the heap during LaPalme's time with them, and he never had a winning season. After he led the league with eight wild pitches in 1954, LaPalme joined the Cardinals where he had his best year in 1955, posting a 4–3 record with a 2.75 ERA. He also played for the Redlegs and White Sox before wrapping up his career in the minors in 1959. After baseball, LaPalme launched a successful engraving business in Leominster, Massachusetts. He passed away in 2010 at the age of 86.

Career Stats

Record:	24–45
ERA:	4.42
IP:	616.1
Ks:	277
Threw:	LH

Teams

Pittsburgh Pirates NL (1951–1954)
St. Louis Cardinals NL (1955–1956)
Cincinnati Redlegs NL (1956)
Chicago White Sox AL (1956–1957)

Don Lenhardt

Don "Footsie" Lenhardt played for four teams in five years. A decent hitter and fielder, he made a bid for Rookie of the Year honors in 1950 with his .273 batting average and 22 dingers. Lenhardt never took it to the next level though, and from that point on he was traded frequently. He finished up his very vanilla playing career with the Boston Red Sox. This turned out to be a providential move as Lenhardt carved out a lengthy career as scout and coach for them. In the early 1970s, he was first-base coach for manager Eddie Kasko. Before and after that, Lenhardt scouted for the Red Sox for many years, signing Dick Mills, Al Nipper, Scott Cooper, and Cory Bailey, among others. Lenhardt continued to work for the Sox until 2004. He passed away at the age of 91 in 2014.

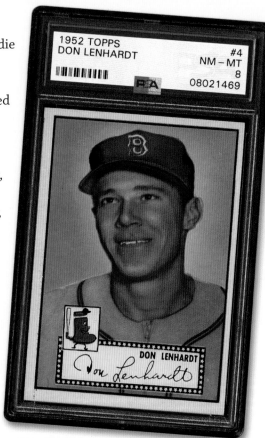

1952 TOPPS #4
DON LENHARDT NM–MT
8
08021469

DON LENHARDT

Career Stats

AB:	1,481	HR:	61
R:	192	RBI:	239
H:	401	OPS:	.815
BA:	.271		

Teams

St. Louis Browns/Baltimore Orioles AL (1950–1951, 1952–1954)
Chicago White Sox AL (1951)
Boston Red Sox AL (1952, 1954)
Detroit Tigers AL (1952)

Ted Lepcio

On Opening Day of his rookie season with the 1952 Red Sox, Ted Lepcio had the honor of fielding the pitch thrown by President Harry Truman. A versatile infielder, Lepcio played seven seasons in Boston and his stats mirrored the so-so performance of the franchise during that era. His best season was 1956, when the Sox won 84 games to finish a respectable fourth in the AL, while Lepcio slugged 15 home runs with 51 RBI. A decent doubles man, Lepcio was a free swinger who also missed often and had some high strikeout totals for a part-time player. The close pal and warm-up partner of Ted Williams enjoyed a much more productive post-baseball career. A Seton Hall grad, Lepcio became a successful businessman in Massachusetts and always maintained close ties with the Red Sox organization. Lepcio was 90 years old when he died in 2019.

Career Stats

AB:	2,092	HR:	69
R:	233	RBI:	251
H:	512	OPS:	.715
BA:	.245		

Teams

Boston Red Sox AL (1952–1959)
Detroit Tigers AL (1959)
Philadelphia Phillies NL (1960)
Chicago White Sox AL (1961)
Minnesota Twins AL (1961)

Johnny Lipon

A marginal hitter and mediocre fielder, shortstop Johnny Lipon had much more success as a manager and coach than as a Major League ballplayer. Signed out of the Detroit sandlots by the Tigers in 1941, Lipon came up to the big club in 1942 but missed the next few seasons to service in the US Navy. Detroit's starting shortstop from 1948 through 1951, Lipon had some pretty good seasons. The high water mark of his career was 1950, when he batted .293 with 176 hits. Traded to the Red Sox in 1952, Lipon also played for the Browns before ending his playing years with the Cincinnati Redlegs in 1954. A baseball lifer, Lipon managed in the Cleveland, Detroit, and Pittsburgh minor-league systems for 30 years. He also coached for the Indians and was their interim manager in 1971. Lipon died in 1998 at the age of 75.

Career Stats

AB:	2,661	HR:	10
R:	350	RBI:	266
H:	690	OPS:	.671
BA:	.259		

Teams

Detroit Tigers AL (1942, 1946–1952)
Boston Red Sox AL (1952–1953)
St. Louis Browns AL (1953)
Cincinnati Redlegs NL (1954)

Turk Lown

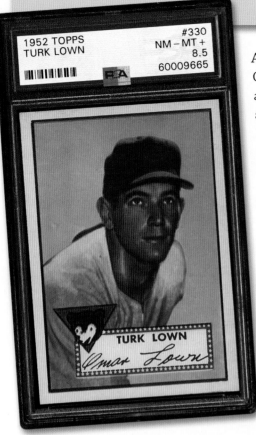

A Brooklyn-born boyhood hoops star, Omar "Turk" Lown embraced baseball and registered some great minor-league seasons before debuting with the Cubs in 1951. Chicago was Lown's kind of town. He sandwiched one season in Cincinnati between seven years with the Cubbies and five with the ChiSox. The City of the Big Shoulders relied heavily on Lown's arm. He was relieving royalty, saving 13 games in 1956, 12 in 1957, and a league-high 15 in 1959. Moreover, he led the league in games finished three times. Lown teamed with Gerry Staley to save a combined 30 games for the 1959 AL Champion White Sox. The hearty pitcher who won many a bullpen battle served in the US Army, was injured in Battle of the Bulge, and received the Purple Heart. After his MLB days, he was a postal carrier for many years. Lown died in 2016 at age 92.

Career Stats

Record:	55–61
ERA:	4.12
IP:	1,032.0
Ks:	574
Threw:	RH

Teams

Chicago Cubs NL (1951–1954, 1956–1958)
Cincinnati Redlegs NL (1958)
Chicago White Sox AL (1958–1962)

Peanuts Lowrey

Nicknamed "Peanuts" as a child for his tiny physique, Harry Lowrey had some pop in his bat despite his diminutive 5-foot-8 and 170-pound frame. Lowrey batted .283 for the 1945 Cubs NL pennant winners and hit .310 in the Series loss to the Tigers. He batted .303 in 1951 and set an MLB record in 1952 with seven consecutive pinch hits. A versatile utility man, Lowrey played every position except catcher and pitcher, but usually patrolled the outfield. He led the league in several defensive categories as left fielder in 1945 and 1949. In the offseason, the 1946 All-Star and California native had bit parts in several baseball movies, including *The Pride of the Yankees*. He later managed in the minors and coached for many years in the majors where he became known as a skilled sign stealer. Lowrey passed away in 1986 at the age of 68.

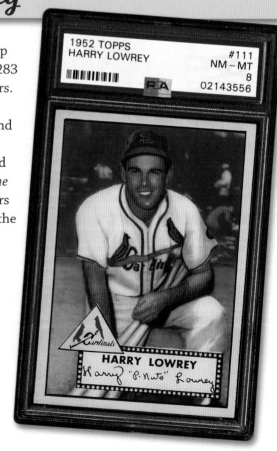

Career Stats

AB:	4,317	HR:	37
R:	564	RBI:	479
H:	1,177	OPS:	.698
BA:	.273		

Teams

Chicago Cubs NL (1942–1943, 1945–1949)
Cincinnati Reds NL (1949–1950)
St. Louis Cardinals NL (1950–1954)
Philadelphia Phillies NL (1955)

Bill MacDonald

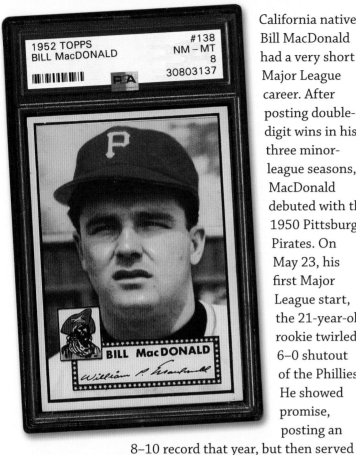

California native Bill MacDonald had a very short Major League career. After posting double-digit wins in his three minor-league seasons, MacDonald debuted with the 1950 Pittsburgh Pirates. On May 23, his first Major League start, the 21-year-old rookie twirled a 6–0 shutout of the Phillies. He showed promise, posting an 8–10 record that year, but then served in the US Army during the Korean War, missing the 1951 and 1952 seasons. Like many other players, MacDonald was not able to regain his form after military service. He tried coming back in 1953 but was ineffective, pitching only seven innings with a 0–1 record. After a brief return to the minors in 1954, MacDonald called it quits. He returned to California, worked as sales manager for the Del Monte Corporation, and later became a volunteer forest ranger in Shasta County. He passed away in 1991 at the age of 62.

Career Stats

Record:	8–11
ERA:	4.66
IP:	160.1
Ks:	64
Threw:	RH

Teams

Pittsburgh Pirates NL (1950, 1953)

Dave Madison

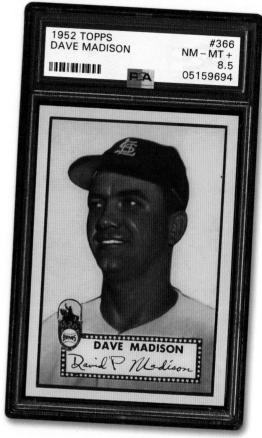

A late season call-up, Dave Madison pitched in one game for the 1950 world champion Yankees. In three innings, he surrendered three hits, two runs, and a home run. After that one game, Madison, a WWII US Army veteran, was re-activated and sent to Korea. He returned in time for the 1952 season and posted a 4–2 record with a 4.38 ERA for the seventh-place Browns, which featured Hall of Famers Bill Veeck as general manager and Rogers Hornsby as manager. A starter and reliever throughout his brief MLB career, Madison was traded to Detroit for, among others, Vic Wertz. After 32 appearances with the Tigers in 1953, Madison was a player-manager in the minors through the 1955 season. The Louisiana State University baseball and football star then launched a lengthy scouting career for the Yankees, Orioles, Athletics, and Mets. He passed away in 1985 at age 64.

Career Stats

Record:	8–7
ERA:	5.70
IP:	158.0
Ks:	70
Threw:	RH

Teams

New York Yankees AL (1950)
St. Louis Browns AL (1952)
Detroit Tigers AL (1952–1953)

Bob Mahoney

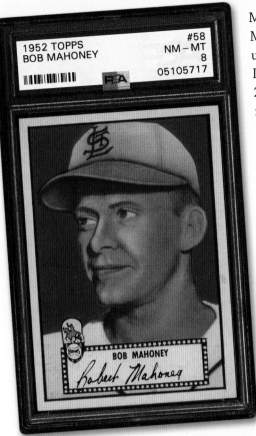

Minnesota native Bob Mahoney had a brief, uneventful Major League career. The 23-year-old rookie right-hander for the 1951 White Sox had worked his way up by posting 17 Class D league wins in 1947, 17 Class C league wins in 1948, and 20 Class A league wins in 1950. After finally making it to the big leagues, Mahoney appeared in three games with no decisions for the White Sox, who promptly shipped him off to the lowly St. Louis Browns.

There he finished the season with a 2–5 record and a 4.44 ERA. In 1952, Mahoney appeared in three games for the Browns with an off-the-charts 18.00 ERA. He was traded to the Dodgers after the 1952 season, but, showing wisdom beyond his 24 years, he retired from the game. A businessman in Lincoln, Nebraska, Bob Mahoney passed away in 2000 at the age of 72.

Career Stats

Record:	2–5
ERA:	4.96
IP:	90.2
Ks:	34
Threw:	RH

Teams

Chicago White Sox AL (1951)
St. Louis Browns AL (1951–1952)

Woody Main

California native Woody Main played four seasons with the Pittsburgh Pirates, posting a 4–13 career mark. The 1952 season was a double-edged sword for Main. He started 11 games for the Bucs and tossed two complete games. He also finished 17 games out of the pen with two saves. Alas, Main's record of 2–12 and his ERA of 4.46, a career best, was hardly the stuff of which All-Stars are made. It wasn't all Main's fault. The 1952 Pirates lost 112 games despite having Branch Rickey as general manager. Originally signed by the Yankees in 1941, Main was acquired by Pittsburgh in 1947, and he made the big club in 1948. Between 1941 and 1954, he played for the Pirates, served three years in the US Marine Corps, and played nine minor-league seasons. He returned to California, where he died in 1992 at age 70.

Career Stats

Record:	4–13
ERA:	5.14
IP:	204.2
Ks:	107
Threw:	RH

Teams

Pittsburgh Pirates NL (1948, 1950, 1952–1953)

Cliff Mapes

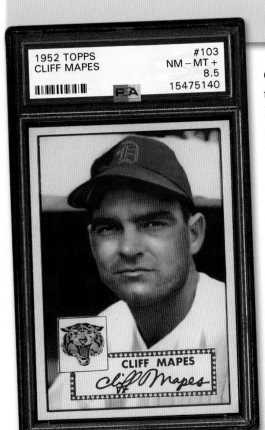

Cliff Mapes and Babe Ruth had one thing in common. No, Mapes did not hit prodigious home runs or hit for average. He was the last player to wear the Bambino's famous number "3" before the Yankees retired it. Otherwise, as backup outfielder, Mapes had a vanilla career for the Yanks. In reality though, he happened to be in the right place at the right time. Mapes had the good fortune to play in both the 1949 and 1950 World Series for the juggernaut Yankees. After number "3," Mapes wore "13" before settling on "7" for the rest of his time in pinstripes. Mapes was traded to the Browns soon after Mickey Mantle joined the Yanks in 1951, freeing up the famous number "7" for The Mick.

His final MLB season was with Detroit in 1952. The WWII veteran passed away in 1996 at the age of 74.

Career Stats

AB:	1,193	HR:	38
R:	199	RBI:	172
H:	289	OPS:	.743
BA:	.242		

Teams

New York Yankees AL (1948–1951)

St. Louis Browns AL (1951)

Detroit Tigers AL (1952)

Fred Marsh

Over the course of his career, Fred Marsh was traded for memorable players like Snuffy Stirnweiss, Merl Combs, Cass Michaels, Earl Rapp, Dixie Upright, Jim Brideweser, Bob Chakales, and Clint Courtney—not exactly household names. A light-hitting third baseman, Marsh played for four different teams over seven years. As a matter of fact, in 1952 he barely had time to unpack his bags. That was the year Marsh got traded from the St. Louis Browns to the Washington Senators in May and back to the Browns in June. In addition to third base, Marsh played shortstop and second base. He was actually pretty good defensively, but he never really made an impact. After Marsh finally hung up his cleats in 1956, he worked for many years as a postal carrier. He passed away at the age of 82 in 2006.

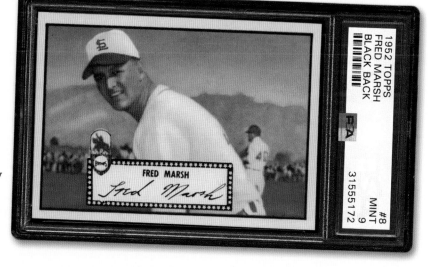

Career Stats

AB:	1,236	HR:	10
R:	148	RBI:	96
H:	296	OPS:	.622
BA:	.239		

Teams

Cleveland Indians AL (1949)

St. Louis Browns/Baltimore Orioles AL (1951, 1952, 1955–1956)

Washington Senators AL (1952)

Chicago White Sox AL (1953–1954)

Cuddles Marshall

1952 TOPPS #174
CLARENCE MARSHALL NM – MT 8
11989412

Bellingham, Washington, native Clarence "Cuddles" Marshall had some memorable moments during his brief Major League career with the Yankees and Browns. On May 28, 1946, Marshall was the Yankees starting pitcher for the first night game ever played at Yankee Stadium. Although he didn't play in the Series, Marshall earned a ring with the 1949 world champion Yankees. That ring was stolen from his home, but it was recast and presented to him years later. The 6-foot-3 and 200-pound Marshall was given his nickname as a gag by Yankees pals Joe Page and Joe DiMaggio. The spot starter and reliever finished in 1950 with a 7–7 MLB record. He served in the Korean War, played one more season in the minors, and retired with a 42–29 minor-league record. After baseball Marshall worked for Douglas Aircraft and Litton Industries. He passed away in 2007 at the age of 82.

Career Stats

Record:	7–7
ERA:	5.98
IP:	185.0
Ks:	69
Threw:	RH

Teams
New York Yankees AL (1946, 1948–1949)
St. Louis Browns AL (1950)

Walt Masterson

Both a starter and reliever, Walt Masterson signed with the Washington Senators at the age of 19 in 1939 and tossed for them for most of his career. Desperate for pitching, the Senators called him up after just one minor-league appearance. After four seasons with the Senators, Masterson served three years in the US Navy and returned to be named an All-Star in 1947 and 1948. Although his stats with the Senators never got close to the .500 mark, he was dependable in his four years with the Red Sox. During that time, he became good friends with future Hall of Famer Ted Williams and eventually became the pitching coach for Williams' Texas Rangers in 1972. Masterson later coached baseball at George Mason University. One of the founding members of the Major League Baseball Players Alumni Association, Masterson died in 2008 at age 87.

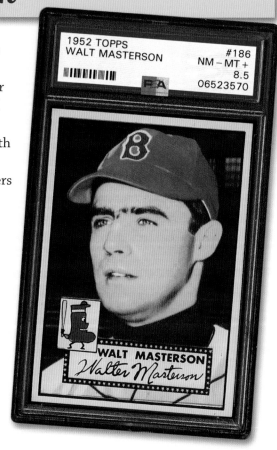

1952 TOPPS #186
WALT MASTERSON NM – MT + 8.5
06523570

Career Stats

Record:	78–100
ERA:	4.15
IP:	1,649.2
Ks:	815
Threw:	RH

Teams
Washington Senators AL (1938–1942, 1945–1949, 1952–1953)
Boston Red Sox AL (1949–1952)
Detroit Tigers AL (1956)

Clyde McCullough

1952 TOPPS #218
CLYDE McCULLOUGH
MINT 9
17226848
PSA

A dependable catcher for the Cubs and the Pirates, Clyde McCullogh was good at handling pitchers and called a good game. The two-time All-Star's 15-season career was interrupted by two years in the US Navy. He returned to the Cubs right after they captured the 1945 NL pennant. Commissioner Happy Chandler allowed McCullough to play in the Series, and he had one at-bat in the seven-game loss to the Tigers. McCullough later coached for the Senators and Mets. He managed 11 seasons in the minors; mostly in the Mets system, where he helped develop future stars Tom Seaver and Nolan Ryan; and led his teams to the league championship four times. In 1982, at age 65, McCullough became a bullpen coach for the San Diego Padres. He was on a road trip with the team in San Francisco when he was found dead in his hotel room.

Career Stats

AB:	3,121	HR:	52
R:	308	RBI:	339
H:	785	OPS:	.672
BA:	.252		

Teams
Chicago Cubs NL (1940–1943, 1946–1948, 1953–1956)
Pittsburgh Pirates NL (1949–1952)

Mickey McDermott

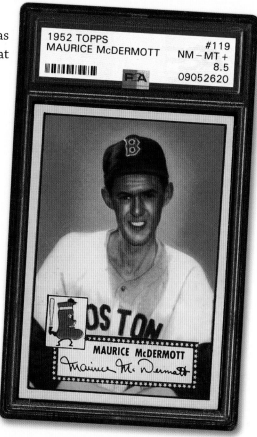

1952 TOPPS #119
MAURICE McDERMOTT
NM – MT + 8.5
09052620
PSA

As a rookie in 1948, Mickey McDermott was touted as the next great lefty. A free spirit, McDermott was more interested in partying than pitching, and he never fulfilled those lofty expectations. Supposedly the subject of Norman Rockwell's painting *The Rookie*, McDermott's best years were with the Red Sox, where in 1953 he was 18–10 with a very nice 3.01 ERA. The next year McDermott went 7–15 for the sixth-place Senators. He played for the 1956 Yankees World Series champs and pitched three innings in relief in Game Two of that fall classic. A career .252 batter, he was often used as a pinch-hitter. A nightclub singer in the offseason, McDermott's late-night antics caused his downfall. After baseball, his drinking hampered his business career. Luckily, he won the lottery for $7 million dollars. He passed away at the age of 74 in 2003.

Career Stats

Record:	69–69
ERA:	3.91
IP:	1,316.2
Ks:	757
Threw:	LH

Teams
Boston Red Sox AL (1948–1953)
Washington Senators AL (1954–1955)
New York Yankees AL (1956)
Kansas City Athletics AL (1957)
Detroit Tigers AL (1958)

Jack Merson

The oldest of nine children, Elkridge, Maryland, native Jack Merson was strongly tied to the community. He was originally signed by the Senators in 1940 and scratched and clawed his way through the minors, semipro ball, and a plethora of baseball outposts. Merson finally made it to the majors with GM Branch Rickey's Pirates in 1951 and batted a blistering .360 with 14 RBI in 13 games. His performance earned him the starting second baseman job in 1952, but he suffered a wrist fracture and batted just .246 for the 42–112 Bucs. His chance lost, Merson played just one game for the Red Sox in 1953, the end of his MLB career. After baseball, he returned to Elkridge, worked for the Maryland House of Corrections, and was a founder of the Elkridge Youth Organization. Merson was 78 years old when he died of stroke complications in 2000.

Career Stats

AB:	452	HR:	6
R:	47	RBI:	52
H:	116	OPS:	.657
BA:	.257		

Teams

Pittsburgh Pirates NL (1951–1952)
Boston Red Sox AL (1953)

Billy Meyer

Catcher Billy Meyer broke into the big leagues with the White Sox in 1913 at age 20. He moved to Philly in 1916, joining one of baseball's worst-ever teams, the 36–117 Athletics. Meyer then played for future Yankees skipper Joe McCarthy at Louisville. McCarthy later hired Meyer to manage in the New York farm system. After 20 years of minor-league managing, Meyer became manager of the Pirates in 1948. That year, he led the Bucs to an 83–71 record and won *The Sporting News* Manager of the Year Award. Meyer managed Pittsburgh through 1952 while battling recurring health problems. He scouted for the Pirates, but retired after suffering a stroke in 1955. Two years later, Meyer died of a heart attack at age 64. His number "1" was retired by the Pirates, an honor Meyer shares with the likes of Honus Wagner, Roberto Clemente, and Willie Stargell.

Career Stats

AB:	301	HR:	1
R:	15	RBI:	21
H:	71	OPS:	.563
BA:	.236		

Teams

Chicago White Sox AL (1913)
Philadelphia Athletics AL (1916–1917)

Russ Meyer

1952 TOPPS
RUSS MEYER
#339
MINT
9
06519378

Fiery Russ Meyer enjoyed a 13-year MLB career, won 94 games, and was a member of the 1955 World Champion Dodgers. After three seasons with the Cubs, Meyer won 17 games with a 3.08 ERA for the Phillies in 1949 and played on the 1950 "Whiz Kids" NL pennant winning team. He debuted in Brooklyn with 15 wins in 1953. With the Dodgers, Meyer had a stretch of 24 consecutive road starts without a loss. The nicknames "Mad Monk" and "Rowdy Russ" fit the hot-tempered Meyer. He slammed the baseball to the dirt when pulled from a game and showed disdain to umpires with certain bodily gestures. He once hit a photographer and even tossed racially charged insults at future teammate Jackie Robinson.

Meyer later coached college and minor-league ball and was bench coach for the Yankees. He died in 1997 at age 74.

Career Stats

Record:	94–73
ERA:	3.99
IP:	1,531.1
Ks:	672
Threw:	RH

Teams

Chicago Cubs NL (1946–1948, 1956)
Philadelphia Phillies NL (1949–1952)
Brooklyn Dodgers NL (1953–1955)
Cincinnati Redlegs NL (1956)
Boston Red Sox AL (1957)
Kansas City Athletics AL (1959)

Eddie Miksis

The consummate utility man, Eddie Miksis played every infield and outfield position during his 14-year Major League career. Signed by the Dodgers in 1944, 17-year-old Miksis came up that year to fill a wartime vacancy at shortstop. After spending 1945 and part of 1946 in the US Navy, Miksis returned to the Dodgers and for the next five years he was backup to Jackie Robinson and Pee Wee Reese. Miksis played in the 1947 and 1949 World Series and batted .273 in eight games as the Dodgers lost to the archrival Yankees in both fall classics. His best season was in 1953 with the Cubs when he batted .251 with 145 hits. A good outfielder but mediocre infielder, Miksis actually got one vote for entry into the Hall of Fame in 1964, something he always joked about. He passed away in 2005 at the age of 78.

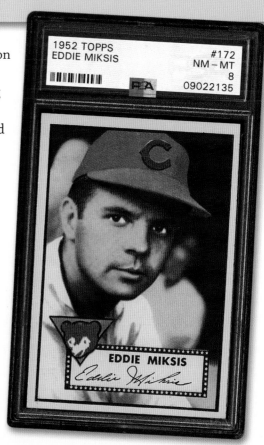

1952 TOPPS
EDDIE MIKSIS
#172
NM – MT
8
09022135

Career Stats

AB:	3,053	HR:	44
R:	383	RBI:	228
H:	722	OPS:	.610
BA:	.236		

Teams

Brooklyn Dodgers NL (1944, 1946–1951)
Chicago Cubs NL (1951–1956)
St. Louis Cardinals NL (1957)
Baltimore Orioles AL (1957–1958)
Cincinnati Redlegs NL (1958)

Bill Miller

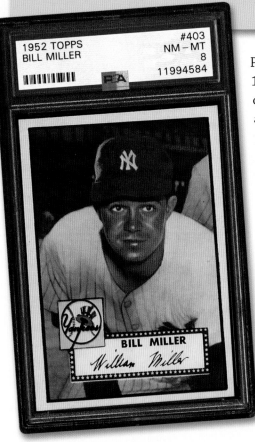

Pennsylvania native Bill Miller spent 12 years in professional baseball, but only four of them in the majors. He was acquired by the Yankees in 1951 after he posted a 16–10 record with a 2.96 ERA in 1951 for the Syracuse Chiefs in the International League. A lefty pitcher, Miller was lucky enough to play for the world champion Yankees in 1952 and 1953, although he never pitched in the fall classic. After the 1954 season, Miller was part of a 17-player swap with the Baltimore Orioles. At the time, it was one of the largest trades in baseball history. Miller was 0–1 for the seventh-place 1955 Orioles, while the Yankees won the pennant that year. He never pitched in the majors again, but Miller continued in the minors through 1956 and finished with an 82–62 minor-league record. He passed away in 2003 at the age of 75.

Career Stats

Record:	6–9
ERA:	4.24
IP:	131.2
Ks:	72
Threw:	LH

Teams

New York Yankees AL (1952–1954)
Baltimore Orioles AL (1955)

Bob Miller

Detroit native Bob Miller made his baseball name in Philadelphia. He served two years in the US Army after high school and was signed by the Phillies in 1948. Miller won 11 games for the 1950 NL Champion Phillies, known as the "Whiz Kids," and ranked second in NL Rookie of the Year voting that year. In 1955, Miller went 8–4 with a 2.41 ERA, but the Phillies finished in fourth place. Blessed with a live fastball and a hook to match it, Miller played in Philly for a decade, posting a 42–42 career mark. He battled injuries throughout his career and eventually became head coach at his alma mater, the University of Detroit Mercy, winning 896 games in 36 years. Miller was inducted into the Detroit Mercy Titans Hall of Fame and the Michigan Sports Hall of Fame. At the time of this writing, he is 93 years old.

Career Stats

Record:	42–42
ERA:	3.96
IP:	822.0
Ks:	263
Threw:	RH

Teams

Philadelphia Phillies NL (1949–1958)

Paul Minner

A hard-luck pitcher who played for weak Chicago Cubs teams, Paul "Lefty" Minner signed with the Dodgers in 1941. After spending time in the minors and in the US Army, he joined the big club for good in 1948. The crafty, soft-throwing junkballer pitched the top of the ninth inning for the Dodgers in Game Five of the 1949 Series, becoming the first to pitch under artificial lights in a World Series game. A starter for the sad-sack Cubbies, Minner was a real workhorse, pitching three 200-inning seasons. He led the NL with 17 losses in 1951, but the next year he went 14–9 with a .500 Cubs team. In his final season, 1956, Minner gave up the first of Frank Robinson's 586 career home runs. He later worked for the Pennsylvania State Insurance Department and passed away in 2006 at the age of 82.

Career Stats

Record:	69–84
ERA:	3.94
IP:	1,310.1
Ks:	481
Threw:	LH

Teams
Brooklyn Dodgers NL (1946, 1948–1949)
Chicago Cubs NL (1950–1956)

Bobby Morgan

A light-hitting infielder for the Dodgers, Phillies, Cardinals, and Cubs, Bobby Morgan enjoyed an eight-year MLB career despite some weak hitting stats. His career batting average was .233 and he dipped below the .200 mark on occasion. The Oklahoma native played on pennant-winners with Brooklyn in 1952 and 1953, but went hitless in two World Series at-bats. Morgan's best year offensively was in 1954 when he hit .262 with 14 home runs and 50 RBI for the Phillies. Signed by the Dodgers out of high school in 1944, Morgan toiled a total of 11 seasons in the minors, interrupted by service in WWII and his MLB career. After his minor-league playing days ended in 1963, when he was 37 years old, he was a minor-league manager for three years and scouted until 1994. At the time of this writing, he is 93 years old.

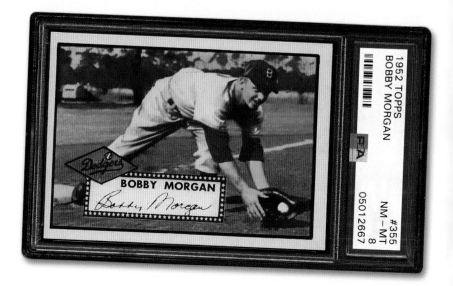

Career Stats

AAB:	2,088	HR:	53
R:	286	RBI:	217
H:	487	OPS:	.704
BA:	.233		

Teams
Brooklyn Dodgers NL (1950, 1952–1953)
Philadelphia Phillies NL (1954–1956, 1957)
St. Louis Cardinals NL (1956)
Chicago Cubs NL (1957–1958)

Tom Morgan

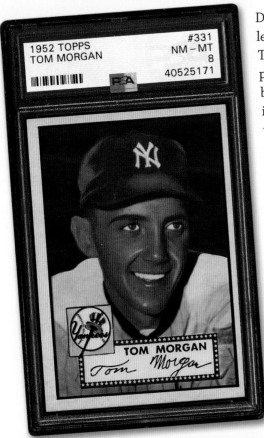

During his 12-year big-league pitching career, Tom "Plowboy" Morgan played for some of the best and worst teams in baseball. He broke in with the Yankees and was a member of the 1951 and 1956 world championship teams, as well as a pennant winner in 1955. Later, he played for the seventh place 1957 Athletics, the sixth place 1960 Tigers, and the eighth place 1961 Angels. He missed the 1953 season serving in the military, but returned in 1954 to post his best season as a Yankee with an 11–5 record and 3.34 ERA. With those woeful 1961 expansion Angels, Morgan posted an 8–2 record, a career-best 2.36 ERA, and ten saves. The California native was known as Plowboy because of his shuffling walk. Morgan eventually became a pitching coach in the majors, but sadly suffered a fatal stroke at the age of 56 in 1987.

Career Stats

Record:	67–47
ERA:	3.61
IP:	1,023.1
Ks:	364
Threw:	RH

Teams

New York Yankees AL (1951–1952, 1954–1956)
Kansas City Athletics AL (1957)
Detroit Tigers AL (1958–1960)
Washington Senators AL (1960)
Los Angeles Angels AL (1961–1963)

Les Moss

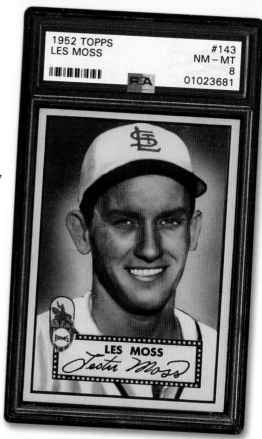

Primarily a backup catcher, Les Moss was a good platoon player for three different organizations. Signed by the Browns in 1941, the 16-year-old backstop played in the minors and served in the US Merchant Marine in the Pacific and in Europe before coming up to the big leagues. A Brownie for most of his MLB career, Moss moved with the team from St. Louis to Baltimore when they became the Orioles. Over his 13 MLB seasons, Moss batted .247 with a .978 fielding percentage, very respectable for a catcher. After his Major League career, Moss went on to scout, coach, and manage in both the minor leagues and Major Leagues. He had short stints as interim manager of the 1968 Chicago White Sox and the 1979 Detroit Tigers. A career baseball guy, Moss retired in 1995 and passed away in 2012 at the age of 87.

Career Stats

AB:	2,234	HR:	63
R:	210	RBI:	276
H:	552	OPS:	.702
BA:	.247		

Teams

St. Louis Browns/Baltimore Orioles AL (1946–1951, 1952–1955)
Boston Red Sox AL (1951)
Chicago White Sox AL (1955–1958)

Joe Muir

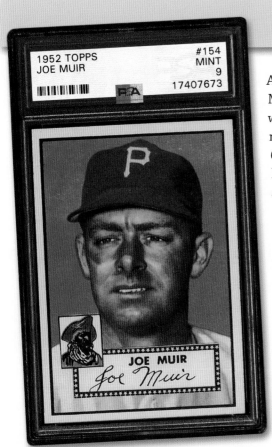

1952 TOPPS   #154
JOE MUIR   MINT
9
17407673

A star pitcher in high school, Maryland native Joe Muir signed with the Pirates in 1947. In seven minor-league seasons, he posted a 62–40 record, earning a couple of looks with the big club. Muir debuted at age 28 and pitched parts of the 1951 and 1952 seasons. The 6-foot-1 and 172-pound southpaw appeared in a total of 21 games for Pittsburgh and posted a 2–5 record with a 5.19 ERA. Keep in mind that the sad-sack Pirates finished in seventh place in 1951, and in 1952 they hit bottom with 112 losses. Although Muir was not a big contributor, he did make it to the majors. He retired in 1953 to join the Maryland State Police before reaching age 30, the cut-off age for recruits. The Marine Corps veteran and 1982 inductee to the Eastern Shore Baseball Hall of Fame died in 1980 at age 57.

Career Stats

Record:	2–5
ERA:	5.19
IP:	52.0
Ks:	22
Threw:	LH

Teams

Pittsburgh Pirates NL (1951, 1952)

Pat Mullin

Born in Trotter, Pennsylvania, Pat Mullin was a top-flight high-school punter and running back, but he dreamed of being a Major Leaguer. He eschewed a football scholarship to Notre Dame to pursue his passion. The converted catcher debuted as outfielder for the Detroit Tigers in 1940, playing just four games. In 1941, Mullin batted .345 with 23 RBI in 54 games. He lost four seasons to US Army service and returned to Detroit in 1946 at 28 years old. Mullin made the All-Star team in 1947 and in 1948 he batted .288, slugged 23 home runs, knocked in 80 runs, and was an All-Star again. After his playing days, Mullin managed in the minors, scouted, and coached for the Tigers, Indians, and Expos. He was inducted into the Pennsylvania Mid Mon Valley All Sports Hall of Fame in 1952 and died in 1999 at age 81.

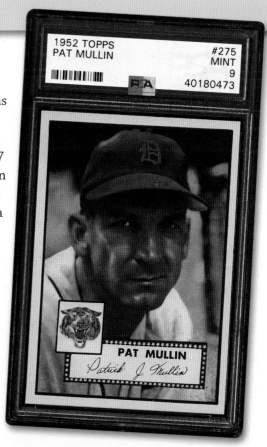

1952 TOPPS   #275
PAT MULLIN   MINT
9
40180473

Career Stats

AB:	2,493	HR:	87
R:	383	RBI:	385
H:	676	OPS:	.811
BA:	.271		

Teams

Detroit Tigers AL (1940–1941, 1946–1953)

Red Munger

A hard-throwing righty from Houston, Texas, Red Munger signed with the Cardinals in 1937 and made his MLB debut in 1943. The three-time All-Star used his fastball, curveball, changeup, slider, and knuckleball to compile 77 wins in ten MLB seasons, interrupted by military service. Part of the occupation forces in Germany in 1946, Second Lieutenant Munger returned in August to help the Cardinals to the World Series championship. In Game Four of that 1946 fall classic, he pitched a complete game win over the Red Sox. In 1947, he posted a 16–5 record with a tidy 3.37 ERA. Arm woes and control problems sent Munger back to the minors late in his career, where he posted double-digit wins in the highly regarded Pacific Coast League. He later worked as a private investigator for the Pinkerton Detective Agency in Houston. Munger died in 1996 at the age of 77.

Career Stats

Record:	77–56
ERA:	3.83
IP:	1,228.2
Ks:	564
Threw:	RH

Teams

St. Louis Cardinals NL (1943–1944, 1946–1952)
Pittsburgh Pirates NL (1952, 1956)

Ray Murray

The ultimate backup backstop, Ray Murray played for three teams in a six-year big-league career. After serving four years in the US Army Air Force, he broke in with Cleveland in 1948, but played in just four games. The Indians won the World Series that season, but Murray saw no postseason action. His best season was 1953, when he batted .284 with six homers and 41 RBI in 84 games for the Athletics. Born and raised in North Carolina, the 6-foot-3, 204-pound Murray

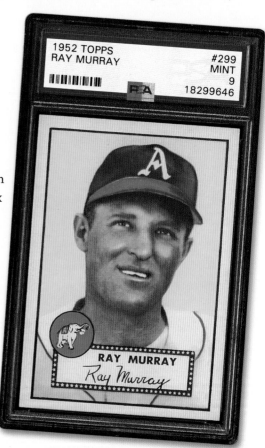

was an ominous figure behind the dish, but was not intimidating at the plate, with just eight career home runs. After his MLB days, Murray was player-manager in the minors for six years and led his 1960 Rio Grande Valley team to the Texas League pennant. After baseball, he was a deputy sheriff in Tarrant County, Texas. Murray died in 2003 at age 85.

Career Stats

AB:	731	HR:	8
R:	69	RBI:	80
H:	184	OPS:	.657
BA:	.252		

Teams

Cleveland Indians AL (1948, 1950–1951)
Philadelphia Athletics AL (1951–1953)
Baltimore Orioles AL (1954)

Rocky Nelson

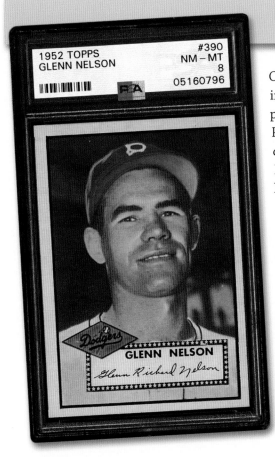

1952 TOPPS
GLENN NELSON
#390
NM – MT
8
05160796

One of the more colorful characters in the Topps set, Rocky Nelson played for the 1960 world champion Pirates. He batted .333 in the fall classic vs. the Yankees, setting up Bill Mazeroski's dramatic Series-winning home run in Game Seven. He also played in the Dodgers' 1952 Series loss to the Yankees. Known for his unusual batting stance, sense of humor, and the cigar hanging out of his mouth, the first baseman was a part-time player throughout his MLB career, which included stops with five teams. Nelson served three years in the military and was a bona fide star in the minors. A popular and gregarious teammate, the three-time International League MVP earned many a trip to the majors but never achieved glory in the Bigs. After baseball, the Portsmouth, Ohio, native returned home to a painting business and passed away in 2006 at the age of 81.

Career Stats

AB:	1,394	HR:	31
R:	186	RBI:	173
H:	347	OPS:	.696
BA:	.249		

Teams

St. Louis Cardinals NL (1949–1951, 1956)
Pittsburgh Pirates NL (1951, 1959–1961)
Chicago White Sox AL (1951)
Brooklyn Dodgers NL (1952, 1956)
Cleveland Indians AL (1954)

Gus Niarhos

A utility backstop with a decent bat, Gus Niarhos came up to the Yankees in 1946 after serving four years in the US Navy. With Yogi Berra as the starting catcher, Niarhos got playing time when Berra played occasionally in the outfield. A good defensive catcher with a career .984 fielding percentage, Niarhos played for four teams in nine seasons. The highlight of his career was in 1949 when the Yankees took the pennant and Niarhos had an opportunity to play in the World Series. He caught the top of the ninth inning in Game Two and thus contributed in a small way to the victory vs. Brooklyn. His days in pinstripes ended in 1950, and he moved on to the White Sox, Red Sox, and Phillies. Niarhos then coached for the Athletics before managing in the minors for eight seasons. He died in 2004 at the age of 84.

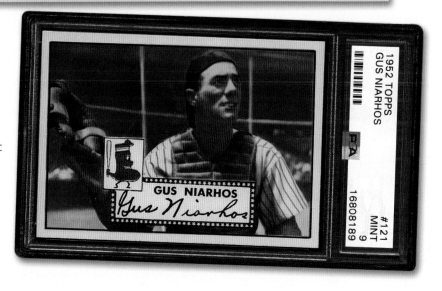

1952 TOPPS
GUS NIARHOS
#121
MINT
9
16808189

Career Stats

AB:	691	HR:	1
R:	114	RBI:	59
H:	174	OPS:	.699
BA:	.252		

Teams

New York Yankees AL (1946, 1948–1950)
Chicago White Sox AL (1950–1951)
Boston Red Sox AL (1952–1953)
Philadelphia Phillies NL (1954–1955)

Chet Nichols

1952 TOPPS #288
CHET NICHOLS MINT 9
30283112

If you ever wondered who finished second to Willie Mays for the 1951 National League Rookie of the Year Award, the answer is Chet Nichols. The Rhode Island native broke in with the Boston Braves and led the NL in ERA with a sparkling 2.88 mark. Nichols won 11 games and hurled three shutouts for the Braves, but his success was halted by a two-year stint in the US Army. In 1959, Nichols returned to Boston, this time with the Red Sox. He won just five games in four seasons, but was a solid reliever in 1961 and 1962. Nichols finished his career with the Reds in 1964. A banker in Rhode Island, Nichols helped save the bankrupt minor-league Red Sox team, the Pawtucket Red Sox, by urging pal Ben Mondor to buy the club in the mid-1970s. Nichols died of cancer in 1995 at age 64.

Career Stats

Record:	34–36
ERA:	3.64
IP:	603.1
Ks:	266
Threw:	LH

Teams

Boston/Milwaukee Braves NL (1951, 1954–1956)
Boston Red Sox AL (1960–1963)
Cincinnati Reds NL (1964)

Willard Nixon

Georgia native Willard Nixon pitched for the Red Sox from 1950 through 1958, posting a 69–72 career record. He hit a career high in wins with a 12–10 mark in 1955. Two years later, he would again win 12 games, while losing 13. Nixon brought value to Boston by gobbling up innings, starting and relieving, and consistently beating the rival Yankees. Four of his 11 wins in 1954 were vs. the Yanks, and he continued his New York dominance over the next two seasons. Originally offered a deal by the Tigers, Nixon instead attended Alabama Polytechnic Institute, now Auburn University. After baseball, he scouted for the Red Sox, was police chief in Floyd County, Georgia, and was a successful amateur golfer. A 1993 inductee to the Georgia Sports Hall of Fame, Nixon succumbed to the effects of Alzheimer's disease seven years later at age 72.

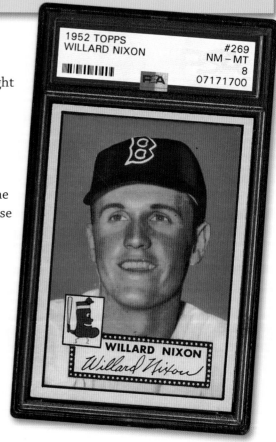

1952 TOPPS #269
WILLARD NIXON NM – MT 8
07171700

Career Stats

Record:	69–72
ERA:	4.39
IP:	1,234.0
Ks:	616
Threw:	RH

Teams

Boston Red Sox AL (1950–1958)

Irv Noren

A good utility player and coach, Irv Noren played on two World Series championship teams and coached two more. As a rookie with the 1950 Senators, Noren batted .295 with 14 home runs and 160 hits. After leaving Washington, Noren had some pretty good years with Casey Stengel's Yankees. He participated in the World Series in 1952, 1953, and 1955 and was an All-Star in 1954. Noren played all three outfield positions and was a valuable asset as a utility player who produced for the Yankees. After his days in pinstripes, he was a journeyman for the Kansas City A's, St. Louis Cards, Chicago Cubs, and Dodgers. Noren was third-base coach for the Oakland A's under Dick Williams when they won the 1972 and 1973 World Series. After baseball, he owned racehorses and was a successful businessman. Noren died in 2019, just two weeks before his 95th birthday.

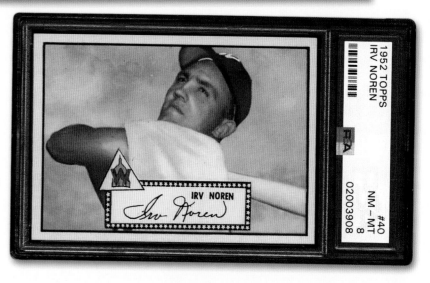

Career Stats

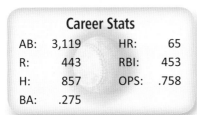

AB:	3,119	HR:	65
R:	443	RBI:	453
H:	857	OPS:	.758
BA:	.275		

Teams

Washington Senators AL (1950–1952)
New York Yankees AL (1952–1956)
Kansas City Athletics AL (1957)
St. Louis Cardinals NL (1957–1959)
Chicago Cubs NL (1959–1960)
Los Angeles Dodgers NL (1960)

Ron Northey

A solid, hardnosed right fielder, Ron Northey would have been welcome on any team. By no means a superstar, the Pennsylvania native always got the job done, whether he was starting or pinch-hitting. Ron had some fine years with the Phillies during the early part of his career, with his best season being 1944 when he batted .288 with 22 home runs and 164 hits. His career was interrupted in 1945 while he served in the US Army. A starter for the first part of his career, Northey battled weight issues and was mostly used as a pinch-hitter towards the end of his career. He was a darn good part-time player for the Reds, Cubs, White Sox, and—ending where he started—for the Phillies. After retirement, he scouted for the White Sox and coached for the Pirates, but died suddenly at the age of 50 in 1971.

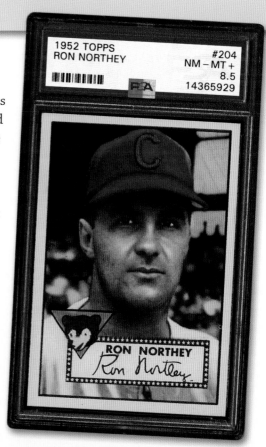

Career Stats

AB:	3,172	HR:	108
R:	385	RBI.	513
H:	874	OPS:	.801
BA:	.276		

Teams

Philadelphia Phillies NL (1942–1944, 1946–1947, 1957)
St. Louis Cardinals NL (1947–1949)
Cincinnati Reds NL (1950)
Chicago Cubs NL (1950, 1952)
Chicago White Sox AL (1955–1957)

Karl Olson

A decent utility guy, Karl Olson enjoyed his best seasons with the Red Sox. Not a power hitter, the outfielder's most productive year was 1954 when he batted .260 with 227 at-bats for Boston. Signed by the Red Sox in 1948, Olson put up some lofty numbers in the minors, but after serving Uncle Sam in the Korean War, he could never get his mojo back. From the Red Sox, Olson went to the Washington Senators in 1956 and wrapped up his Major League career with the Detroit Tigers in 1957. He finished up that season in the minors and retired from the game. After leaving baseball, Olson moved his family to the Lake Tahoe area. He bought a few Hamburger Heaven restaurants and later owned a successful construction company which he operated for 25 years. Karl Olson passed away in 2010 at the age of 80.

Career Stats

AB:	681	HR:	6
R:	74	RBI:	50
H:	160	OPS:	.594
BA:	.235		

Teams

Boston Red Sox AL (1951, 1953–1955)
Washington Senators AL (1956–1957)
Detroit Tigers AL (1957)

Joe Ostrowski

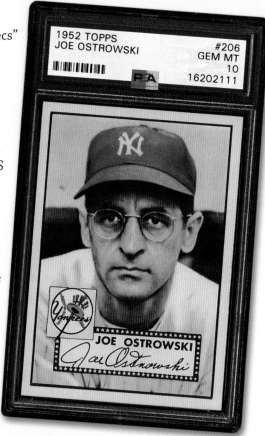

Pennsylvania native Joe "Specs" Ostrowski worked as a high-school teacher, played in the minors, and served as a medic in the US Army Air Force during World War II before making it to the majors at age 31 with the 1948 St. Louis Browns. The lefty pitcher had the good fortune to be traded to the Yankees in 1950 and enjoyed a three-year run with the Pinstripes. He was a reliever on three Yankees World Series championship teams, with his best season in 1951 when he posted a 6–4 record with a 3.49 ERA and pitched two innings in the fall classic. After his tenure with the Yankees, Ostrowski finished in 1953 with the Los Angeles Angels in the Pacific Coast League. He then taught in the high school in his hometown of West Wyoming, Pennsylvania, for 25 years. He died in 2003 at the age of 86.

Career Stats

Record:	23–25
ERA:	4.54
IP:	455.2
Ks:	131
Threw:	LH

Teams

St. Louis Browns AL (1948–1950)
New York Yankees AL (1950–1952)

Stubby Overmire

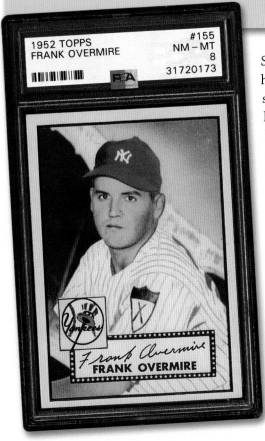

Southpaw Frank "Stubby" Overmire had a ten-year career in the majors with some success, but after his playing days he had a fine 16-year career as a minor-league manager. The Michigan native and product of Western Michigan University signed with the Tigers in 1941 and debuted in 1943 at age 23. At 5-foot-7 and 170 pounds, his nickname was apt. Overmire's best year was 1947, when he posted an 11–5 record with a 3.77 ERA. He picked up a couple of World Series rings playing for the 1945 Tigers and the 1951 Yankees. Overmire went on to manage, coach, and scout in the Detroit Tigers organization until 1976. His 1957 Montgomery Rebels and 1962 Jamestown Tigers finished first in their leagues. The 1976 Grand Rapids Sports Hall of Fame inductee passed away after suffering a stroke in 1977 at the age of 57.

Career Stats

Record:	58–67
ERA:	3.96
IP:	1,130.2
Ks:	301
Threw:	LH

Teams

Detroit Tigers AL (1943–1949)
St. Louis Browns AL (1950–1951, 1952)
New York Yankees AL (1951)

Erv Palica

He broke in with the Brooklyn Dodgers in 1947, played for their 1949 NL championship team, and went 13–8 in 1950, but Erv Palica's nine-year MLB pitching career was defined by one outing. On July 18, 1951, in a game vs. the lowly Pirates, Brooklyn manager Charlie Dressen tabbed Palica for relief duty. It was the fifth inning and the Dodgers trailed the Pirates 10–6. Amazingly, Brooklyn came back to take a 12–11 lead, but Palica blew it in the eighth and the Pirates won 13–12. After this performance, Dressen lost confidence in Palica, considering him to be an oft-injured and soft choker. Palica spent 1952 and most of 1953 in military service. He returned to Brooklyn in 1954, spent two seasons with Baltimore, and played until 1963 in the minors. A longshoreman after baseball, Palica died of a heart attack in 1982 at age 54 while working.

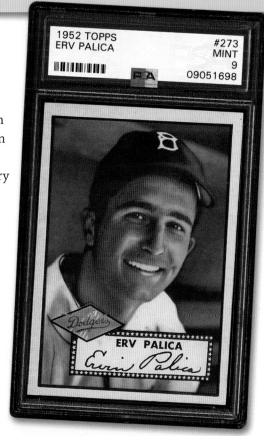

Career Stats

Record:	41–55
ERA:	4.22
IP:	839.1
Ks:	423
Threw:	RH

Teams

Brooklyn Dodgers NL (1947–1951, 1953–1954)
Baltimore Orioles AL (1955–1956)

Eddie Pellagrini

1952 TOPPS #405
EDDIE PELLAGRINI
NM – MT 8
02178315

Boston native Eddie Pellagrini broke in with the 1946 AL Champion Red Sox and hit a home run in his first MLB at-bat, the second Red Sox player to achieve that feat. Before he played at Fenway Park, Pellagrini played for the Great Lake Bluejackets military team while serving in the US Navy from 1942 to 1945. The versatile infielder was dealt to the Browns in 1947 and also played for the Phillies, Reds, and Pirates. After his playing days, Pellagrini was the head coach at Boston College where in 31 years he won a school-record 359 games and made three trips to the College World Series. Before his death at age 88 in 2006, he was active in the Red Sox boosters' BoSox Club. Pellagrini is a member of the Boston College Varsity Club Athletic Hall of Fame and the American Baseball Coaches Association Hall of Fame.

Career Stats

AB:	1,423	HR:	20
R:	167	RBI:	133
H:	321	OPS:	.611
BA:	.226		

Teams

Boston Red Sox AL (1946–1947)
St. Louis Browns AL (1948–1949)
Philadelphia Phillies NL (1951)
Cincinnati Reds NL (1952)
Pittsburgh Pirates NL (1953–1954)

Harry Perkowski

After one minor-league season, Harry Perkowski served almost four years in the US Navy in Europe and the Pacific. Drafted by the Reds in 1946, the southpaw from West Virginia excelled in their farm system. After a brief look with the big club in 1947, Perkowski went 22–10 for the 1948 Tulsa Oilers and was named Texas League Pitcher of the Year. Back with the Reds in 1949, his best seasons were 1952 and 1953, when he went 12–10 and 12–11, respectively, but he only posted 33 total wins in his eight-year MLB career. Perkowski continued in the minors until 1960, finishing with a 117–63 minor-league record. After baseball, he worked as an ambulance driver, constable, chief of police, deputy sheriff, and bus driver before working for the West Virginia Highway Department weight enforcement division. Perkowski died in 2016 at the age of 93.

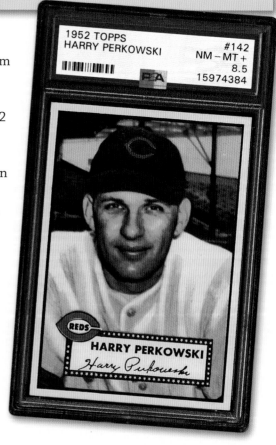

1952 TOPPS #142
HARRY PERKOWSKI
NM – MT + 8.5
15974384

Career Stats

Record:	33–40
ERA:	4.37
IP:	697.2
Ks:	296
Threw:	LH

Teams

Cincinnati Reds/Redlegs NL (1947, 1949–1954)
Chicago Cubs NL (1955)

Dave Philley

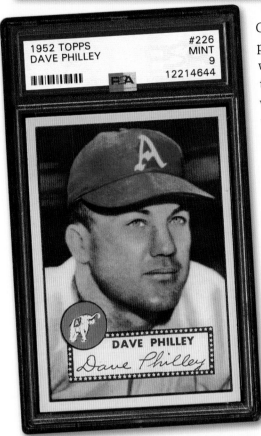

1952 TOPPS #226
DAVE PHILLEY MINT 9
12214644

One of those players everyone wanted on their team, Dave Philley was a good hitter, versatile defensive outfielder, and a clutch player. A tough competitor, the switch-hitting Philley would ignite the rally and finish it with a clutch hit. Over his 18-year career he played for eight teams. Philley started with the White Sox in 1941, lost three seasons to military service, and returned to play all outfield positions. He batted .303 for the 1953 Athletics and led the league with 157 games played. A member of the 1954 Indians AL pennant-winning squad, Philley played in the Series loss to the Giants. With the Orioles in 1955, he was voted Baltimore's Most Valuable Player. A record-setting pinch-hitter at the end of his career, Philley later managed in the minors. He retired to his ranch in Paris, Texas, where he died at the age of 91 in 2012.

Career Stats

AB:	6,296	HR:	84
R:	789	RBI:	729
H:	1,700	OPS:	.710
BA:	.270		

Teams

Chicago White Sox AL (1941, 1946–1951, 1956–1957)
Philadelphia Athletics AL (1951–1953)
Cleveland Indians AL (1954–1955)
Baltimore Orioles AL (1955–1956, 1960–1961)
Detroit Tigers AL (1957)
Philadelphia Phillies NL (1958–1960)
San Francisco Giants NL (1960)
Boston Red Sox AL (1962)

Jack Phillips

1952 TOPPS #240
JACK PHILLIPS MINT 9
05424333

First baseman Jack Phillips broke in with the World Champion Yankees in 1947, playing in 16 games. In 1949, he was hitting .308 for the Yanks when he was sold to the Pirates. The next season, he batted .293 for the Bucs and even pitched five innings for the Pirates in a lopsided loss to the Braves. Phillips was traded to the Tigers in 1954 and batted .316 and .295, respectively, in 1955 and 1956. Nicknamed "Stretch," the 6-foot-4 and 193-pound Phillips starred on the Clarkson College baseball and basketball teams and served in the US Navy during World War II. After five seasons as a minor-league manager, Phillips returned to Clarkson in 1965 as head baseball coach, a position he held for 24 years. One of the original inductees into Clarkson's Athletic Hall of Fame, Phillips passed away in 2009 at age 87.

Career Stats

AB:	892	HR:	9
R:	111	RBI:	101
H:	252	OPS:	.740
BA:	.283		

Teams

New York Yankees AL (1947–1949)
Pittsburgh Pirates NL (1949–1952)
Detroit Tigers AL (1955–1957)

Duane Pillette

Duane Pillette came up with the Yankees in 1949 and contributed two wins for the World Series champs that year. The son of former Major League pitcher Herman Pillette, Duane was traded to the Browns in 1950 and stayed on when the team became the Baltimore Orioles. While in St. Louis, Pillette was befriended by teammate Satchel Paige, who knew Pillette's father from the winter leagues and barnstorming. In 1951, Pillette unfortunately led the American League with 14 losses and 106 earned runs allowed. The last Brownie to pitch in St. Louis and the first pitcher to win a game for the Orioles, Pillette never had a winning season. He retired in 1956 after posting a career 38–66 record in eight seasons. Pillette continued in the minors through 1960 and later was owner-manager of a mobile home dealership. He passed away at the age of 88 in 2011.

Career Stats

Record:	38–66
ERA:	4.40
IP:	904.0
Ks:	305
Threw:	RH

Teams

New York Yankees AL (1949–1950)
St. Louis Browns/Baltimore Orioles AL (1950–1955)
Philadelphia Phillies NL (1956)

Jake Pitler

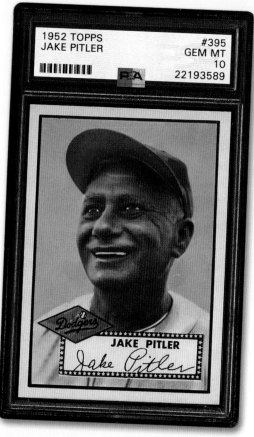

Second sacker Jake Pitler played briefly in the majors, batting .232 for his career, but he achieved lasting fame as a coach. When he was a child, Pitler's family moved from New York City to Beaver Falls, Pennsylvania, the home of future NFL legend Joe Namath. There Pitler befriended another NFL icon, future Pittsburgh Steelers owner Art Rooney. Pitler played four years in the minors before making it with his hometown Pirates in 1917. He was demoted in 1918 but left baseball to support the war effort by working in the aluminum business. Pitler played semipro and minor-league ball before managing in Brooklyn's farm system, where he developed a host of Dodgers stars including Duke Snider. Named Brooklyn's first-base coach in 1947, Pitler stayed in that role for a decade. One of the architects of the Dodgers' winning tradition, Pitler died at age 73 in 1968.

Career Stats

AB:	383	HR:	0
R:	40	RBI:	23
H:	89	OPS:	.578
BA:	.232		

Teams

Pittsburgh Pirates NL (1917–1918)

Bud Podbielan

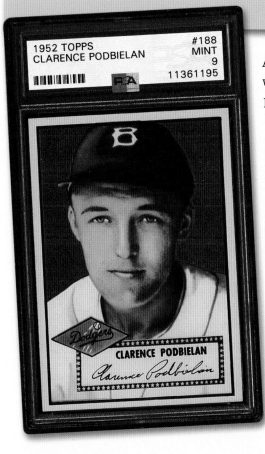

A World War II veteran at age 25 when he started with the 1949 NL pennant-winning Dodgers, Bud Podbielan pitched 12 innings in seven appearances during his rookie year. The bright spot in his career was 1950, when he posted a 5–4 record for the second-place Dodgers. Traded to the sixth-place Cincinnati Reds in June of 1952, Podbielan missed the Dodgers pennant run that year. On May 18, 1953, facing Preacher Roe and his former Dodgers teammates, Podbielan walked a Reds franchise record 13 batters in a ten-inning game, but held on for the 2–1 win. That same year, he lost 16 games. A .500 pitcher for the Dodgers and sub-.500 pitcher for Cincinnati and Cleveland, Podbielan had better success in the minors, where he finished in 1961 with a 111–81 record compiled in 12 minor-league seasons. He died in 1982 at the age of 58.

Career Stats

Record:	25–42
ERA:	4.49
IP:	641.0
Ks:	242
Threw:	RH

Teams

Brooklyn Dodgers NL (1949–1952)
Cincinnati Reds NL (1952–1955, 1957)
Cleveland Indians AL (1959)

Tom Poholsky

Detroit native Tom Poholsky compiled a record of 31–52 in six Major League seasons. Originally signed by the Red Sox, he played five years with the Cardinals, interrupted by Korean War service. An imposing figure on the hill at 6-foot-3 and 205 pounds, he never had a winning record, but he did finish his career with a respectable 3.93 ERA. Poholsky had excellent control. After his first two seasons, he mastered the art of location and his strikeout-to-walk ratio increased. Poholsky won nine games for the Cards in both 1955 and 1956. In the latter season, he logged 203 innings pitched with a 3.59 ERA. Traded to the Cubs in a multi-player deal, Poholsky left St. Louis after the 1956 season. His final season in the majors was 1957, when he went 1–7 with a 4.93 ERA. He died at age 71 in 2001.

Career Stats

Record:	31–52
ERA:	3.93
IP:	753.2
Ks:	316
Threw:	RH

Teams

St. Louis Cardinals NL (1950–1951, 1954–1956)
Chicago Cubs NL (1957)

Bob Porterfield

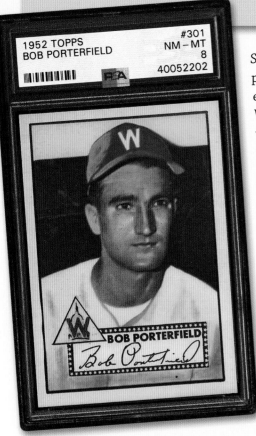

1952 TOPPS
BOB PORTERFIELD
#301
NM – MT
8
40052202

Star-crossed and oft-injured Bob Porterfield played 12 Major League seasons and enjoyed most of his success with the Washington Senators. In five seasons with the Senators, he won 67 games, and in 1953 he led the league with 22 wins, 24 complete games, and nine shutouts. Porterfield was an All-Star in 1954 despite a losing record and a league-leading 249 hits allowed. The 6-foot, 190-pound right-hander broke in with the Yankees in 1948, but health woes plagued his early career. The US Army veteran experienced freak accidents, arm soreness, and, in 1950, a vicious beaning that broke his jaw. Porterfield also spent time with the Red Sox, Pirates, and Cubs before wrapping it up in 1959. He pitched in the minors through 1961 and coached at the pro and college level. Porterfield later worked as a welder in North Carolina, where he died at age 56 in 1980.

Career Stats

Record:	87–97
ERA:	3.79
IP:	1,567.2
Ks:	572
Threw:	RH

Teams

New York Yankees AL (1948–1951)
Washington Senators AL (1951–1955)
Boston Red Sox AL (1956–1958)
Pittsburgh Pirates NL (1958–1959)
Chicago Cubs NL (1959)

Bill Posedel

San Francisco-born Bill Posedel won 15 games for the 1939 Boston Bees, the high point of a five-year Major League career interrupted by military service. He won 41 career games and was known for his powerful, yet wild, arm. Posedel was born just months after the cataclysmic 1906 San Francisco earthquake, and with more career walks than strikeouts, his control was almost as shaky. As a 31-year-old rookie in 1938, he butted heads with Brooklyn teammate and future manager Leo Durocher. The next season, Posedel moved on to Boston and a better rapport with manager Casey Stengel. He served in the US Navy before his MLB career and re-enlisted after the bombing of Pearl Harbor, serving from 1942 through 1945. Posedel eventually became a renowned pitching coach for the Oakland A's, grooming such stars as Catfish Hunter and Rollie Fingers. He died of cancer in 1989 at 83 years old.

1952 TOPPS
BILL POSEDEL
#361
MINT
9
04030342

Career Stats

Record:	41–43
ERA:	4.56
IP:	679.1
Ks:	227
Threw:	RH

Teams

Brooklyn Dodgers NL (1938)
Boston Bees/Braves NL (1939–1941, 1946)

Johnny Pramesa

Like many others over the years, Johnny Pramesa was a marginal MLB performer who enjoyed a successful minor-league career. Drafted in 1943, the Barton, Ohio, native worked in the New York Giants farm system until 1948, interrupted by two years of US Marine Corps service during WWII. As backup catcher for the Cincinnati Reds from 1949 to 1951, Pramesa's best year was 1950 when he batted .307 in 228 at-bats. Pramesa played out the string with the Chicago Cubs in 1952, his final MLB season, finishing with a lifetime .268 average and 141 hits. He continued to play in the minors and retired at age 30 in 1956 with a .311 BA compiled over nine minor-league seasons. A salesman after baseball, Pramesa passed away in 1996 at the age of 71. In July 2019, Barton, Ohio, dedicated a ballpark in his honor, which is now called Pramesa Park.

Career Stats

AB:	526	HR:	13
R:	29	RBI:	59
H:	141	OPS:	.696
BA:	.268		

Teams
Cincinnati Reds NL (1949–1951)
Chicago Cubs NL (1952)

Joe Presko

Known as "Baby Joe," Joe Presko was used primarily as a spot starter for the St. Louis Cardinals. After posting three double-digit win seasons in the minors, Presko got his opportunity with the Cards and put together a six-year Major League career. In 1951, his rookie season, he went 7–4 with a 3.45 ERA, which proved to be his best season in the majors. Along the way Presko played with future Hall of Famers Stan Musial, Enos Slaughter, and Red Schoendienst. Acquired by Detroit in 1955, Presko played out his career moving between their Charleston farm team and the Tigers. The Kansas City native returned home to work in security for the Brinks Armored Car Company. He coached American Legion and Ban Johnson League baseball for nearly 30 years and mentored future Cy Young Award winner and All-Star pitcher David Cone. Presko passed away in 2019 at age 90.

Career Stats

Record:	25–37
ERA:	4.61
IP:	490.1
Ks:	202
Threw:	RH

Teams
St. Louis Cardinal NL (1951–1954)
Detroit Tigers AL (1957–1958)

Ken Raffensberger

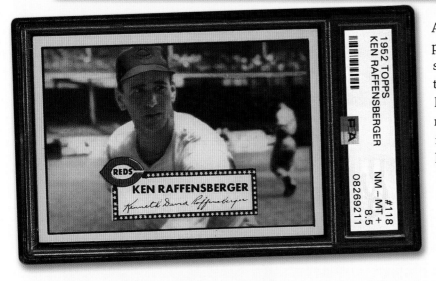

A pretty good pitcher on some very bad teams, Ken Raffensberger's record is not indicative of his talent. Had he pitched for first-division teams, he would have fared much better than his dismal 119–154 career record. His 3.60 ERA is a much better indicator. While playing for the eighth-place 1944 Phillies, Raffensberger made the All-Star team even though he led the National League with 20 losses. He paced the league in losses again in 1951 with 17. A lefty with excellent command, Raffensberger's arsenal included a nasty curveball, slider, and forkball. His best season was with the 1952 Cincinnati Reds when, at age 34, he went 17–13 with a 2.81 ERA, twirled 18 complete games, and led the league with six shutouts. After baseball, the dependable lefty became a bartender in his hometown of York, Pennsylvania, and died in 2002 at the age of 85.

Career Stats

Record:	119–154
ERA:	3.60
IP:	2,151.2
Ks:	806
Threw:	LH

Teams

St. Louis Cardinals NL (1939)
Chicago Cubs NL (1940–1941)
Philadelphia Phillies NL (1943–1947)
Cincinnati Reds/Redlegs NL (1947–1954)

Bob Ramazzotti

If Bob Ramazzotti didn't have bad luck, he would have had no luck at all. A very good prospect coming up the ranks, his career was derailed by a series of injuries, some life-threatening. After serving three years in the US Army, 29-year-old Ramazzotti came up to Brooklyn in 1946 with good potential. Back in the minors in 1947, he was beaned at the plate. His skull was fractured and he developed a blood clot on his brain. In critical condition, Ramazzotti soldiered through operations, a long hospital stay, and rehab to make it back to the majors. The infielder had decent seasons with the Cubs batting .262 in 1950 and .284 in 1952, but was plagued by a series of injuries that kept him from reaching his potential. After retiring from the game, Ramazzotti worked with youth baseball groups. He died in 2000 at age 83.

Career Stats

AB:	851	HR:	4
R:	86	RBI:	53
H:	196	OPS:	.562
BA:	.230		

Teams

Brooklyn Dodgers NL (1946, 1948–1949)
Chicago Cubs NL (1949–1953)

Willie Ramsdell

A colorful knuckleballer with no idea where his knuckleball was going to go, "Willie the Knuck" Ramsdell had a very good minor-league career. Acquired by Brooklyn in 1941, Ramsdell went 17–7 in 1946 and 21–5 in 1947 for the Fort Worth Cats, earning two brief stops with the big club. After his 18–12 season for the 1949 Hollywood Stars, he returned to the Dodgers in 1950. He also played briefly for the Reds and the Cubs, without much success. Ramsdell knuckled his way to ten complete games and one shutout for the 1951 Reds, but also led the league with 17 losses and nine wild pitches that year. A happy-go-lucky party guy, Ramsdell finished in the minors in 1954 with a 153–92 record from his 12 minor-league seasons. Ramsdell died in 1969 at the relatively young age of 53, which some attribute to his hard living.

Career Stats

Record:	24–39
ERA:	3.83
IP:	479.2
Ks:	240
Threw:	RH

Teams

Brooklyn Dodgers NL (1947, 1948, 1950)
Cincinnati Reds NL (1950–1951)
Chicago Cubs NL (1952)

Del Rice

A fine defensive catcher, Del Rice had a long 17-year Major League career. A member of the 1946 world champion St. Louis Cardinals, Rice led the National League in fielding percentage in 1948, double plays in 1951, putouts in 1952, and he made the All-Star team in 1953. With the Cardinals for 12 years, Rice's ability to call a great game was evident as the pitching staff was often among the league ERA frontrunners. Rice became backup catcher for the Milwaukee Braves in 1955, but was starter Bob Buhl's personal catcher and a contributor on the 1957 world champion Braves team. After his playing career, Rice coached and managed in both the majors and the minors, including a stint as manager of the 1972 California Angels. He was 60 years old and scouting for the San Francisco Giants when he died in 1983 at a banquet held in his honor.

Career Stats

AB:	3,826	HR:	79
R:	342	RBI:	441
H:	908	OPS:	.668
BA:	.237		

Teams

St. Louis Cardinals NL (1945–1955, 1960)
Milwaukee Braves NL (1955–1959)
Chicago Cubs NL (1960)
Baltimore Orioles AL (1960)
Los Angeles Angels (1961)

Hal Rice

Signed by St. Louis in 1941, outfielder Hal "Hoot" Rice broke in with the Cardinals in 1948 and hit .323 in eight games. He reached the .300 mark again in 1953, batting .310 while splitting time between St. Louis and Pittsburgh. Inconsistent at the plate, Rice twice saw his average dip below the .200 mark. He never played in a World Series, but he did play alongside future Hall of Famers Stan Musial with the Cards and Ernie Banks with the Cubs.

Rice hailed from a hardworking, coal-mining family. He entered the US Army in 1943 and suffered leg injuries in battle but rose to the rank of second lieutenant. After baseball, Rice resided in Muncie, Indiana. He was inducted into the Delaware County Athletic Sports Hall of Fame in 1981. Rice passed away in 1997 at age 73 and is buried at Arlington National Cemetery.

Career Stats

AB:	1,183	HR:	19
R:	129	RBI:	162
H:	307	OPS:	.686
BA:	.260		

Teams

St. Louis Cardinals NL (1948–1953)
Pittsburgh Pirates NL (1953–1954)
Chicago Cubs NL (1954)

Marv Rickert

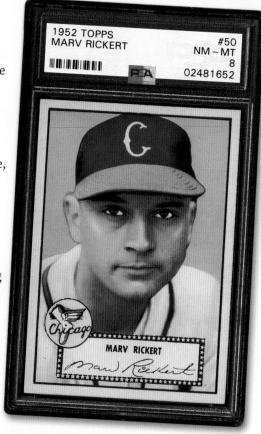

The highlight of journeyman Marv Rickert's career took place in 1948. The Boston Braves called Rickert up from their Triple-A affiliate, the Milwaukee Brewers, after their starting left-fielder, Jeff Heath, broke his ankle sliding into home plate on September 29. Rickert played the last three games of the season and started five games in the World Series, registering four hits. Rickert earned a place on the 1949 Braves roster, and he batted .292 in 100 games that year. He played for the Cubs from 1942 through 1947, interrupted by three years of US Coast Guard service. After a brief stint with the Reds and his time with the Braves, Rickert finished up with the Pirates and White Sox in 1950. He became a charter-boat operator and then worked for the Pierce County Parks and Recreation Department. Marv Rickert died in 1978 at the age of 57.

Career Stats

AB:	1,149	HR:	19
R:	139	RBI:	145
H:	284	OPS:	.653
BA:	.247		

Teams

Chicago Cubs NL (1942, 1946–1947)
Cincinnati Reds NL (1948)
Boston Braves NL (1948–1949)
Pittsburgh Pirates NL (1950)
Chicago White Sox AL (1950)

Sherry Robertson

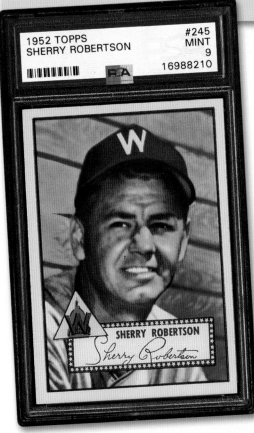

1952 TOPPS
SHERRY ROBERTSON
#245
MINT
9
16988210

Montreal native Sherrard "Sherry" Robertson spent a decade in the big leagues as an infielder, outfielder, and pinch-hitting specialist. His best year was 1949 when he played in 110 games and batted .251 with 11 home runs and 42 RBI for Washington. Signed by the Athletics in 1952, Robertson played just 43 games in Philly before his release. Robertson, however, had family connections in baseball. One of seven children, Robertson and his siblings were the nieces and nephews of Senators owner Clark Griffith. Two siblings, Thelma and Calvin, were raised by the Griffith's in Washington, and took their last name. After Clark died in 1955, Calvin Griffith became president of the ballclub. Robertson became assistant farm director, a position he held throughout the club's move to Minnesota and until his death in 1970. He died in a car crash during a hunting trip at age 51.

Career Stats

AB:	1,507	HR:	26
R:	200	RBI:	151
H:	346	OPS:	.664
BA:	.230		

Teams

Washington Senators AL (1940–1941, 1943, 1946–1952)

Philadelphia Athletics AL (1952)

Saul Rogovin

Brooklyn native Saul Rogovin had a few good seasons and a few bad seasons. Hence the .500 lifetime record. His best year was 1951, a season split between the Tigers and White Sox, when he led the American League with his 2.78 ERA and posted a 12–8 record. He had another good year in 1952, posting a 14–9 record with a nice 3.85 ERA for Chicago. One interesting little tidbit is that Rogovin suffered from a sleep disorder and sometimes dozed off in the dugout. Not an overpowering pitcher, Rogovin had decent command using his slider and curveball. After baseball, he worked in sales and later got his degree at City College of New York. At age 57, Rogovin found his niche as a high-school English literature teacher in Manhattan and Brooklyn. He died from bone cancer at the age of 72 in 1995.

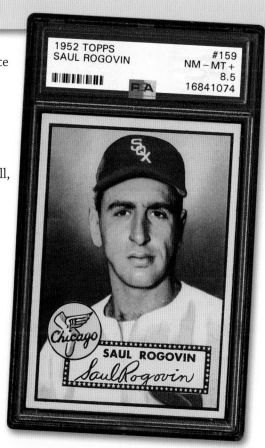

1952 TOPPS
SAUL ROGOVIN
#159
NM – MT +
8.5
16841074

Career Stats

Record:	48–48
ERA:	4.06
IP:	883.2
Ks:	388
Threw:	RH

Teams

Detroit Tigers AL (1949–1951)
Chicago White Sox AL (1951–1953)
Baltimore Orioles AL (1955)
Philadelphia Phillies NL (1955–1957)

Stan Rojek

A nice little shortstop, Stan "Happy Rabbit" Rojek started with the Dodgers, flourished with the Pirates, and finished with the Browns. He debuted in 1942, and after one game in Dodger blue, he served three years in the US Army Air Force. As backup to Pee Wee Reese after the war, Rojek was a member of the 1947 Dodgers NL pennant-winning team, but he did not play in the Series. That year, Rojek's locker was next to Jackie Robinson's, and he was one of the guys who was very supportive of his new teammate. With the Pirates in 1948, Rojek had his best year, batting .290 in a league-leading 641 at-bats. He also played eight seasons in the minors, before and after his MLB career. After baseball, Rojek worked in the family dairy business and operated a bowling alley. He died in 1997 at age 78.

Career Stats

AB:	1,764	HR:	4
R:	225	RBI:	122
H:	470	OPS:	.653
BA:	.266		

Teams

Brooklyn Dodgers NL (1942, 1946–1947)
Pittsburgh Pirates NL (1948–1951)
St. Louis Cardinals NL (1951)
St. Louis Browns AL (1952)

Bob Ross

California-born Bob Ross played three seasons of big-league ball, posting a career record of 0–2 with a 7.17 ERA. Originally signed by the Dodgers in 1945, he debuted with the Senators in 1950. Ross joined the Phillies in 1956, appeared in three games, and posted an 8.10 ERA. His time in the Bigs was brief, but Ross had some unique baseball experiences. In 1951, he was a minor-league teammate of Mickey Mantle. Their manager, George Selkirk, was the player who replaced Babe Ruth in right field for the Yankees. In 1952, Ross was drafted into the US Army and played on several military teams. Back in the minors in 1957, he was a teammate of future broadcasting legend Bob Uecker. Ross earned his teaching degree and served as a teacher, principal, and administrator in the Anaheim, California, area until 1984. At the time of this writing, he is 91 years old.

Career Stats

Record:	0–2
ERA:	7.17
IP:	47.2
Ks	29
Threw:	LH

Teams

Washington Senators AL (1950–1951)
Philadelphia Phillies NL (1956)

Joe Rossi

Oakland, California, native Joe Rossi played just one season in Major League Baseball. He batted .221 with the 1952 Reds, breaking into the Bigs at age 31. Rossi played 55 games for Cincy as a backup catcher to starter Andy Seminick. In 1952, Rossi's Reds were a mess. They had three managers, including Hall of Famer Rogers Hornsby, but even "The Rajah" could not keep his club from finishing in sixth place. Their best player was Ted Kluszewski, the only Cincy starter to hit over .300. In October of 1952, Rossi was traded with Cal Abrams and Gail Henley to the Pirates for future Reds Hall of Famer, Gus Bell. Rossi never reached the big club in Pittsburgh and after 14 seasons in the minors he returned home to Oakland where, in 1999, he passed away at the age of 77.

Career Stats

AB:	145	HR:	1
R:	14	RBI:	6
H:	32	OPS:	.574
BA:	.221		

Teams
Cincinnati Reds NL (1952)

Dick Rozek

We have all heard the phrase "claim to fame." Well, Iowa native Dick Rozek has a claim to someone else's fame, but first, his career. After serving in the military, Rozek played five MLB seasons, mostly as a reliever. He broke in with the Indians in 1950 and finished up with the Athletics in 1954. Along the way, Rozek compiled a 4.55 ERA and walked twice as many batters than he K'd. His career was essentially uneventful, save for one event, that claim to fame. On May 16, 1951, Rozek made baseball history by surrendering Mickey Mantle's first-ever Yankee Stadium home run. The "Commerce Comet" would smash 266 home-field homers, but Rozek, whose career pitching line shows just one victory, will always hold this part of diamond history. After baseball, Rozek returned to Iowa to operate a manufacturing company. He died in 2001 at the age of 74.

Career Stats

Record:	1–0
ERA:	4.55
IP:	65.1
Ks:	26
Threw:	LH

Teams
Cleveland Indians AL (1950–1952)
Philadelphia Athletics AL (1953–1954)

Bob Rush

A Cubs pitching-rotation mainstay in the 1950s, Bob Rush relied on a sinking fastball to baffle opposing batters and had eight 200-innings-pitched seasons. An All-Star in 1950, he lost 12 games after the midsummer break and ended up with a league-leading 20 losses. The Cubs were woeful during this era, and Rush would likely have fared better pitching for better teams. In 1952, his second All-Star season, Rush posted a 17–13 record with four shutouts, a 2.70 ERA, and a .292 BA.

He finally got to play for a contender with the 1958 NL pennant-winning Braves. Rush did his part, going 10–6 that year, but he took the loss in Game Three of World Series. The World War II US Army veteran worked in sales after baseball. The 2008 inductee to the Indiana Sports Hall of Fame died in 2011 at the age of 85.

Career Stats

Record:	127–152
ERA:	3.65
IP:	2,410.2
Ks:	1,244
Threw:	RH

Teams

Chicago Cubs NL (1948–1957)
Milwaukee Braves NL (1958–1960)
Chicago White Sox AL (1960)

Jim Russell

A steady ballplayer and lifetime .267 hitter, Jim Russell had several good years with the Pirates and Braves. In 1944, his most productive season, the switch-hitting outfielder batted .312 with 181 hits. Known for his defensive ability, Russell led the league in assists, putouts, and double plays turned as left fielder for the Pirates during World War II. An offseason trade brought him to the Boston Braves as starting center fielder in 1948. Russell was batting .264 in mid-July when a blood infection damaged his heart, causing him to miss the rest of the season and the World Series. He returned to Boston for the 1949 season, but was never the same. Russell ended his Major League career with the Brooklyn Dodgers in 1951. He later scouted for the Dodgers and Senators and also owned a beer distributorship. Jim Russell passed away in 1987 at the age of 69.

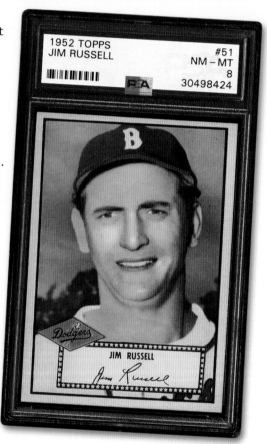

Career Stats

AB:	3,595	HR:	67
R:	554	RBI:	428
H:	959	OPS:	.760
BA:	.267		

Teams

Pittsburgh Pirates NL (1942–1947)
Boston Braves NL (1948–1949)
Brooklyn Dodgers NL (1950–1951)

Johnny Rutherford

Unlike his auto racing namesake, Johnny Rutherford's career passed by quickly. In 1952, his only big-league season, the Canadian-born righty was part of a Brooklyn Dodgers pitching staff that included Carl Erskine, Joe Black, Clem Labine, Ralph Branca, and Preacher Roe. There was some symmetry to Rutherford's mediocrity. In 1952, he surrendered 97 hits in 97.1 innings. He had seven wins and seven losses. He posted 29 walks and 29 strikeouts, and his 22 games were split evenly between starting and relieving. Because of shoulder troubles, Johnny "Doc" Rutherford made just one lap around the track before the checkered flag signaled his early MLB finish. He played a total of eight minor-league seasons, retiring in 1955 with a 76–55 minor-league record. Rutherford then became a doctor of osteopathic medicine with a practice in Detroit. He died in 2016 at age 91.

Career Stats

Record:	7–7
ERA:	4.25
IP:	97.1
Ks:	29
Threw:	RH

Teams

Brooklyn Dodgers NL (1952)

Connie Ryan

A versatile infielder, Connie Ryan was a starter and utility player during his 12-year Major League career. The dependable 1944 All-Star second baseman never had glitzy numbers, but he was smart, tough, and competitive. Ryan's best season was 1947, when he batted .265 with 144 hits for the Boston Braves, and he was a member of the 1948 Braves' NL pennant-winning team. A bit of a prankster, he got tossed from a game in 1949 for wearing a raincoat over his Braves uniform in the on-deck circle because he thought the game should be called due to heavy rain. After playing, Ryan used his baseball IQ to his advantage for more than 20 years as manager, coach, and scout. The interim manager of the 1975 Atlanta Braves, interim manager of the 1977 Texas Rangers, and US Navy WWII veteran passed away in 1996 at the age of 75.

Career Stats

AB:	3,982	HR:	56
R:	535	RBI:	381
H:	988	OPS:	.694
BA:	.248		

Teams

New York Giants NL (1942)
Boston Braves NL (1943–1944, 1946–1950)
Cincinnati Reds/Redlegs NL (1950–1951, 1954)
Philadelphia Phillies NL (1952–1953)
Chicago White Sox AL (1953)

Ray Scarborough

1952 TOPPS #43
RAY SCARBOROUGH NM – MT
8
05052982

A decent pitcher at the beginning of his career, Ray Scarborough's most productive year was 1948 for the Senators when he compiled a 15–8 record with a 2.82 ERA. The 1950 All-Star was also part of the 1952 World Series champion New York Yankees. However, over his ten-year Major League career, Ray had some vanilla numbers, compiling a sub-.500 won-lost record. In those days, many players worked in the offseason to supplement their MLB salary. When Scarborough played for Boston, the press discovered his pickle salesman job and dubbed him "the pitching pickle peddler." In retirement, Scarborough started an oil and supply business in his native North Carolina, and he helped to establish the Mount Olive College baseball program. He was on the 1968 Baltimore Orioles coaching staff and scouted for several different MLB teams until he suffered a heart attack and died in 1982 at age 64.

Career Stats

Record:	80–85
ERA:	4.13
IP:	1,428.2
Ks:	564
Threw:	RH

Teams

Washington Senators AL (1942–1943, 1946–1950)
Chicago White Sox AL (1950)
Boston Red Sox AL (1951–1952)
New York Yankees AL (1952–1953)
Detroit Tigers AL (1953)

Carl Scheib

One of the youngest players to appear in a Major League game, Carl Scheib left high school to join the Philadelphia Athletics, making his debut in 1943 at 16 years old. The youngster developed under the watchful eye of Connie Mack, but as soon as Scheib turned 18, he was drafted. He returned from the US Army in 1947 and enjoyed his best season in 1948, posting a 14–8 record and batting .298 as a pinch-hitter. Overall, Scheib was a .250 career hitter and was called upon on many occasions to show his offensive chops. Both a starter and reliever, Scheib's 1953 shoulder injury caused the end of his MLB career. He worked in the minors until 1957, trying to get back into form. After baseball, Scheib operated a service station and car wash in San Antonio, Texas, where he passed away at the age of 91 in 2018.

Career Stats

Record:	45–65
ERA:	4.88
IP:	1,070.2
Ks:	290
Threw:	RH

Teams

Philadelphia Athletics AL (1943–1945, 1947–1954)
St. Louis Cardinals NL (1954)

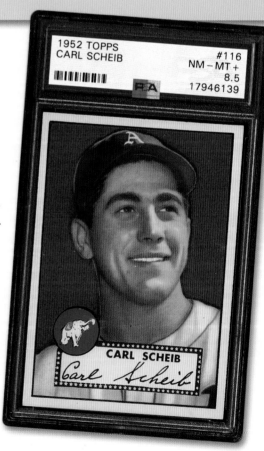

1952 TOPPS
CARL SCHEIB #116
NM – MT +
8.5
17946139

Johnny Schmitz

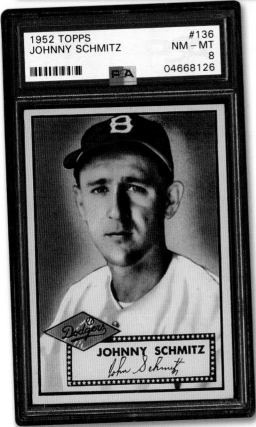

1952 TOPPS #136
JOHNNY SCHMITZ NM – MT
8
04668126
PSA

A pretty good pitcher for some pretty bad teams, southpaw Johnny Schmitz should have had a more successful career. With the Cubs for eight seasons interrupted by three years in the US Navy, Schmitz returned in 1946 to lead the league with 135 strikeouts and make the All-Star team. In 1948, Schmitz won 18 games for the eighth-place Cubbies and was an All-Star again. Nicknamed "Bear Tracks" for his signature shuffle to the mound, Schmitz had brief stops with six more teams after Chicago. In 1954 at age 33, he had a resurrection of sorts, posting an 11-8 record with a sparkling 2.91 ERA for the Senators. Johnny wrapped up his 13-year MLB career with the Orioles in 1956, finishing with a 93–114 record and a good 3.55 ERA. A golfer and greenskeeper in Wisconsin after baseball, Schmitz passed away in 2011 at the ripe old age of 90.

Career Stats

Record: 93–114
ERA: 3.55
IP: 1,812.2
Ks: 746
Threw: LH

Teams

Chicago Cubs NL (1941–1942, 1946–1951)
Brooklyn Dodgers NL (1951–1952)
New York Yankees AL (1952, 1953)
Cincinnati Reds NL (1952)
Washington Senators AL (1953–1955)
Boston Red Sox AL (1956)
Baltimore Orioles AL (1956)

Bob Schultz

In 1951, 27-year-old rookie left-hander "Bullet Bob" Schultz posted a 3–6 record with a 5.24 ERA for the Cubs. The next season, Schultz reversed that record to 6–3 and lowered his ERA to 4.01. He moved on to Pittsburgh and Detroit but would never win another game at the Major League level. Schultz played ten seasons in the minors around his MLB career. His 25–6 season with the Nashville Volunteers in 1950 paved the way for his MLB call-up. Nicknamed for his fastball and known for his fiery, competitive spirit, Schultz's lack of control held him back from stardom. Born in Kentucky, Schultz served in the US Army Air Force in World War II and was a house painter in the Nashville area after baseball. In 1979, at age 55, "Bullet Bob" died of gunshot wounds stemming from a bar fight at the VFW Club in Nashville.

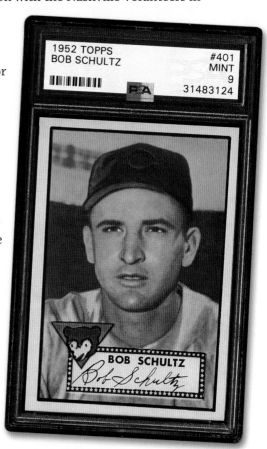

1952 TOPPS #401
BOB SCHULTZ MINT
9
31483124
PSA

Career Stats

Record: 9–13
ERA: 5.16
IP: 183.0
Ks: 67
Threw: LH

Teams

Chicago Cubs NL (1951–1953)
Pittsburgh Pirates NL (1953)
Detroit Tigers AL (1955)

Bill Serena

1952 TOPPS
BILL SERENA

#325
NM – MT
8
05261177

Bill Serena's Major League career is a study in opportunity. When he was able to play a significant amount of games, he produced. Serena, a California native, spent his entire six-year career with the Cubs. The 5-foot-9, 175 pounder was built low to the ground, a fact which served him well as a third baseman for most of his career. In 1950, playing in 127 games, he had 17 homers and 61 RBI. Similarly, he played in 122 games in 1952 and had 15 dingers, 61 RBI, and batted .274. Out of MLB two years later, Serena scouted for the Indians, Braves, Rangers, Tigers, and Marlins, retiring in 1994. His baseball legacy lived on through his grandson, Kevin Cassidy, who played at Centenary College and for several independent level teams. Serena was 71 when he died of lung cancer in 1996.

Career Stats

AB:	1,239	HR:	48
R:	154	RBI:	198
H:	311	OPS:	.787
BA:	.251		

Teams

Chicago Cubs NL (1949–1954)

Spec Shea

A rookie All-Star with the 1947 world champion Yankees, Spec Shea went 14–5 and won two games in the World Series as the Yanks topped Brooklyn. Shea had 13 complete games and an ERA of 3.07, but alas, his time as a star was short-lived. In 1948, the Naugatuck, Connecticut, native came back to earth with a 9–10 record. In 1952, he was traded to the Senators and was reborn, winning 23 games over the next two seasons. Once again, the run did not last, and Shea's MLB career ended after the 1955 season. The extroverted Shea served in the US Army Air Corps in WWII and was dubbed by Yankees broadcaster Mel Allen as the "Naugatuck Nugget." After baseball, he worked on behalf of retired ballplayers and taught Robert Redford how to pitch for the film *The Natural*. Shea passed away at age 81 in 2002.

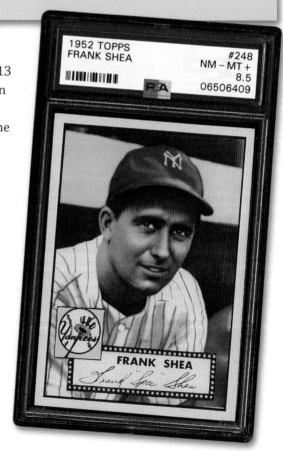

1952 TOPPS
FRANK SHEA

#248
NM – MT +
8.5
06506409

FRANK SHEA

Career Stats

Record:	56–46
ERA:	3.80
IP:	943.2
Ks:	361
Threw:	RH

Teams

New York Yankees AL (1947–1949, 1951)
Washington Senators AL (1952–1955)

George Shuba

Charlie Silvera

Outfielder George Shuba played seven seasons for the Brooklyn Dodgers and had 211 hits, but his best moment at home plate came as a minor leaguer in 1946. On April 18 of that year, Jackie Robinson became the first African American to play pro baseball in the International League with the Montreal Royals. Robinson smashed a three-run homer that day, and as he approached home plate, Shuba, the on-deck hitter, shook Robinson's hand. The impactful Associated Press photo of this gesture became a symbol of changing racial relations. Known as "Shotgun," Shuba was the first National League player to hit a World Series pinch-hit homer in 1953. He was also a member of the fabled 1955 world champion Dodgers. After retiring in 1955, Shuba returned to Ohio, worked for the US Postal Service, and spoke at area schools about racial tolerance. He died in 2014 at age 89.

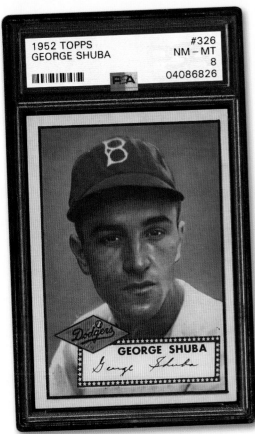

As backup catcher to Yogi Berra for most of his ten-year MLB career, Charlie "Swede" Silvera didn't get much playing time, but he did get six World Series rings. His most active season was 1949, his first full season in New York. That year, Silvera played in 58 games, batted .315 with 130 at-bats, and played in Game Two of the World Series. The Yankees were world champs from 1949 through 1953 and again in 1956, when Silvera warmed up Don Larson before Game Five, his perfect game. Silvera served three years in the US Army Air Force in the Pacific during his minor-league days. He finished his career with the Cubs in 1957 and then managed in the minors. He was bullpen coach for Billy Martin's Twins, Tigers, and Rangers, and he continued on as a Major League scout until 2011. Silvera passed away in 2019 at age 94.

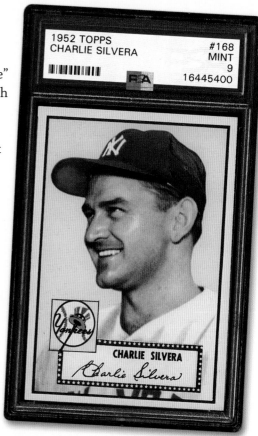

Career Stats

AB:	814	HR:	24
R:	106	RBI:	125
H:	211	OPS:	.771
BA:	.259		

Teams
Brooklyn Dodgers NL (1948–1950, 1952–1955)

Career Stats

AB:	482	HR:	1
R:	34	RBI:	52
H:	136	OPS:	.683
BA:	.282		

Teams
New York Yankees AL (1948–1956)

Chicago Cubs NL (1957)

Al Sima

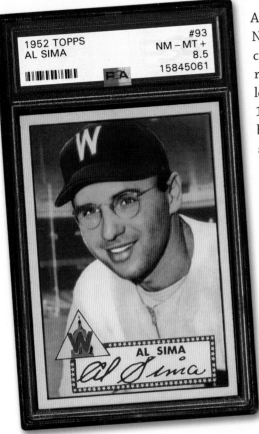

A big lefty from New Jersey, Al Sima compiled a 111–103 record in 14 minor-league seasons (1942–1959), interrupted by WWII military service. After the Washington Senators called Sima up in 1950, the 28-year-old rookie went 4–5 before returning to the Chattanooga Lookouts in the Southern Association. He split time between both clubs again in 1951, and, after going 24–9 for the 1952 Lookouts, he earned another look with the Senators in 1953. He split time between the White Sox and Philadelphia Athletics in 1954 and wrapped up his MLB career with a 11–21 record and 4.61 ERA. On September 19, 1954, his last MLB game, Sima had the distinction of being the last A's pitcher to take the mound at the old Connie Mack Stadium in Philly before the franchise moved to Kansas City. He passed away in 1993 at the age of 71.

Career Stats

Record:	11–21
ERA:	4.61
IP:	308.2
Ks:	111
Threw:	LH

Teams

Washington Senators AL (1950, 1951, 1953)
Chicago White Sox AL (1954)
Philadelphia Athletics AL (1954)

Harry Simpson

One of the first African American ballplayers in the American League, Harry "Suitcase" Simpson was an outstanding outfielder with an average bat. The 1956 All-Star played for five teams over his eight-year Major League career. Very well-liked, Simpson had the reputation as a diligent, hard worker. As a matter of fact, Hall of Famer Casey Stengel once referred to Harry as the best defensive right fielder in the American League. Simpson's best offensive seasons were with the Kansas City Athletics. In 1956, he batted .293 with 21 home runs, 11 triples, and 105 RBI for the Athletics. With the Yankees in 1957, Simpson played in five games of the World Series loss to the Milwaukee Braves. After his MLB days, Simpson continued in the minors until 1964 and then worked as a machinist in the aerospace industry. He died in 1979 at the age of 53.

Career Stats

AB:	2,829	HR:	73
R:	343	RBI:	381
H:	752	OPS:	.739
BA:	.266		

Teams

Cleveland Indians AL (1951–1953, 1955)
Kansas City Athletics AL (1955–1957, 1958–1959)
New York Yankees AL (1957–1958)
Chicago White Sox AL (1959)
Pittsburgh Pirates NL (1959)

Dick Sisler

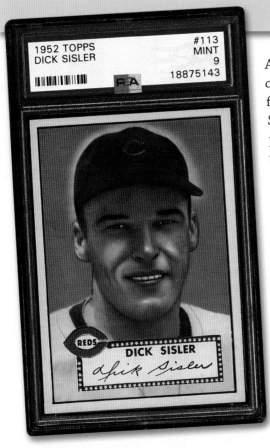

1952 TOPPS #113
DICK SISLER
MINT 9
18875143

Although Dick Sisler never came close to matching the numbers of his famous father, Hall of Famer George Sisler, he enjoyed a long career as player, manager, and coach. After three years in the US Navy, young Sisler joined his hometown Cardinals in 1946, which was perfect timing as St. Louis won the World Series that year. However, his best season was 1950 with the Phillies, when he slammed 13 homers, had 155 hits, batted .296, and made the All-Star team. That year the pennant race between "The Whiz Kids" and Brooklyn came down to the last game of the season. Tied 1–1 in the top of the 10th with two men on base, Sisler famously hit one out of the park for the pennant win.

Sisler went on to coach and manage in the minors and the majors through the 1980s. He died in 1998 at age 78.

Career Stats

AB:	2,606	HR:	55
R:	302	RBI:	360
H:	720	OPS:	.743
BA:	.276		

Teams

St. Louis Cardinals NL (1946–1947, 1952–1953)
Philadelphia Phillies NL (1948–1951)
Cincinnati Reds NL (1952)

Sibby Sisti

Sebastian "Sibby" Sisti played 13 seasons in the majors interrupted by three years of military service. Sisti spent his entire career with the Braves, played every infield and outfield position except pitcher and catcher, and moved with the team from Boston to Milwaukee in 1953. He played on the Braves 1948 NL pennant-winning team, but unfortunately he bunted into a double play in the final inning of the final game of the Series, and Cleveland won the 1948 Championship. After his playing days, Sisti coached and managed and eventually became a truck driver. A member of the Boston Braves Hall of Fame inaugural class alongside legends Warren Spahn, Johnny Sain, and Tommy Holmes, Sisti later served as technical advisor for the film *The Natural* and had a bit role as the Pirates manager in the film. He died in 2006 at age 85.

1952 TOPPS #293
SIBBY SISTI
NM – MT + 8.5
07063147

Career Stats

AB:	2,999	HR:	27
R:	401	RBI:	260
H:	732	OPS:	.637
BA:	.244		

Teams

Boston/Milwaukee Bees/Braves NL (1939–1942, 1946–1954)

Lou Sleater

```
1952 TOPPS          #306
LOU SLEATER         MINT
                      9
              01448049
                RA
```

LOU SLEATER
Louis Sleater Jr.

Lefty knuckleballer Lou Sleater made his debut in 1950 with his hometown St. Louis Browns, but soon moved on to the Senators, Athletics, Braves, Tigers, and Orioles. A star pitcher for Mount St. Joseph High School in Baltimore and the University of Maryland, Sleater signed with the Boston Braves in 1946 and spent time in the Cubs and Giants organizations before his MLB debut. With the Senators in 1952, Sleater stopped a record 12-consecutive-hit streak by Walt Dropo. His career-best ERA was 3.15 with the 1956 Braves. Sleater appeared in a career-high 41 games for Detroit in 1957, posted three wins and two saves, and slammed a walk-off home run in May. He finished in 1958 with a 12–18 Major League record. Sleater then worked in steel industry sales and became an avid golfer. The journey of this ultimate journeyman ended with his passing in 2013 at age 86.

Career Stats

Record:	12–18
ERA:	4.70
IP:	300.2
Ks:	152
Threw:	LH

Teams

St. Louis Browns AL (1950–1952)
Washington Senators AL (1952)
Kansas City Athletics AL (1955)
Milwaukee Braves NL (1956)
Detroit Tigers AL (1957–1958)
Baltimore Orioles AL (1958)

Roy Smalley Jr.

```
1952 TOPPS          #173
ROY SMALLEY         NM – MT
                      8
              02306580
                RA
```

ROY SMALLEY
Roy Smalley

US Navy veteran Roy Smalley Jr. was starting shortstop for the Cubs from 1948, his rookie season, through 1953, when future Hall of Famer Ernie Banks came on board. A decent shortstop, Smalley slammed 21 home runs in 1950, but led the league with 114 strikeouts. He also led the league in assists, putouts, and double plays that year. Unfortunately, Smalley also led the NL in errors for three seasons. Cubbie fans were merciless, but Smalley was stalwart through the boos. In 1954, he was traded to Milwaukee, and he also played with the Phillies for several seasons before retiring in 1958. He then managed in the minors and operated a janitorial service in Los Angeles. His son, Roy Smalley III, followed in his footsteps to become an All-Star MLB shortstop. Roy Smalley Jr. retired to Arizona, where he passed away in 2011 at age 85.

Career Stats

AB:	2.644	HR:	61
R:	277	RBI:	305
H:	601	OPS:	.660
BA:	.227		

Teams

Chicago Cubs NL (1948–1953)
Milwaukee Braves NL (1954)
Philadelphia Phillies NL (1955–1958)

Frank Smith

Right-handed reliever Frank Smith pitched for six of his seven Major League seasons with the Cincinnati Reds. Considered one of the better relievers in the game, he had an effective sidearm delivery and became one of baseball's first closers. Coming out of the bullpen in late innings was his specialty. Smith's best season was 1952, when he posted a 12–11 record. In 1954, he went 5–8 with 20 saves and a 2.67 ERA. Consistent throughout his career, Smith compiled a 35–33 record with a nice 3.81 ERA and 44 saves. After retiring as a player, Smith worked in sales for automotive and boat dealerships and ran baseball clinics. He succumbed to leukemia in 2005 at the age of 77 in Malone, Florida. In 2016, the baseball field at his high school alma mater, LaFargeville (NY) Central School, was named Frank Smith Memorial field in his honor.

Career Stats

Record:	35–33
ERA:	3.81
IP:	495.2
Ks:	277
Threw:	RH

Teams

Cincinnati Reds/Redlegs NL (1950–1954, 1956)
St. Louis Cardinals NL (1955)

Bud Souchock

Steve "Bud" Souchock broke in with the Yankees in 1946, batting .302 in 47 games. After a 1947 stint in the minors, he returned to New York in 1948, but batted just .203. That offseason, the Yanks dealt Souchock to the White Sox. He eventually landed in Detroit, where he spent the rest of his career. In 1952, Souchock gained a measure of revenge against the Yankees. He drove in the winning run as Virgil Trucks no-hit the Bombers. It was Trucks' iconic second no-no of the season. A first baseman and outfielder, Souchock batted .302 for the Tigers in 1953. Before making it to the majors, he served in the US Army in World War II and was awarded the Silver Star. After his playing days, Souchock managed in the minors and served as a scout for the Yankees and Tigers. He died in 2002 at 83 years old.

Career Stats

AB:	1,227	HR:	50
R:	163	RBI:	186
H:	313	OPS:	.764
BA:	.255		

Teams

New York Yankees AL (1946, 1948)
Chicago White Sox AL (1949)
Detroit Tigers AL (1951–1955)

George Spencer

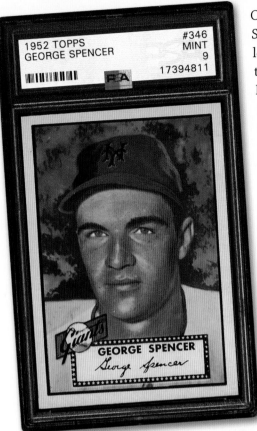

Ohio native, George Spencer had eight big-league seasons with the Giants and Tigers. His best season was 1951, his rookie year, when he had a 10–4 record and 3.75 ERA for Leo Durocher's pennant-winning Giants. Spencer was one of the top rookie pitchers in baseball that season. He had an astronomical 18.90 ERA in the 1951 World Series versus the Yankees, but Spencer did retire Joe DiMaggio twice. Before entering pro ball, he played baseball and football for Ohio State. Spencer played in the minors before, during, and after his MLB career, compiling a 105–73 record over 15 seasons. He roomed with Roger Maris one summer while with Indianapolis in the American Association. Spencer became a pitching coach in the Tigers organization and a sheet metal worker after his baseball career ended. He died in 2014 at 88 years old.

Career Stats

Record:	16–10
ERA:	4.05
IP:	251.1
Ks:	82
Threw:	RH

Teams

New York Giants NL (1950–1955)
Detroit Tigers AL (1958, 1960)

Ebba St. Claire

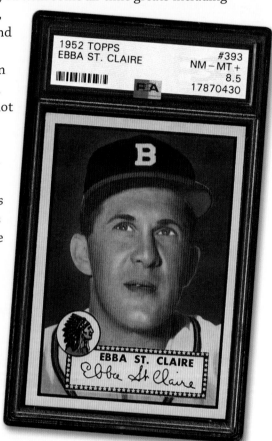

A solid defensive catcher, Ebba St. Claire played for the Braves and Giants in the early 1950s. An imposing 6-foot-1 and 219 pounds, the switch-hitting St. Claire batted .282 in 1951, his rookie year with Boston. In 1954, he was traded to New York along with Johnny Antonelli, Billy Klaus, and Don Liddle for Sam Calderone and 1951 pennant-winning hero Bobby Thomson. St. Claire was a standout player at Whitehall High School in New York and at Colgate University. A career backup, he played with some all-time greats including Warren Spahn, Willie Mays, and Monte Irvin. With just seven career homers, St. Claire did not produce a lot of offense, but he did produce some solid ballplayers. His son Randy was a Major League pitcher from 1984 to 1994, and son Steve played minor-league ball. Ebba St. Claire passed away in 1982 at age 61.

Career Stats

AB:	450	HR:	7
R:	39	RBI:	40
H:	112	OPS:	.662
BA:	.249		

Teams

Boston/Milwaukee Braves NL (1951–1953)
New York Giants NL (1954)

Virgil Stallcup

The starting shortstop for the Cincinnati Reds from 1948 through 1951, Virgil "Red" Stallcup was decent from the defensive perspective. As a matter of fact, he led the league in fielding percentage at the shortstop position in both 1950 and 1951. Signed by the Boston Red Sox in 1941, Stallcup spent the next several years between the minors and US Naval service, and he finally broke into the Major Leagues in 1947 at age 25 with the Reds. At best, Stallcup was an average to below-average hitter. His best offensive season was 1949, when he batted .254 and registered 146 hits. In 1952, Stallcup was traded to the St. Louis Cardinals, where he finished out his Major League career. He then played and managed in the minors through 1955. After baseball, Stallcup was a supervisor for a chemical company. Tragically, Virgil Stallcup committed suicide in 1989 at 67 years old.

Teams
Cincinnati Reds NL (1947–1952)
St. Louis Cardinals NL (1952–1953)

Career Stats
AB:	2,059	HR:	22
R:	171	RBI:	214
H:	497	OPS:	.595
BA:	.241		

Bud Stewart

California native Bud Stewart broke in with the Pirates in 1941 and enjoyed a nine-year big-league career that included stops with the Yankees, Senators, and White Sox. As a rookie outfielder, Stewart batted .267 and led the National League with ten pinch hits. After the 1942 season, he served in the US Army, played in the minors, and resurfaced with the Yankees in 1948. Stewart played just six games for New York before being dealt to Washington for Leon Culberson. He experienced one of his best seasons with the 1949 Senators, playing in 118 games and batting .284 with 43 RBI. Stewart played all three outfield positions and batted a career .268. Released by the White Sox in June of 1954, he finished the season as manager of Colorado in the Western League. After baseball, Stewart returned to the West Coast. He passed away in 2000 at age 84.

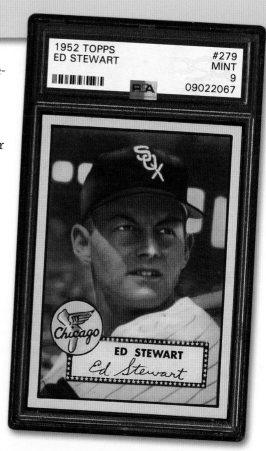

Career Stats
AB:	2,041	HR:	32
R:	288	RBI:	260
H:	547	OPS:	.744
BA:	.268		

Teams
Pittsburgh Pirates NL (1941–1942)
New York Yankees AL (1948)
Washington Senators AL (1948–1950)
Chicago White Sox AL (1951–1954)

Chuck Stobbs

A bonus baby, Chuck Stobbs was 18 years old when he debuted for the Red Sox in 1947. He got into the rotation in 1949, posting 11 wins that year, 12 wins in 1950, and ten wins in 1951. With the Washington Senators for most of his career, Stobbs had the dubious distinction of giving up probably the longest home run ever hit in the annals of baseball. It was April 17, 1953, Stobbs' first game for the Senators, and he faced a young Mickey Mantle who smashed a home run right out of Griffith Stadium. It landed 565 feet away, in a back yard across the street. Although he played 15 Major League seasons, Stobbs is remembered for that one pitch. After retiring in 1961, he coached at George Washington University and worked for the Royals and Indians. He died in 2008 at the age of 79.

Career Stats

Record:	107–130
ERA:	4.29
IP:	1,920.1
Ks:	897
Threw:	LH

Teams

Boston Red Sox AL (1947–1951)
Chicago White Sox AL (1952)
Washington Senators/Minnesota Twins AL
(1953–1958, 1959–1961)
St. Louis Cardinals NL (1958)

George Strickland

New Orleans native George "Bo" Strickland was a good infielder for the Pittsburgh Pirates and Cleveland Indians over his ten seasons as a ballplayer. The US Navy veteran did not have a great bat, but he did have a nice season in 1953 when he batted .284 for the Indians. Strickland's strength was his glove. The shortstop led the league in double plays in 1953 and fielding percentage in 1955. A member of the 1954 Indians AL pennant-winning team, Strickland played in three games of the World Series loss to the New York Giants. Strickland later coached for the Indians and was interim manager in 1964 and 1966. He also coached for the Twins and the Royals until 1972. After baseball, he went into the horse-racing business. A member of the Louisiana Sports Hall of Fame, Strickland passed away in 2010 at the age of 84.

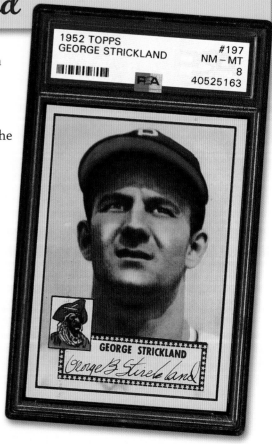

Career Stats

AB:	2,824	HR:	36
R:	305	RBI:	284
H:	633	OPS:	.624
BA:	.224		

Teams

Pittsburgh Pirates NL (1950–1952)
Cleveland Indians AL (1952–1957, 1959–1960)

Marlin Stuart

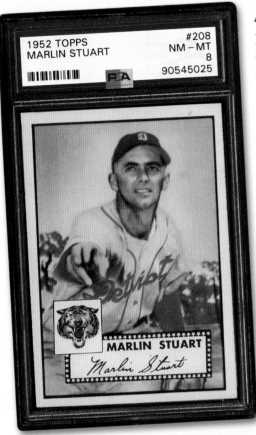

1952 TOPPS
MARLIN STUART
#208
NM – MT
8
90545025

Accustomed to playing barefoot sandlot baseball, Arkansas native Marlin Stuart got permission to play barefoot in the last game of 1940, his first season in the minors, and he pitched a complete game victory. After losing three years to military service, Stuart returned to the minors before making his Major League debut with Detroit in 1949. Back in the minors in 1950, Stuart pitched a perfect game for the Toledo Mud Hens with his signature screwball. In 1953, he led the St. Louis Browns pitching staff with the most victories when he went 8–2 with a 3.94 ERA. Stuart retired in 1954 after a brief stint with the Yankees. He returned to farming in Arkansas and later became a heavy equipment operator. Sadly, an aneurysm and stroke in 1980 left him wheelchair-bound and unable to speak. Stuart passed away in 1994 at the age of 75.

Career Stats

Record:	23–17
ERA:	4.65
IP:	485.2
Ks:	185
Threw:	RH

Teams

Detroit Tigers AL (1949–1952)
St. Louis Browns/Baltimore Orioles AL (1952–1954)
New York Yankees AL (1954)

Pete Suder

1952 TOPPS
PETE SUDER
#256
MINT
9
19460937

Aliquippa, Pennsylvania, native Pete "Pecky" Suder enjoyed a solid career with the Philadelphia Athletics interrupted by US Army service. He joined the club in 1941 and finished in 1955, the team's first season in Kansas City. Decent offensively, Suder batted .281 with 50 RBI in 1946 and .286 with 130 hits in 1953. A dependable glove man, Suder played second base on the famous Athletics infield that included third sacker Hank Majeski, shortstop Eddie Joost, and first baseman Ferris Fain. Together, they set a Major League record for double plays with 217 in 1949, a 154-game season. They also logged more than 200 double plays in 1950 and 1951, inspiring the poem *Joost to Suder to Fain*. After managing in the minors and scouting, Suder returned to Aliquippa, served on the school board, and was warden of the Beaver County Jail. He died at age 90 in 2006.

Career Stats

AB:	5,085	HR:	49
R:	469	RBI:	541
H:	1,268	OPS:	.627
BA:	.249		

Teams

Philadelphia/Kansas City Athletics AL (1941–1943, 1946–1955)

Max Surkont

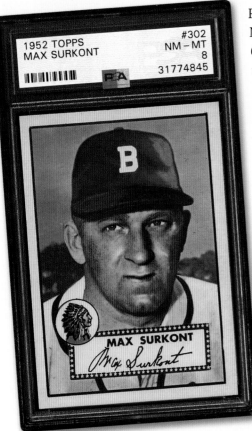

Right-handed pitcher Max Surkont won 61 career games in nine Major League seasons. He debuted with the White Sox in 1949, but it was with the Braves that he thrived. Surkont won 40 games in four seasons and, in 1953, shut out the Reds for the team's first win as the Milwaukee Braves. A starter and reliever, Surkont also pitched for the Pirates, Cardinals, and Giants. The Rhode Island native had some sparkling moments as a minor leaguer, but never really produced at the big-league level. He served three years in the US Navy during World War II and battled control issues on the mound. Injuries stalled and eventually ended Surkont's career in 1957. He returned to Rhode Island, opened a popular bar, and contributed to many charitable causes. In 1986, he was inducted into the Pawtucket, Rhode Island, Hall of Fame. Later that year, he passed away at age 64.

Career Stats

Record:	61–76
ERA:	4.38
IP:	1,194.1
Ks:	571
Threw:	RH

Teams

Chicago White Sox AL (1949)
Boston/Milwaukee Braves NL (1950–1953)
Pittsburgh Pirates NL (1954–1956)
St. Louis Cardinals NL (1956)
New York Giants NL (1956–1957)

Bob Swift

In one of the most unusual baseball photos of all time, Detroit catcher Bob Swift was pictured on his knees behind the dish when Eddie Gaedel stepped up to the plate on August, 19, 1951. In a publicity stunt by St. Louis Browns owner Bill Veeck, the 3-foot-7 Gaedel was sent in as pinch-hitter. Told not to swing, Gaedel walked on four straight pitches. A good defensive catcher, Swift played for the Tigers for ten of his 14 MLB seasons. He won a ring with the 1945

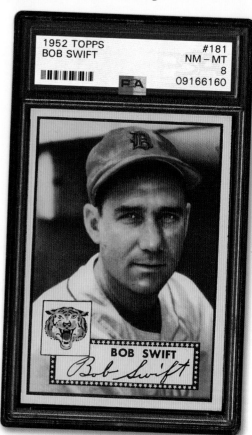

world champion Tigers, batting .250 in the Series win vs. the Cubs. After retiring as a player in 1953, Swift managed in the minors and coached in the majors. He skippered the Detroit Tigers for part of 1965 and 1966. Sadly his managerial tenure was cut short when he succumbed to lung cancer in 1966 at the age of 51.

Career Stats

AB:	2,750	HR:	14
R:	212	RBI:	238
H:	635	OPS:	.592
BA:	.231		

Teams

St. Louis Browns AL (1940–1942)
Philadelphia Athletics AL (1942–1943)
Detroit Tigers AL (1944–1953)

Bob Thorpe

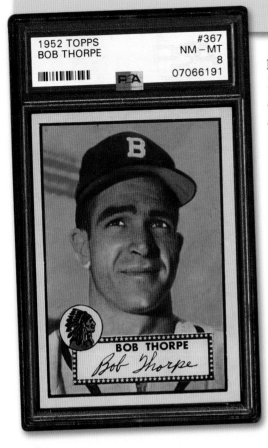

1952 TOPPS   #367
BOB THORPE   NM – MT
            8
07066191

Florida native Bob Thorpe joined the Boston Braves in 1951 and hit .500 with a slugging percentage of 1.500—he had a triple in two at-bats. An outfielder, Thorpe batted .260 with three home runs and 26 RBI in 292 at-bats with Boston in 1952. The aggressive right-hander struck out 42 times with just five walks that season. Thorpe moved with the Braves to Milwaukee in 1953, and the team won 92 games, finishing second in the National League. That year, Thorpe played alongside Eddie Mathews, who smacked 47 home runs, and Warren Spahn, who won 23 games. Thorpe's 1953 stats were slightly more modest. His average dipped to .162 in just 27 games. Around his MLB appearances, Thorpe played a total of 14 seasons in the minors and wrapped it up in 1961. A business owner in Waveland, Mississippi, Thorpe died in 1996 at age 69.

Career Stats

AB:	331	HR:	3
R:	22	RBI:	32
H:	83	OPS:	.590
BA:	.251		

Teams

Boston/Milwaukee Braves NL (1951–1953)

Faye Throneberry

Baseball has had some legendary families, including the Griffeys, Bonds, and Niekros. In the realm of mediocrity, however, it is hard to beat the Throneberrys. Faye and his younger brother Marv were baseball "everymen," hardly the stuff of legend. Fisherville, Tennessee, native Faye Throneberry was 20 years old when he joined the Red Sox in 1952. He had a decent rookie year, batting .258 with 23 RBI and 16 steals. After serving in the US Army in 1953 and 1954, Throneberry returned to Boston and was eventually dealt to the Senators in 1957. The outfielder hit ten homers for the 1959 Senators and ended his career with the expansion Angels in 1961. While Marv would be known for his future beer commercials, Faye became an award-winning bird-dog trainer. He died in 1999 at the age of 67, joining brother Marv on the bench somewhere in baseball heaven.

1952 TOPPS   #376
FAYE THRONEBERRY   NM – MT
            8
31809254

Career Stats

AB:	1,302	HR:	29
R:	152	RBI:	137
H:	307	OPS:	.665
BA:	.236		

Teams

Boston Red Sox AL (1952, 1955–1957)
Washington Senators AL (1957–1960)
Los Angeles Angels AL (1961)

Joe Tipton

After his minor-league seasoning was interrupted by three years in the US Navy, where he saw action in the Pacific, Joe Tipton came back to win the 1947 Eastern League batting championship. A rookie with the 1948 World Series champion Cleveland Indians, Tipton batted .289 in 47 games but only had one pinch-hit appearance in the Series. Strictly a backup catcher in the majors, Tipton was adequate, but his .236 lifetime average was so-so. Somewhat better defensively than he was with the bat, Tipton was never a front line player. He was part of one of the most lopsided trades in baseball history in 1949 when the White Sox traded him to the Philadelphia Athletics straight up for future Hall of Famer Nellie Fox. After baseball, Tipton owned and operated an automotive dealership in Birmingham, Alabama, until he passed away in 1994 at age 72.

Career Stats

AB:	1,117	HR:	29
R:	116	RBI:	125
H:	264	OPS:	.706
BA:	.236		

Teams

Cleveland Indians AL (1948, 1952–1953)
Chicago White Sox AL (1949)
Philadelphia Athletics AL (1950–1952)
Washington Senators AL (1954)

Earl Torgeson

Known as "The Earl of Snohomish," Earl Torgeson had a successful 15-year Major League career. Very good offensively and defensively, the bespectacled Torgeson was a walking machine with a great eye and was speedy on the basepaths. The competitive first baseman was known for his aggressive play and brawling, but his engaging personality made him a fan favorite. The high-water mark of his career was 1950 with the Boston Braves when he batted .290 and scored a league-leading 120 runs. That year he banged out 23 home runs, which he followed in 1951 with 24 homers. Torgeson played on the 1948 Boston Braves NL pennant winners and the 1959 Chicago White Sox AL pennant winners before finishing his career with the 1961 world champion Yankees.

The Snohomish, Washington, native and World War II US Army veteran passed away in 1990 at the age of 66.

Career Stats

AB:	4,969	HR:	149
R:	848	RBI:	740
H:	1,318	OPS:	.802
BA:	.265		

Teams

Boston Braves NL (1947–1952)
Philadelphia Phillies NL (1953–1955)
Detroit Tigers AL (1955–1957)
Chicago White Sox AL (1957–1961)
New York Yankees AL (1961)

Jim Turner

After 14 years in the minors, Jim Turner was a ripe 33 years old when he joined the Boston Bees in 1937. That season, although he won 20 games and led the league with his 2.38 ERA and 24 complete games, he reaped no All-Star recognition. Oddly, Turner was an All-Star in 1938 despite losing 18 games and surrendering a league-high 21 home runs. Such is the nature of the midseason classic. Turner won 14 games for the 1940 world champion Reds and finished his career with a league-leading ten saves for the 1945 Yanks. As Yankees pitching coach under Casey Stengel (1949–1959), Turner won seven World Series titles. He coached the Reds pitching staff to the 1961 NL flag and continued coaching for the Reds and Yankees until 1973. Turner died in 1998 after spending more than half of his 95 years in his beloved baseball.

Career Stats

Record:	69–60
ERA:	3.22
IP:	1,132.0
Ks:	329
Threw:	RH

Teams

Boston Bees NL (1937–1939)
Cincinnati Reds NL (1940–1942)
New York Yankees AL (1942–1945)

Tom Upton

Belying his nickname, Tom "Muscles" Upton was a fairly weak hitter. Over his three years in the majors, Upton had 525 at-bats, an anemic .225 lifetime batting average, and two career home runs, not exactly Major League material. Not a total disaster, Upton did bat .237 with 389 at-bats as starting shortstop for the St. Louis Browns in 1950, his rookie season. From that point on, it was all downhill for

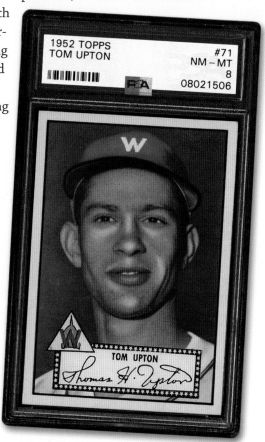

Upton. He wasn't much better in his six minor-league seasons, batting .239 with 464 hits and 22 runs in 1,943 at-bats. It's not surprising Upton's career in the majors was not lengthy. His brother, Bill Upton, also made it to the Bigs, but the extent of his career was pitching five innings for the Athletics in 1954, so big brother Tom was the star of the family. Tom Upton passed away in 2008 at the age of 81.

Career Stats

AB:	525	HR:	2
R:	60	RBI:	42
H:	118	OPS:	.600
BA:	.225		

Teams

St. Louis Browns AL (1950–1951)
Washington Senators AL (1952)

Bob Usher

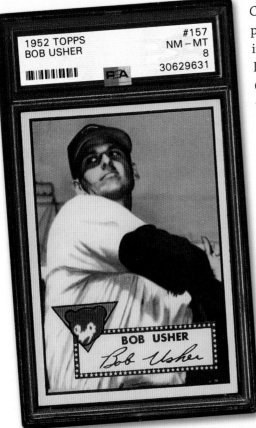

Centerfielder Bob Usher played for four teams in six mediocre Major League seasons. The California native signed with the Reds in 1943, before his two-year stint in the US Navy, where he played ball in the Hawaii and Oahu service leagues. He debuted with Cincinnati in 1946 and had a good year in 1950, batting .259 with six home runs in 321 at-bats. Traded to the Cubs in 1952, Usher had just one appearance in Chicago followed by five seasons in the Pacific Coast League. In 1957, he had one more shot in the Bigs, starting with the Indians and moving on to the Senators, where he batted a career-high .261. The San Diego State University graduate then worked for US Naval Intelligence and later served in the Bay Area Coast Guard Auxiliary, where he was Vice-Commodore. Usher died in 2014 at the age of 89.

Career Stats

AB:	1,101	HR:	18
R:	133	RBI:	102
H:	259	OPS:	.623
BA:	.235		

Teams
Cincinnati Reds NL (1946–1947, 1950–1951)
Chicago Cubs NL (1952)
Cleveland Indians AL (1957)
Washington Senators AL (1957)

Elmer Valo

A fearless outfielder, Elmer Valo often injured himself colliding with ballpark walls to make heroic catches, robbing the likes of Ted Williams and Yogi Berra of home runs. Most of his 20-year career was with the Philadelphia Athletics, where he had some fine offensive seasons. An aggressive player, Valo was a line-drive hitter who hit for average. In 1955, he batted a lofty .364, although he had only 283 at-bats. Valo emigrated from Czechoslovakia when he was six years old and soon developed a love for baseball. During World War II, his baseball career was interrupted when he served in the US Army. After retiring as a player, Valo managed in the minors, and coached and scouted for several organizations. In 1990, he was chosen for the Philadelphia Wall of Fame. Elmer Valo passed away in 1998 at the age of 77.

Career Stats

AB:	5,029	HR:	58
R:	768	RBI:	601
H:	1,420	OPS:	.790
BA:	.282		

Teams
Philadelphia/Kansas City Athletics AL (1940–1943, 1946–1956)
Philadelphia Phillies NL (1956, 1961)
Brooklyn/Los Angeles Dodgers NL (1957–1958)
Cleveland Indians AL (1959)
New York Yankees AL (1960)
Washington Senators/Minnesota Twins AL (1960–1961)

Chris Van Cuyk

1952 TOPPS
CHRIS VAN CUYK
#53
MINT
9
09003318

Wisconsin native Chris Van Cuyk was more a career minor leaguer than a Major League ballplayer. The 6-foot-6, 215-pound left-handed pitcher compiled a 7–11 record to go along with his 5.16 ERA in three short seasons in the majors. Signed in 1946 by the Brooklyn Dodgers, Van Cuyk put together a 103–61 record in 11 minor-league seasons spent mostly in the Dodgers farm system. In 1947, playing in the D leagues, the 20-year-old southpaw posted a sparkling 25–2 record with a 1.93 ERA. At the AA level, Van Cuyk had three 14-win seasons. Unfortunately, he could not duplicate that success in the majors. Interestingly, Van Cuyk's older brother, Johnny, was also signed by the Dodgers in 1946, and his pitching career was no better. Chris Van Cuyk retired to Hudson, Florida, and passed away at the age of 65 in 1992.

Career Stats

Record:	7–11
ERA:	5.16
IP:	160.1
Ks:	103
Threw:	LH

Teams

Brooklyn Dodgers NL (1950–1952)

Clyde Vollmer

Clyde Vollmer was a 6-foot-1 and 185-pound outfielder who showed flashes of power throughout his ten-year career. He came up with his hometown Cincinnati Reds in 1942 and on the first pitch thrown to him smacked a home run off of Pittsburgh's Max Butcher. Vollmer missed the next three seasons serving in the US Army. He returned to Cincy after the war but never batted higher than .219 for them. Dealt to Washington in 1948, Vollmer had a breakout season in 1949 with 14 home runs and 59 RBI. That season, he slammed a home run in every American League ballpark. He joined the Red Sox in 1950 and enjoyed his best career season in 1951 with 22 home runs and 85 RBI in 115 games. After baseball, Vollmer settled in Kentucky, owned a bar, and was active in civic organizations. He died in 2006 at age 85.

1952 TOPPS
CLYDE VOLLMER
#255
NM – MT +
8.5
17221330

Career Stats

AB:	2,021	HR:	69
R:	283	RBI:	339
H:	508	OPS:	.737
BA:	.251		

Teams

Cincinnati Reds NL (1942, 1946–1948)
Washington Senators AL (1948–1950, 1953–1954)
Boston Red Sox AL (1950–1953)

Ben Wade

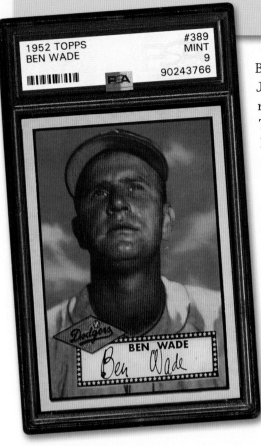

1952 TOPPS
BEN WADE
#389
MINT
9
90243766

Ben Wade's claim to fame occurred on July 6, 1952, when he hit two home runs against the great Warren Spahn. That season, Wade won 11 games for Brooklyn but was hard-pressed to make his mark on a pitching staff that included Carl Erskine, Preacher Roe, and Joe Black. After his playing career, however, Wade would leave an indelible impact on the Dodgers organization. As the team's scouting director, he played a role in signing players such as Mike Piazza, Rick Sutcliffe, Dave Stewart, and Orel Hershiser, along with seven Rookies of the Year including Fernando Valenzuela, Raul Mondesi, and Eric Karros. Wade did not always hit on draft picks though. In 1983, he selected a pitcher named Erik Sonberg one pick before Boston chose Roger Clemens. Wade's death in 2002 at age 80 signaled the passing of a true baseball game changer.

Career Stats

Record:	19–17
ERA:	4.34
IP:	371.1
Ks:	235
Threw:	RH

Teams

Chicago Cubs NL (1948)
Brooklyn Dodgers NL (1952–1954)
St. Louis Cardinals NL (1954)
Pittsburgh Pirates NL (1955)

Herm Wehmeier

1952 TOPPS
HERMAN WEHMEIER
#80
NM – MT
8
03445288

Eighteen-year-old Cincinnati native Herm Wehmeier's dream came true when he was signed by his hometown Reds in 1945. Unfortunately, Wehmeier struggled as a big-league pitcher and the dream became more of a nightmare. All over the place as a pitcher, between 1949 and 1952 Wehmeier led the National League in walks three times, wild pitches twice, and also led the league in hit batsman and earned runs allowed. The Cincinnati fans were merciless. They booed him constantly, whether he won or lost, and this took a toll on Wehmeier. After nine years of abuse by his hometown fans, Wehmeier had a few better seasons for the Phillies and Cards before retiring in 1958. He was working as an executive for a trucking company in Texas when he died of a heart attack in 1973 at 46 years old.

Career Stats

Record:	92–108
ERA:	4.80
IP:	1,803.0
Ks:	794
Threw:	RH

Teams

Cincinnati Reds NL (1945, 1947–1954)
Philadelphia Phillies NL (1954–1956)
St. Louis Cardinals NL (1956–1958)
Detroit Tigers AL (1958)
Pittsburgh Pirates NL (1955)

Bill Werle

Bill "Bugs" Werle got his nickname as an entomology major at the University of California. In the majors, Werle bugged a lot of his managers with his pitching. Used mostly as a reliever after his rookie year, Werle's best year was 1949, when the 28-year-old rookie won 12 games for the Pittsburgh Pirates.

Unfortunately, he also lost 13 games that year. In 1950, he lost 16 games, but in 1951 the left-hander posted an 8–6 record with six saves for the Pirates. Werle was traded to the St. Louis Cardinals in 1952 and was claimed off of waivers later that season by the Boston Red Sox. By 1954, Werle was back in the minors where he played until 1961. He managed in the minors for nine seasons and then scouted for the Orioles and Indians until 1999. Werle passed away in 2010 at the age of 89.

Career Stats

Record:	29–39
ERA:	4.69
IP:	665.1
Ks:	283
Threw:	LH

Teams
Pittsburgh Pirates NL (1949–1952)
St. Louis Cardinals NL (1952)
Boston Red Sox AL (1953–1954)

Wally Westlake

Outfielder Wally Westlake was actually a good utility player who managed to make the All-Star team in 1951. Westlake had stops with six different teams, but his best years were with the Pittsburgh Pirates at the beginning of his career. Mentored by Casey Stengel in the minors, Westlake initially had some pop in his swing. The right-hander averaged about 20 home runs per season during his five years with the Pirates, but his power diminished after that. Cleveland Indians GM and former Pirates teammate Hank Greenburg brought Westlake on board in 1952. He appeared in the 1954 World Series as part of the Indians 111-wins team that was swept by the New York Giants. A career .272 hitter, Westlake ended his playing days in 1956 with the Phillies. After baseball, he worked in construction and enjoyed hunting and fishing. Wally Westlake passed away in 2019 at age 98.

Career Stats

AB:	3,117	HR:	127
R:	474	RBI:	539
H:	848	OPS:	.795
BA:	.272		

Teams
Pittsburgh Pirates NL (1947–1951)
St. Louis Cardinals NL (1951–1952)
Cincinnati Reds NL (1952)
Cleveland Indians AL (1952–1955)
Baltimore Orioles AL (1955)
Philadelphia Phillies NL (1956)

Al Widmar

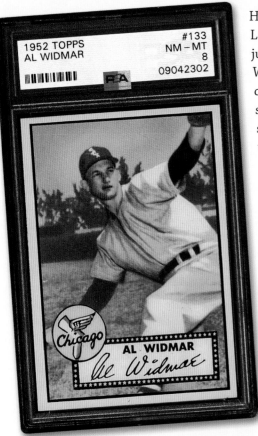

His career as a Major League pitcher lasted just five years, but Al Widmar's career as a coach and manager spanned 45 years. A starter and reliever with an overall sub-.500 record, Widmar played for the Red Sox, Browns, and White Sox from 1947 to 1952. The low point of his career came in 1950 when Widmar lost 15 games while pitching for the St. Louis Browns. Named player-manager of AA level Tulsa Oilers in 1955, Widmar later became pitching coach for the Phillies, Brewers, Orioles, and Blue Jays. Known as a skilled developer of young baseball talent, as pitching coach for Toronto from 1980 to 1989, he helped lead the Blue Jays to a division title. He then worked until 2000 as a special assistant to the Blue Jays general manager. Widmar succumbed to colon cancer in 2005 at the age of 80.

Career Stats

Record:	13–30
ERA:	5.21
IP:	388.1
Ks:	143
Threw:	RH

Teams

Boston Red Sox AL (1947)
St. Louis Browns AL (1948, 1950–1951)
Chicago White Sox AL (1952)

Bill Wight

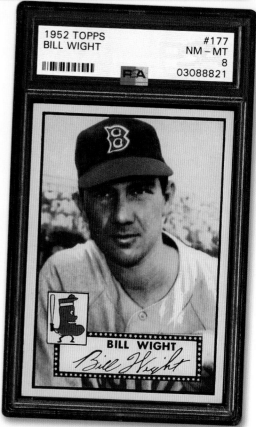

Signed by the Yankees in 1941, while he was still in high school, California native Bill Wight barely got his feet wet in the minors before serving three years in the US Navy. A sub-.500 pitcher in the majors, Wight played for eight teams in twelve seasons. Used as a starter at the beginning of his career, Wight morphed into a reliever, which helped extend his playing time. With the White Sox in 1948, Wight lost 20 games. He bounced back the next season with a 15–13 record, but lost another 16 games in 1950. Wight's career 3.95 ERA indicates that he played for some dreadful teams and was given very little support. After retiring as a player, Wight scouted for Houston and signed future Hall of Famer Joe Morgan. He then scouted for the Braves until 1998. Wight passed away in 2007 at the age of 85.

Career Stats

Record:	77–99
ERA:	3.95
IP:	1,563.0
Ks:	574
Threw:	LH

Teams

New York Yankees AL (1946–1947)
Chicago White Sox AL (1948–1950)
Boston Red Sox AL (1951–1952)
Detroit Tigers AL (1952–1953)
Cleveland Indians AL (1953, 1955)
Baltimore Orioles AL (1955–1957)
Cincinnati Redlegs NL (1958)
St. Louis Cardinals NL (1958)

Del Wilber

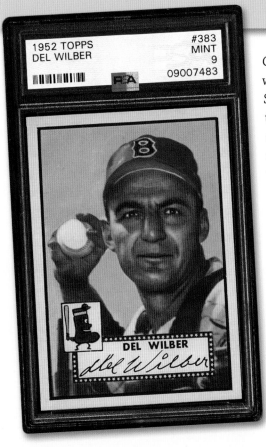

1952 TOPPS #383
DEL WILBER
MINT 9
09007483

Catcher Del Wilber played eight years with the Cardinals, Phillies, and Red Sox. On August 27, 1951, he slugged three home runs in three at-bats, accounting for all of the Phillies' runs in a 3–0 win vs. Cincinnati, the first player to accomplish that feat. In the US Army, Wilber played vs. Negro League legends Josh Gibson and Satchel Paige. An accomplished minor-league manager, he was hired as bullpen coach by his good friend, Senators manager Ted Williams, in 1970. This enabled Wilber to accrue enough time to earn a big-league pension. Ironically, Wilber would pass away at age 83 in 2002, just two weeks after the death of Williams. In 1973, Wilber was the meat in a legendary manager sandwich. The Rangers fired Whitey Herzog and Wilber was named interim manager. He defeated the A's and was abruptly replaced by Billy Martin that same night.

Career Stats

AB:	720	HR:	19
R:	67	RBI:	115
H:	174	OPS:	.675
BA:	.242		

Teams

St. Louis Cardinals NL (1946–1949)
Philadelphia Phillies NL (1951–1952)
Boston Red Sox AL (1952–1954)

Ted Wilks

He broke into the majors like a comet, compiling a 17–4 record with four shutouts and a 2.64 ERA for the 1944 St. Louis Cardinals, helping them to the World Series championship. After that first impressive year, Ted Wilks developed arm problems and his days as a starter were over. After elbow surgery, Wilks resurfaced as a relief pitcher and won another World Series ring with the 1946 Cards. Nicknamed "The Cork" by catcher and teammate Joe Garagiola for his uncanny ability to stop rallies, Wilks was considered one of the better relievers of the era. He had an impressive career 3.26 ERA, and led the NL with nine saves in 1949 and 13 saves in 1951. In retirement, Wilks coached in the Major and minor leagues, and later worked for the Harris County Sheriff's Office in Houston, Texas. He died in 1989 at the age of 73.

Career Stats

Record:	59–30
ERA:	3.26
IP:	913.0
Ks:	403
Threw:	RH

Teams

St. Louis Cardinals NL (1944–1951)
Pittsburgh Pirates NL (1951–1952)
Cleveland Indians AL (1952–1953)

1952 TOPPS #109
TED WILKS
NM – MT 8
15531362

Davey Williams

Davey Williams will forever be known for catching the relay throw from Willie Mays after his legendary over-the-shoulder catch off the bat of Vic Wertz in the 1954 World Series. Williams played second base for six seasons with Leo Durocher's Giants and was an All-Star in 1953. He saw action in the 1951 World Series loss to the Yankees and was clearly a defensive force in the Giants' unexpected World Series win over Cleveland in 1954. Troubled by back pain throughout his career, Williams was diagnosed with an arthritic spinal condition in 1955, which caused his early retirement from the game. He coached for the Giants for two seasons before returning to his native Texas to manage the Texas League's Dallas Rangers in 1958. Williams then left baseball for good to work in law enforcement in Dallas County. He died in 2009 at 81 years old.

Career Stats

AB:	1,785	HR:	32
R:	235	RBI:	163
H:	450	OPS:	.672
BA:	.252		

Teams

New York Giants NL (1949, 1951–1955)

Archie Wilson

California native and USC Trojan, Archie Wilson served in the US Navy from 1943 to 1945. After the war, he played minor-league ball in the United States and Canada before joining the Yankees late in their 1951 world championship season, logging a mere five plate appearances. Wilson played all three outfield positions and holds one of those obscure but interesting baseball distinctions. On September 30, 1951, Mickey Mantle famously replaced Joe DiMaggio in center field in the fourth inning. It was Wilson who moved into Mantle's spot in right field and replaced DiMaggio in the batting order. Wilson's last year in the majors, 1952, saw him move from the Yanks to the Senators to the Red Sox. After playing and managing in the minors into the early 1960s, Wilson worked for Fruehauf Corporation in Decatur, Alabama. He died in 2007 at 83 years old.

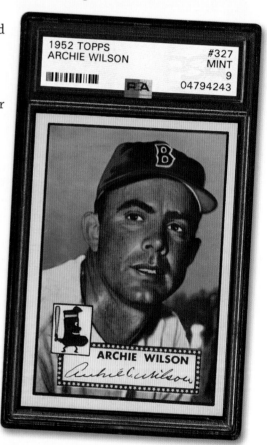

Career Stats

AB:	140	HR:	0
R:	9	RBI:	17
H:	31	OPS:	.568
BA:	.221		

Teams

New York Yankees AL (1951–1952)

Washington Senators AL (1952)

Boston Red Sox AL (1952)

Jim Wilson

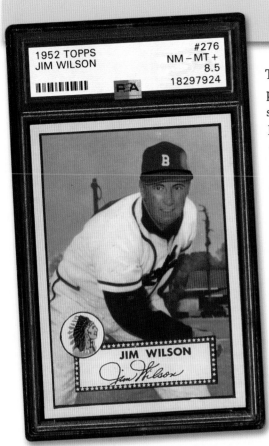

The circuitous baseball journey of pitcher Jim Wilson was a series of starts and stops. He played at San Diego State in 1941 but took 1942 off to work on a ferry boat. Wilson joined the Red Sox in 1945, but that season ended in August when his skull was fractured by a line drive off the bat of Detroit's Hank Greenberg. He returned briefly in 1946, spent time in the minors, and resurfaced with the 1948 Browns and the 1949 A's. Wilson came back again in 1951 to become a three-time All-Star while playing for three different clubs. His best season was 1957 when, at age 35, he posted a 15–8 record and 3.48 ERA for the White Sox. A scout after his playing days, Wilson became the first executive director of the Major League Scouting Bureau. He passed away in 1986 at age 64.

Career Stats

Record:	86–89
ERA:	4.01
IP:	1,539.0
Ks:	692
Threw:	RH

Teams

Boston Red Sox AL (1945–1946)
St. Louis Browns/Baltimore Orioles AL (1948, 1955–1956)
Philadelphia Athletics AL (1949)
Boston/Milwaukee Braves NL (1951–1954)
Chicago White Sox AL (1956–1958)

Ken Wood

Outfielder Ken Wood had a rifle for an arm, but that was about it. The North Carolina native made a splash when he threw out two runners at home plate in the same inning on August 11, 1950. Other than that, his six-year MLB career was fairly uneventful. Wood started in the minors at the young age of 16 in 1941, and after serving two years in the US Coast Guard during World War II, he finally debuted with the St. Louis Browns in 1948. His high mark offensively was in 1951 when he batted .237 for the eighth-place Brownies. After stints with the Red Sox and Senators, Wood finished up in the minors in 1956. After baseball, he returned to North Carolina and a career with the Prudential Life Insurance Company. Wood retired to Myrtle Beach where he passed away in 2007 at the age of 83.

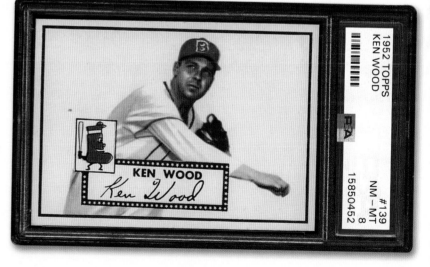

Career Stats

AB:	995	HR:	34
R:	110	RBI:	143
H:	223	OPS:	.691
BA:	.224		

Teams

St. Louis Browns AL (1948–1951)
Boston Red Sox AL (1952)
Washington Senators AL (1952–1953)

Ed Wright

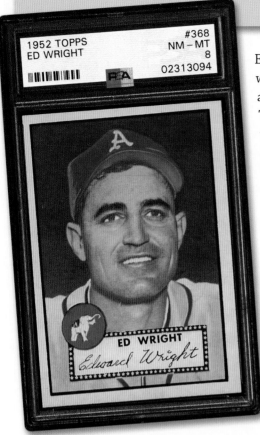

1952 TOPPS #368
ED WRIGHT
NM – MT 8
02313094

Ed Wright's first two seasons in the Bigs were quite promising. He went 8–3 with a 2.54 ERA for the 1945 Boston Braves. The next season, he won 12 games for the Braves as part of the rotation with Spahn and Sain. Unfortunately, from there it all went wrong for Wright. Born in Dyersburg, Tennessee, Wright fired a no-hitter as a minor leaguer with Indianapolis in 1945. Following four seasons in Boston, he toiled in the Phillies and Giants organizations before finishing up with the Athletics in 1952. After allowing 208 men to go home during his MLB pitching career, Wright did the same. A businessman and alderman in Dyersburg, Wright coached his hometown youth league team to the 1964 Connie Mack state championship. Wright passed away at the age of 76 in 1995, but his legacy remains in the Dyersburg Youth Baseball park that bears his name.

Career Stats

Record:	25–16
ERA:	4.00
IP:	398.1
Ks:	93
Threw:	RH

Teams
Boston Braves NL (1945–1948)
Philadelphia Athletics AL (1952)

Bobby Young

Slick-fielding second baseman Bobby Young had his best success as the starter for the St. Louis Browns. The Maryland native led the league in double plays in 1951 and 1952 and was considered one of the better fielding second baseman in the majors. The last second sacker in the Browns history, Young moved with the team to Baltimore and became the first-ever second baseman for the Orioles in 1954. Offensively, Young had no power and was at best a mediocre singles hitter, but he did score the first run in Orioles history. Up and down between the majors and minors towards the end of his career, Young wrapped it up with the Phillies in 1958. After baseball, he owned a janitorial service and worked in the construction business in Baltimore. Young suffered a heart attack and died in 1985 at the age of 60.

1952 TOPPS #147
BOB YOUNG
MINT 9
11593941

Career Stats

AB:	2,447	HR:	15
R:	244	RBI:	137
H:	609	OPS:	.626
BA:	.249		

Teams
St. Louis Cardinals NL (1948)
St. Louis Browns/Baltimore Orioles AL (1951–1955)
Cleveland Indians AL (1955–1956)
Philadelphia Phillies NL (1958)

Eddie Yuhas

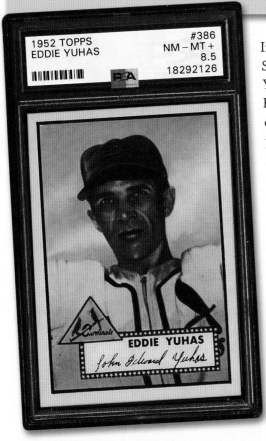

1952 TOPPS
EDDIE YUHAS
#386
NM – MT +
8.5
18292126

In 1952, Cardinals manager Eddie Stanky paired 27-year-old rookie Eddie Yuhas with fellow relief pitcher Al Brazle to form one of the best bullpen combos in the National League. Yuhas posted a 12–2 record with a 2.72 ERA. He finished 30 games and recorded six saves for the third place Cards. Originally drafted by the Yankees in 1942, Yuhas served in the military from 1943 to 1946. He played at Winston-Salem in 1947 and continued to toil in the minors until his 1952 call-up with St. Louis. Soon after that sparkling rookie campaign, the Ohio native retired from baseball and returned to Winston-Salem, where he died in 1986 at age 61. In 2008, he was posthumously inducted into the Greater Winston-Salem Professional Baseball Hall of Fame along with 1967 Red Sox Cy Young Award winner Jim Lonborg and former team player, manager, and owner Nelson Petree.

Career Stats

Record:	12–2
ERA:	2.87
IP:	100.1
Ks:	39
Threw:	RH

Teams

St. Louis Cardinals NL (1952–1953)

Sal Yvars

A tough kid from New York who fought for all that he achieved, Sal Yvars played for his hometown Giants from 1947 to 1953. He batted .317 in 25 games for the iconic 1951 pennant winners. As a bullpen catcher, Yvars was in the center of the Giants' sign-stealing scandal for which many credit Bobby Thomson's 1951 pennant-winning homer against the Dodgers. In that 1951 World Series, Yvars was a near-hero when he launched a ninth-inning Game Six blast to right field. Alas, the Yankees Hank Bauer made a sublime catch, propelling the Bronx Bombers to the title. Before baseball, Yvars served three years in the US Army Air Force and allegedly punched a sergeant. After baseball, he enjoyed a 50-year career as an investment broker and was very involved in charity work. He died in 2008 at the age of 84.

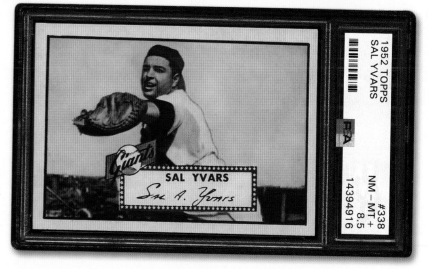

1952 TOPPS
SAL YVARS
#338
NM – MT +
8.5
14394916

Career Stats

AB:	418	HR:	10
R:	41	RBI:	42
H:	102	OPS:	.659
BA:	.244		

Teams

New York Giants NL (1947–1953)
St. Louis Cardinals NL (1953–1954)

Al Zarilla

A dependable outfielder with a strong arm, Al "Zeke" Zarilla had some very productive seasons with the St. Louis Browns and the Boston Red Sox. Zarilla was called up by the sixth-place Browns in 1943. He batted .299 in 1944, helping the hapless Brownies to the National League pennant. In 1948, Zarilla batted an impressive .329 and made an All-Star appearance. As right fielder, Zarilla led the league in double plays and fielding percentage on a few occasions and batted .325 in 1950 for the Red Sox. Zarilla then played for the White Sox, but he returned to both the Browns and Red Sox before finishing up in 1953. He continued in the minors through 1956 and then scouted for the Athletics, Reds, and Senators. Zarilla continued to scout and coach after moving to Hawaii in the 1970s. He died in 1996 in Honolulu at the age of 77.

Career Stats

AB:	3,535	HR:	61
R:	507	RBI:	456
H:	975	OPS:	.761
BA:	.276		

Teams

St. Louis Browns AL (1943–1944, 1946–1949, 1952)
Boston Red Sox AL (1949–1950, 1952–1953)
Chicago White Sox AL (1951–1952)

Sam Zoldak

With an odd motion where he would raise his arms over his head three times before throwing a pitch, Sam Zoldak won 43 games with a 3.54 ERA in nine seasons. His best season was in 1948, when he won 11 games splitting time between the Browns and Indians. Imagine his joy when, on June 15 of that year, Zoldak was traded from the woeful Brownies to the eventual world champion Indians. Zoldak won nine games down the stretch for Cleveland with a 2.81 ERA. The truth is that when Zoldak debuted for the Browns in 1944, they were anything but woeful. St. Louis topped the American League that year, winning 89 games and losing to the rival Cardinals in the World Series. A starter and reliever, Zoldak finished his career in 1952 with the Athletics. The Brooklyn native died at the young age of 47 in 1966.

Career Stats

Record:	43–53
ERA:	3.54
IP:	929.1
Ks:	207
Threw:	LH

Teams

St. Louis Browns AL (1944–1948)
Cleveland Indians AL (1948–1950)
Philadelphia Athletics AL (1951–1952)

George Zuverink

1952 TOPPS #199
GEORGE ZUVERINK
NM – MT +
8.5
16730808

Lanky 6-foot-4 and 195-pound Michigan native George Zuverink had marginal success as a starter, but he enjoyed several seasons as one of the better relievers in the American League. In 1956, he posted a 7–6 record for Baltimore and led the league with 16 saves and 40 games finished. Zuverink and catcher Frank Zupo were nicknamed "The Z Battery." His best year was 1957, when he logged a 10–6 record with a tidy 2.48 ERA for the Orioles. Before the majors, Zuverink served in the US Army Air Force in the Pacific and launched his career like comet, winning 18, 16, and 20 games in the minors. Shoulder woes curtailed his MLB career in 1959, and Zuverink finished with a 32–36 record and 40 saves. He later worked in the insurance business and refereed at the college and high-school level. Zuverink died in 2014 at age 90.

Career Stats

Record:	32–36
ERA:	3.54
IP:	642.1
Ks:	223
Threw:	RH

Teams

Cleveland Indians AL (1951–1952)
Cincinnati Redlegs NL (1954)
Detroit Tigers AL (1954–1955)
Baltimore Orioles AL (1955–1959)

A New Era Begins

The Elements that Make the 1952 Topps Baseball Card Set the Most Iconic of the Postwar Age

In this final chapter, Joe Orlando, president and CEO of Collectors Universe, parent company of Professional Sports Authenticator (PSA), breaks down the overwhelming appeal of the 1952 Topps baseball card set, from composition to design to its place in pop culture. This section is dedicated to the collector and to those who might consider taking their swing at building this masterpiece, a set that includes the most recognizable baseball card ever made.

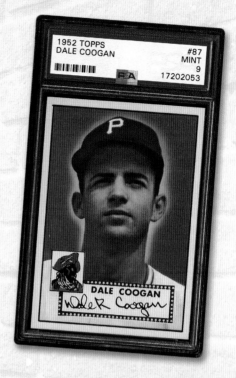

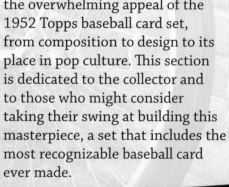

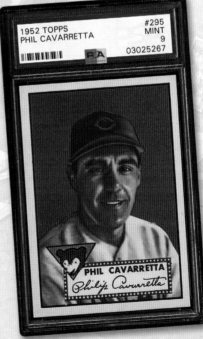

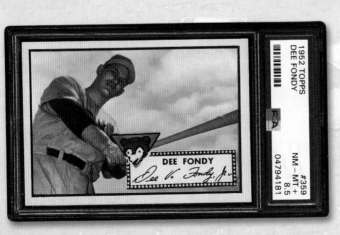

Testing the Waters

Before Topps decided to jump into the market with both feet, the manufacturer tested the waters with a handful of baseball-only releases in 1951. This included the Blue and Red Backs, Connie Mack's All-Stars, Major League All-Stars and Topps Teams. Today, each issue varies in popularity, scarcity, and value. Although every one of these Topps productions predate the 1952 creation, with some of them considered very desirable, their overall popularity pales in comparison to their successor. This is due, in part, to the limited size and scope of each 1951 set, as well as a more limited distribution. In fact, the first baseball collectibles issued by Topps were technically produced in 1948, when the company included a subset of 19 baseball subjects inside their 252-piece issue called "Magic Photos."

Preparing for a Fight

When Topps entered the fold in 1951, they were already preparing for a fight with Bowman, the reigning baseball card powerhouse. Bowman released their first baseball card set in 1948 and had taken the early lead by signing many active players to exclusive contracts. In anticipation of a baseball card battle, Topps began to sign players to deals a couple of years prior to their major move in 1952. As the two primary trading-card manufacturers in the market, Topps and Bowman went head-to-head from 1952 through 1955.

The two companies traded blows during that period, especially as it related to legal matters, namely regarding player contracts. Bowman had exclusives with certain megastars during specific years, while Topps had the same advantage with some other noteworthy players. This resulted in some baseball legends being noticeably absent from one brand or the other while the battle raged on. By 1956, however, that fight officially ended when Topps purchased Bowman and emerged as the new mainstream powerhouse in the card manufacturing world.

The Set that Turned the Tide

Years earlier, prior to the buyout of Bowman, Topps announced their presence with authority when they rolled out their 1952 baseball card set. They assigned Sy Berger the task of creating a look that would grab the attention of youngsters across the country. So, what did the company do to help make a big impression and distinguish itself from Bowman? First, the manufacturer clearly made the decision to go big or go home. That year, Topps unleashed a set that was superior to anything Bowman issued in terms of size and scope. At 407 total cards, the Topps issue was larger than anything Bowman had ever released. This included Bowman's biggest set in 1951, which totaled 324 cards. In 1952, Bowman only issued 252 cards in their set, which was significantly smaller than the one furnished by the new kid on the block.

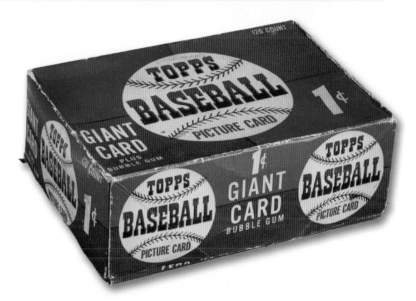

The Topps cards themselves were also larger and, as a result, more eye-catching. In 1952, the Topps cards measured 2-5/8" by 3-6/8" versus Bowman's 2-1/8" by 3-1/8". While the difference in size doesn't sound consequential, it amounted to an increase of nearly 50% and Topps certainly took advantage of their bigger format by touting it on the packaging. On the front and back of the wax packs containing the cards, Topps reiterated this feature. On the front of the packs, the phrase "GIANT SIZE" appears, while Topps used wording like "Giant Baseball Picture Cards," "New Big Size," and "INSIST ON TOPPS GIANT-SIZE BASEBALL CARDS" in all caps on the reverse. Let's just say Topps wanted to make it very clear they had the size advantage in this fight.

Each Topps card showcased color-tinted photos, so they retained a photographic feel along with a touch of art applied through the Flexichrome process. In addition to being

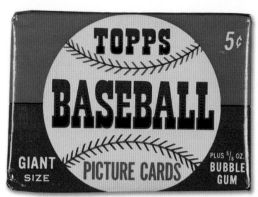

slightly smaller, Bowman's design had a different feel. Even though the artwork was created from black-and-white photographs like Topps, the colorful images contained on the front of each card resembled traditional paintings because they were, in fact, hand-painted color reproductions of the original photos. Some collectors prefer the "painted" Bowman design over the color-tinted Topps look, but both sets offer great eye appeal for the collector.

The Topps cards were also unique in that each one contained stats from the previous year, along with career stats, for every player. Keep in mind that statistics of this nature were not widely available, so the effort Topps made was appreciated in a way that is hard to fathom today. By 1957, Topps expanded the idea by including annual player stats for each year, along with the career totals. While both Topps and Bowman incorporated facsimile signatures into the design on their cards in 1952, this feature was absent on previous Bowman releases. Furthermore, the face of each Topps card was graced with colorful team logos for the first time, which further distinguished the Topps product from Bowman.

The Bookends – Andy Pafko and Eddie Mathews

Long ago, before the advent of third-party grading or even three-ring binders used to house baseball cards in plastic sheets, the first and last cards were often put in harm's way far more than those cards located elsewhere. Whether the damage was caused by rubber bands, which wrapped themselves around the first and last cards like a boa constrictor at the end of a stack, or general exposure to potential blunt force trauma, the bookends of sets often had to contend with increased handling abuse compared to the rest of the cards. While many of them are not technically rare, they can become condition rarities due to the difficulty of locating examples in high grade.

Over time, several classic first and last cards have been identified as especially desirable based on their scarcity, popularity, and their association with iconic sets. In the world of baseball cards, there are several cards that fit this description, from common names to the biggest stars in the game. Some noteworthy #1 cards include the extremely tough 1933 Goudey Benny Bengough and the 1951 Bowman Whitey Ford rookie card, but none of them are more recognizable or talked about than the 1952 Topps #1 Andy Pafko.

To begin with, while Pafko is not a Hall of Famer, he was also no slouch. Pafko was a five-time All-Star who hit over 200 home runs during his 17-year career. He also happened to be playing for the Brooklyn Dodgers when this card was created. At the time of this writing, PSA had graded slightly more than 2,000 Topps Pafko cards in their nearly 30-year history, yet only 10 examples have reached the grade of PSA NM-MT 8 or better during that time. That's right, less than 1% of the Pafko cards submitted to PSA have qualified for what most collectors consider high grade for the period. Poor centering and general wear from handling are usually the two main culprits which prevent more Pafkos from reaching the promised land.

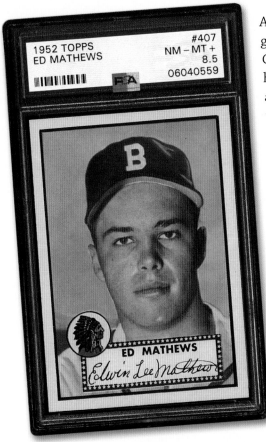

Amazingly, PSA has graded one PSA Gem Mint 10 in its history, and there's a story that goes with the incredible discovery. In the 1990s, a collector decided to do what many view as unthinkable due to the risks involved. That collector, one who happened to own an unopened pack of 1952 Topps baseball cards, made the decision to open the vintage treasure.

The 5-Cent pack contained five cards and, more importantly, a minefield of potential obstacles to overcome if one is looking for exceptional quality. Putting Pafko aside, centering is a problem for many cards in the set. In addition, cards that are pulled from these packs are sometimes found with what are referred to as corner pulls, where the paper near the tips appears to be hanging off the edge of the card. The cards must also contend with wax and gum staining. Remember, that pink-colored brick has been sitting inside that pack for decades.

Despite the pitfalls and the slim chance of finding anything inside that would be considered more valuable than the intact pack itself, the collector decided to open it. After carefully removing the wax paper surrounding the cards, which included that petrified stick of gum that attached itself like an alien facehugger to the back of the last card in the stack, the collector revealed the cards within.

After removing the first two cards from the group, a gorgeous Pafko card was resting comfortably right in the middle. Protected from the elements, which included no direct exposure to wax or gum, the Pafko was perfectly preserved. After receiving the grade of PSA 10, the card sold for a record $83,970 shortly thereafter. The sale and lore of this exact card was referenced in a 2010 movie entitled *Cop Out*, starring Bruce Willis and Tracy Morgan. Willis' character, Jimmy, was on a mission to retrieve the 1952 Topps Pafko card that was stolen from him. He planned on using the proceeds from the sale of the card to finance his daughter's wedding.

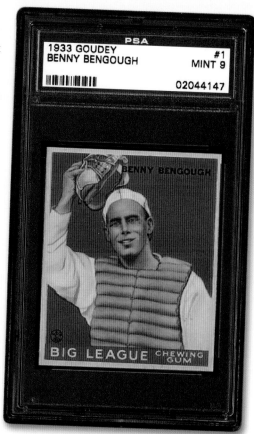

The real card, which is worth significantly more today, remains the finest example in the hobby.

Now let's turn our sights to the other half of this dynamic duo, the last card in the 1952 Topps set. While one could at least make an argument for another #1 card being more important than the 1952 Topps Pafko, even though it would be a difficult task, I am not sure any viable argument can be made for a final card in any set being more desirable than the #407 Eddie Mathews.

Let's go through the checklist. Is this card a bona fide condition rarity? Check...PSA has graded only fourteen 8s, one 8.5, two Mint 9s and zero 10s since 1991. Does the card feature a notable name? Check...Mathews was a premier slugger in his day, part of a devastating 1-2 punch along with teammate Hank Aaron, and is a Hall of Famer. Does this card offer any other appealing features? Check...Not only does the last card in the set feature a Hall of Famer, it just happens to be Mathews' only true rookie card. Add to all of this the fact that the Mathews is the final piece in a set that the hobby at large considers the most important issue of the postwar era, and you have quite a card.

When the hobby transitioned from a semi-esoteric endeavor in previous decades to a nationwide phenomenon in the 1980s, few would argue that the poster child or symbol of the baseball-card-collecting world at that time was anything other than the 1909-11 T206 Honus Wagner. The card combines the appeal of an all-time great with an unparalleled set, not to mention meaningful scarcity and an intriguing story behind it. There is no doubting the importance of the T206 Wagner, which was long referred to as the *Mona Lisa* of baseball cards. In the eyes of many collectors, it still is.

That said, while the T206 Wagner may still be the *Mona Lisa* of baseball cards, no card in our hobby possesses a more recognizable or iconic image than the 1952 Topps Mickey Mantle. Furthermore, no single card elicits more emotion from an entire generation of children than this card. Mantle was the idol of all idols to so many young boys who grew up during the 1950s.

Even as recently as 2018, the ever-popular Mantle card was referenced in a Netflix movie called *The Christmas Chronicles*, starring Kurt Russell as Santa Claus himself. In a comedic and somewhat heartbreaking scene for collectors, Santa approaches a couple seated in a restaurant, hoping to trade a "Mint" condition 1952 Topps Mantle for their Porsche which was parked with the valet. The husband (Larry) quickly accepted since he always wanted the coveted Mantle card. Unfortunately, Larry's wife intercepts the card and rips it in half at the table not realizing that the card was worth far more than the car was.

When the hobby reached new heights in the 1980s, no generation was more responsible for that success than the baby boomers. These hobbyists were able to recapture parts of their youth, and perhaps part of their collections that mom threw away years ago, by engaging in a hobby that brought back so many memories. Mantle was the pulse of an entire era and the 1952 Topps card that bears his likeness remains the heart of this hobby staple.

The player and the card are almost too good to be true. The unforgettable pose, the beautiful blue and yellow colors, and even the name "Mickey Mantle" all combine to create a card that only a Hollywood casting executive could dream up. The image has become more akin to pop culture art than a mere baseball card, which is why it has such powerful symbolic value alone. The 1951 Bowman Mantle may be his true rookie, but the 1952 Topps is *THE* Mantle card. In Mantle's prime, no player was more explosive or dynamic, and he just happened to play centerfield for the most dominant team in the league. For nearly two decades, more young boys wanted to be like Mickey Mantle than any other human on earth.

The card itself has its share of condition obstacles, namely poor centering. As expected, most of the high-grade examples that exist today originate from the famous find of the 1980s. There are a couple of interesting aspects to the card worth mentioning. First and foremost, the card was double printed in the final series, along with cards of Jackie Robinson and Bobby Thomson. This means there are two slightly different versions, but no difference in value has been established by the market at this point.

> *"A significant percentage of Mantle cards exhibit a small, white print dot to the left of his head, towards the left border."*

A significant percentage of Mantle cards exhibit a small, white print dot to the left of his head, towards the left border. Since this print dot is so common, and so minor, its presence has no effect on grading or value. In addition, the line surrounding the Yankees logo is solid black on the Mantle without the white print dot, while the "white dot" variety has a line that is only partially filled. Furthermore, the two versions showcase subtle contrasts in color and focus to further distinguish the two Mantle variations.

Mantle's skin tone is slightly darker and less "red" on the card featuring the white print dot. Even Mantle's autograph offers a subtle distinction. The "e" in the facsimile signature of "Mantle" finishes pointing downward on the "white dot" version. On the other version, the "e" curls up at the end of the signature. Finally, the stitching of the baseball on the reverse points to the right on the "white dot" Mantle, yet the stitching points to the left on the other version.

In 1952, Mantle also appeared in the Bowman set on card #101, but it is currently worth significantly less than the legendary Topps card, the undisputed postwar king.

F.W. WOOLWORTH & CO.
FORDHAM RD. STORE.

"When the Topps cards initially hit stores in March of 1952, sales were reportedly terrific."

If the stories of moms throwing out collections of baseball cards from past generations makes your stomach churn, then you might want to skip over the next few paragraphs. When the Topps cards initially hit stores in March of 1952, sales were reportedly terrific. Over time, however, demand started to wane. In 1952, the cards were distributed in six separate series, which started in the spring and lasted until the baseball season reached its homestretch.

Series	Range	# of Cards
1	1–80	80
2	81–130	50
3	131–190	60
4	191–250	60
5	251–310	60
6	311–407	97

During the last few decades, those series have been consolidated by the hobby for simplicity purposes in price guides and other references. In 1952, cards 81–250 were released in three different waves, which included Series 2 (81–130), Series 3 (131–190) and Series 4 (191–250). Since the scarcity of the cards were about equal and the commons commanded about the same price, the three series were rolled into one group. By the time Topps decided to print and distribute their last run, Series 6 (311–407), the baseball season was quickly coming to an end and kids were headed back to school if they hadn't started already. Consequently, less product was ordered, and many of the cases were returned unsold by retailers to Topps headquarters.

Here's the part that makes most collectors queasy. According to hobby lore, around 1960, Topps allegedly decided to load pallets of the unwanted high-number inventory on a garbage barge and then proceeded to dump them into the ocean to make room for newer product in their Brooklyn warehouse. That's right. Berger, the man who designed the cards, was on the barge and had to watch hundreds of cases sink to the bottom of the Atlantic like Big Pussy from *The Sopranos*. They tried to sell the cards at a major discount. In fact, they tried to basically give the cards away. According to Berger, he even tried offering the cards at "10 for a penny" at amusement parks and carnivals, but no one wanted them. I am sure it was a painful experience for Berger, but the company felt like they ran out of options.

After you are finished drying the tears from your eyes, keep in mind that part of the reason high-grade vintage cards are worth so much today is because of stories like this. If moms kept all their children's cards, kids never put them in their bicycle spokes and Topps archived everything that didn't sell, then scarcity would play a much more limited role. Like the sport of baseball itself, part of the appeal is that it's not easy. It's hard to hit a Major League breaking ball and it's hard to find top-quality collectibles. The truth is that no one knows how the preservation of all those cards would have impacted the market today. What we do know is that collectors may decide to cut moms across the country a little more slack for cleaning out their rooms and taking out the trash. Remember, it wouldn't be considered treasure today if it was common.

Over the past few decades, there have been some major hobby finds that have captured the imaginations of hardcore collectors and the general public all over the world. Some of the more noteworthy baseball card discoveries include the vast *Black Swamp Find* of 1910 E98 cards in 2012 and the diminutive yet remarkable *Lucky Seven Find* of 1909-11 T206 Ty Cobb back rarities in 2016. There is something about the idea that buried treasure still exists, even in cardboard form, that brings out the dreamer in all of us. While these two finds were extraordinary by any definition, no single revelation is referred to more as *THE* find than the 1952 Topps event of the 1980s.

In the spring of 1986, Alan Rosen, the self-proclaimed "buying machine" and perhaps the most recognizable industry figure of the day, received a call from the Boston area that would change his life and the hobby forever. Lying forgotten in an attic for decades was an entire case of uncirculated 1952 Topps cards. The owner, whose father originally acquired the case through his line of work, served Rosen with the contents on a silver platter...literally.

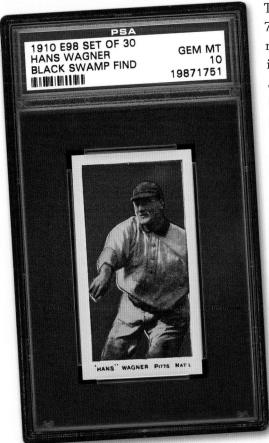

When it was all tallied, about 5,500 Topps cards were unearthed, with nearly 75% of them from the coveted high-number series. This immense group included about 75 or so Mantles and Jackie Robinson cards, but Willie Mays (#261) had the greatest presence at nearly 200 cards. Some of the cards were centered, some were not, but they all retained a fresh appearance since they were tucked away like a vampire in a deep sleep. As a result, not only can current collectors buy some exquisite examples today, the unforgettable event raised the profile of the entire hobby.

"Lying forgotten in an attic for decades was an entire case of uncirculated 1952 Topps cards."

Like many baseball card issues of the era, the 1952 Topps set offers its share of variations and error cards which enhance the intrigue and difficulty of the issue. As we covered earlier in the chapter, the Basic set contains 407 total cards. For those tackling the greater challenge of the Master set, there are many additions to consider, and some of them will cost you a pretty penny if you decide to take collecting 1952 Topps cards to another level. Before we proceed, please keep in mind that while we cover most of this historic set's major components, not every variation is covered in this book. Hobbyists continue to uncover new distinctions and debate which ones should be cast as mere printing errors or unworthy anomalies versus collectible variations.

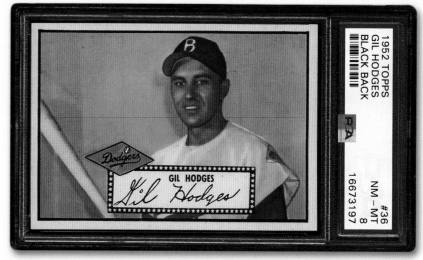

First, let's start with Series 1. The low-number series, which is considered the second toughest group in the set, next to the high-number run, contains a nice mix of stars, errors, condition rarities, and variations. For example, cards 1–80 can be found with either black or red printing on the reverse. That means you already need 80 more cards, one of each color, to complete the Master version of the set. The red backs have better print quality than the black backs, which makes sense since the black backs were made first and Topps was able to improve the quality on the second try during the red back run. It's important to note that all the cards from Series 1 were printed on gray stock.

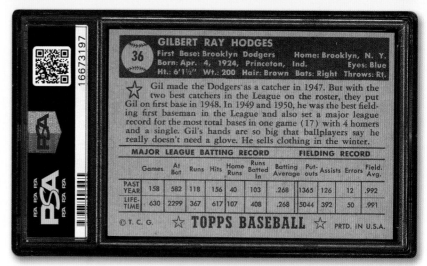

". . . cards 1–80 can be found with either black or red printing on the reverse."

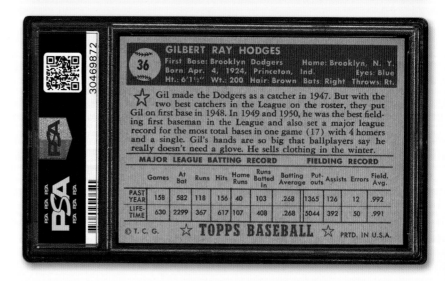

The Pafko card, the leadoff man for the set, and #80 Herman Wehmeier are two of the more challenging cards in high grade. Since one series was issued at a time, Pafko and Wehmeier were often at the top and bottom of the stack, which meant more potential exposure to the elements and rubber bands. Several Hall of Famers appear in Series 1, including the likes of Phil Rizzuto (#11), Warren Spahn (#33), and Duke Snider (#37). The series also includes a fun card of Gus Zernial (#31) where his bat appears to have six gravity-defying baseballs attached to it. Even though this group has its fair share of stars, some of the most desirable cards in the run belong to names that the average person may not be familiar with.

"Gus Zernial's . . . bat appears to have six gravity-defying baseballs attached to it."

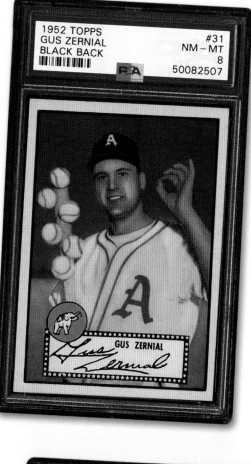

Two of the more valuable cards from Series 1 are the Joe Page and Johnny Sain errors. Some of Page's cards (#48) were printed with Sain's information on the back, while the same fate impacted a small percentage of Sain's cards (#49), with Page's information appearing on the reverse. It's important to note that these error cards can only be found with black backs since they were corrected in time for the red back print run. For Master set builders, these two errors rank near the top of the set in terms of elusiveness.

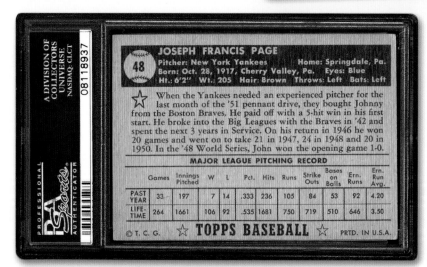

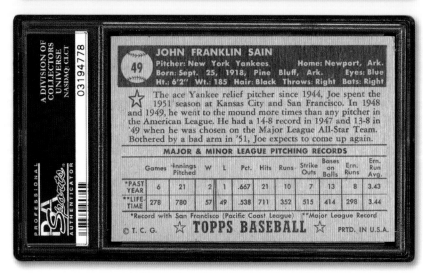

"Two of the more valuable cards from Series 1 are the Joe Page and Johnny Sain errors."

Series 2–4 (81–250) have been consolidated into one by many hobbyists today, and it's often referred to as the easiest of the major card groups to find. From this point forward, all the card backs were printed in red after Topps achieved the print improvement during Series 1 production. Like Series 1, all the cards in the 81–130 and 191–250 ranges were made with gray stock.

In between, cards 131–190 were primarily created using cream-colored stock, but some gray backs are known to exist. Different theories have been tossed about over the years regarding their genesis. From the cards being a Canadian version, like the 1954 Topps gray backs, to being distributed by tissue brands Kleenex and Doeskin, to the factory simply running out of cream-colored stock, definitive proof of their origin still eludes the hobby. For those collectors who seek ultimate completeness, finding these mysterious oddities can be extremely challenging.

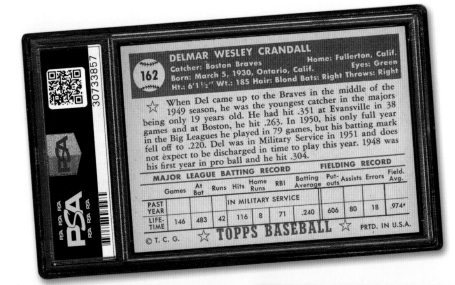

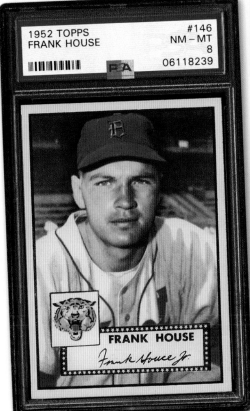

Inside this series lies one of the more elusive and slightly controversial variations. The Frank House card (#146) is normally found with a Detroit Tigers graphic containing a combination of orange, red, and yellow colors. The tougher variation, however, showcases an almost completely yellow tiger with only trace amounts of additional color visible. To be clear, there are varying degrees of orange or red hue present on these "yellow" tigers. Their appearance ranges from mostly yellow, with hints of orange or red sprinkled in, to an almost completely yellow look, absent any orange or red to the naked eye, but all of them are distinctly different from the intended design.

At one point, some hobbyists dismissed the card's variation status as simply missing the red color application on the overall card, but that argument was quickly rebutted. Even on the House cards featuring the primarily yellow tiger, red color can be found inside the "D" on his cap and within the tone of his skin, which provides strong evidence that this wasn't a mere product of missing ink on the entire card. The clear color variation is concentrated within the tiger depiction. As is the case with other Series 3 cards (131–190), both House "Tiger" variations can be found with either cream-colored or gray backs.

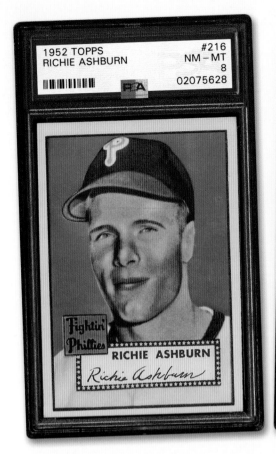

Within this portion of the set, collectors will also find more big names, such as Bob Feller (#88), Yogi Berra (#191), and Richie Ashburn (#216). The 1952 Topps set isn't known for having an extensive rookie card selection, at least as it relates to Hall of Famers, but this series does contain key first issues of players like Billy Martin (#175) and Minnie Minoso (#195).

Series 5 (251–310) is considered slightly tougher than Series 2–4 and all the cards from this point onward were made using gray stock. While Series 5 doesn't contain as many Hall of Famers as the previous group (81–250), it does offer one major star card and one variation of significance. Mays (#261) is one of only a few stars to appear in this series. Even though this is Mays' first Topps card, it doesn't garner the same kind of attention that the Mantle card does. Mays and Mantle both have rookie cards in the 1951 Bowman set. While the Mays card has risen in value during the past several years, it still falls short of his Bowman rookie. In the case of Mantle, of course, the exact opposite is true, which is further proof that the appeal of the Mantle card goes far beyond the basic elements of the issue.

"Even though this is Mays' first Topps card, it doesn't garner the same kind of attention that the Mantle card does."

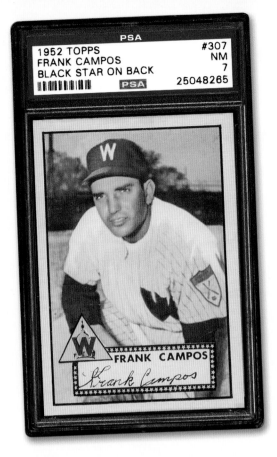

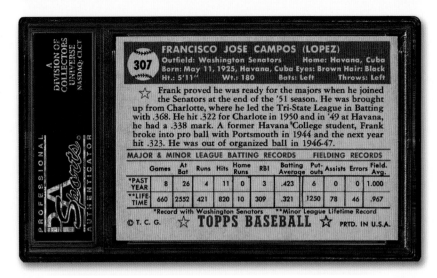

At card #307, the relatively unknown Frank Campos resides, but a variation of the card exists for those seeking ultimate completion. One of the normal red stars that appear on the back next to "TOPPS BASEBALL" near the bottom was overprinted in black on a small percentage of Campos cards. The overprinting affected the star located to the immediate right of the "TOPPS BASEBALL" text. PSA has graded roughly 100 examples since 1991, which is far fewer than the regular Campos card, and none of the "Black Star" variations have graded higher than PSA 8. This semi-scarce Campos variation, in high grade, has sold well into five figures during the past 10–15 years.

Last, but not least, we come to the high-number run, the final card series in the set (311–407). Due to the reasons noted earlier regarding greater scarcity because of fewer orders and weaker sales at the time, this is the toughest series in the whole set today despite the find in 1986. Strangely enough, the very first card in the series is that of Mantle. You just can't make this stuff up. The stars align on the Mantle card in a way that is hard to believe. In fact, four out of the first five cards in the series are those of Hall of Famers. Robinson (#312), Roy Campanella (#314), and Leo Durocher (#315) follow Mantle.

The one non-Hall of Famer in that first five is by no means a common name, either, in Bobby Thomson (#313), who played the leading role in one of the greatest walk-offs in baseball history. Once you get past that first five, there are a few other cards in the series that feature Hall of Famers as well, including Pee Wee Reese (#333) and a trio of rookie cards.

John Rutherford (#320) is regarded as one of the toughest commons in the entire set to find in high grade. Out of 500 or so total specimens submitted to PSA, only 16 Rutherford cards have reached PSA 8, with none higher. At the tail end of the series, the following rookie cards help finish the 1952 Topps set with a bang. Inaugural issues of knuckleballer Hoyt Wilhelm (#392), manager Dick Williams (#396), and super slugger Mathews (#407) close the show in spectacular fashion.

The Cards that Never Were

At 407 cards, versus only 252 included in the Bowman set the same year, Topps certainly had the advantage when it came to player/coach/manager inclusion. That said, even though Topps offered north of 150 more cards in their set, there were a few noticeable omissions. These are often referred to as *The Cards that Never Were*. No matter how great a set may be, many vintage baseball card issues leave collectors wondering what might have been. For example, Stan Musial appeared in the 1952 Bowman set on card #196 and had an exclusive contract, which prevented him from appearing in the Topps release as well.

The two superstars that were missing in action, quite literally, from the Bowman and Topps sets were Whitey Ford and Ted Williams. Both were absent from each set because they were serving

our country in the military, a hard picture to imagine in present times. Ford missed the entire 1951 and 1952 seasons while serving in the armed forces. Williams played a full season in 1951, but he played only six games the next season before leaving on his final tour of duty. Williams missed the rest of the 1952 season and most of the 1953 season before returning to baseball.

Interestingly, it is rumored that Williams may have had an exclusive contract with Bowman at the time, like Musial, yet they decided not to include him in the set. A 1952 Topps

card of any member of this Hall of Fame threesome would be unquestionably desirable, but a Williams card would be one of the most significant *Cards that Never Were* from any set, in any era.

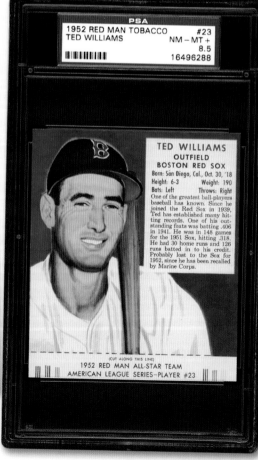

After hearing about the 2018 sale of the PSA Mint 9 Mantle card for nearly $3 million, a New Jersey resident named John decided to sift through his childhood collection, a collection that laid tucked away in an attic for almost seven decades. Only recently did John decide to take those cards, which were sitting loosely stored in a large box, and place the better ones in plastic sheets. There were a few thousand cards in the box.

Luckily for John, his mother was one of the few matriarchs who *didn't* throw away her son's cards. John and his brother Ed collected cards right around the time the Topps Mantle made its debut. There was everything from 1948 Leaf Babe Ruth cards to 1951 Bowman Mays rookies, but almost all the value resided in the 1952 Topps cards. In some cases, there were multiple examples of each card, from Robinson to Campanella to Mays. The real game changer, however, was the presence of five 1952 Topps Mantles. After being sent to PSA for grading, the Mantle cards ranged from PSA EX 5 to PSA NM-MT + 8.5 and eventually sold for a combined $1,273,200 at auction.

It's hard to define events like this as true finds since the cards were collected years ago by the same person who rediscovered them later, but the impact to the hobby and the person who owns them is the same. There are finds or rediscoveries like this all the time. Some change the collectibles market forever, like the 1952 Topps find of 1986, while others are smaller in size and scope. What they all have in common is that the stories inspire collectors to keep up the hunt, and they also help entice those who are not yet collectors to join the hobby.

There are collections like John's that have remained in a sleeping state for a long time. This includes those that were built in the 1980s, prior to the advent of third-party grading, and were suddenly buried for one reason or another. Many collectors go through periods of inactivity. In some cases, that temporary inactivity morphs into something more permanent, like in the case of John.

For collectors who dream of tracking down buried treasure, one thing is for sure—buried treasure still exists and the 1952 Topps issue has been a gift that seems to keep on giving, long after the set was originally unveiled.

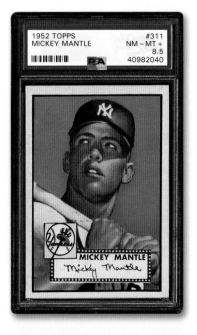
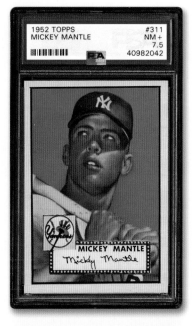

"The real game changer . . . was the presence of five 1952 Topps Mantles."

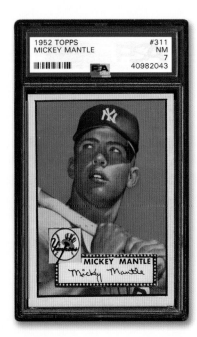
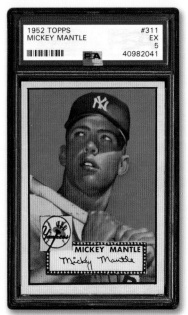
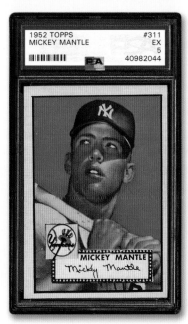

1952 TOPPS #315
LEO DUROCHER MINT 9
05025840

LEO DUROCHER

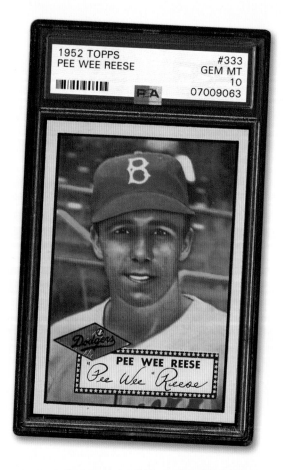

1952 TOPPS #333
PEE WEE REESE GEM MT 10
07009063

PEE WEE REESE
"Pee Wee" Reese

1952 TOPPS
BOBBY THOMSON
#313
MINT
9
17115124

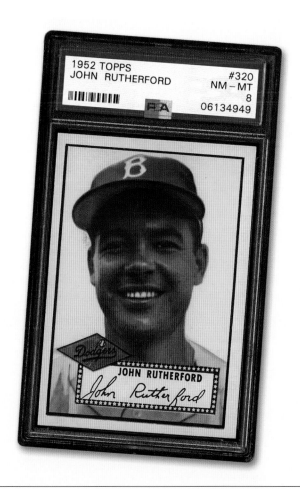

1952 TOPPS
JOHN RUTHERFORD
#320
NM – MT
8
06134949

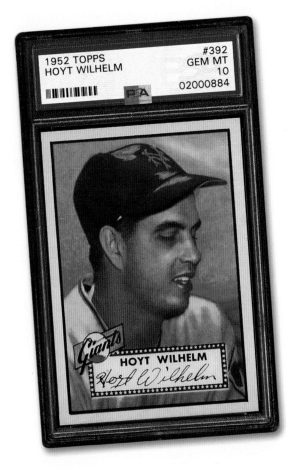

1952 TOPPS
HOYT WILHELM
#392
GEM MT
10
02000884

HOYT WILHELM
Hoyt Wilhelm

Jansen, Larry, 47
Jeffcoat, Hal, 139
Jensen, Jackie, 48
Jethroe, Sam, 48
Johnson, Billy, 139
Johnson, Don, 140
Jones, Nippy, 140
Jones, Sam, 49
Jones, Sheldon, 141
Jones, Willie, 49
Joost, Eddie, 141
Judson, Howie, 142
Kazak, Eddie, 50
Kell, George, 6
Kellner, Alex, 142
Kelly, Bob, 143
Kennedy, Bill, 143
Kennedy Bob, 50
Kennedy, Monty, 144
Kiely, Leo, 144
Kinder, Ellis, 51

King, Clyde, 51
Klippstein, Johnny, 145
Kluszewski, Ted, 52
Kluttz, Clyde, 145
Kolloway, Don, 146
Koshorek, Clem, 146
Koslo, Dave, 147
Konstanty, Jim, 147
Kretlow, Lou, 148
Kryhoski, Dick, 148
Kucab, Johnny, 149
Kuzava, Bob, 149
Labine, Clem, 52
Lanier, Max, 53
LaPalme, Paul, 150
Lavagetto, Cookie, 53
Law, Vern, 54
Lemon, Bob, 7
Lenhardt, Don, 150
Leonard, Dutch, 54
Lepcio, Ted, 151

Lipon, Johnny, 151
Loes, Billy, 55
Lollar, Sherm, 55
Lopat, Eddie, 56
Lown, Turk, 152
Lowrey, Peanuts, 152
MacDonald, Bill, 153
Madison, Dave, 153
Mahoney, Bob, 154
Main, Woody, 154
Majeski, Hank, 56
Mantle, Mickey, 7
Mapes, Cliff, 155
Marrero, Connie, 57
Marsh, Fred, 155
Marshall, Cuddles, 156
Marshall, Willard, 57
Martin, Billy, 58
Martin, Morrie, 58
Masi, Phil, 59
Masterson, Walt, 156
Mathews, Eddie, 8
Maxwell, Charlie, 59
Mays, Willie, 8
McCosky, Barney, 60
McCullough Clyde, 157
McDermott, Mickey, 157
McDougald, Gil, 60
McMillan, Roy, 61
Mele, Sam, 61
Merson, Jack, 158
Metkovich, George, 62
Meyer, Billy, 158
Meyer, Russ, 159
Michaels, Cass, 62
Miksis, Eddie, 159
Miller, Bill, 160
Miller, Bob, 160
Minner, Paul, 161
Minoso, Minnie, 63
Mitchell, Dale, 63

Mize, Johnny, 9
Mizell, Vinegar Bend, 64
Morgan, Bobby, 161
Morgan, Tom, 162
Moss, Les, 162
Mueller, Don, 64
Muir, Joe, 163
Mullin, Pat, 163
Munger, Red, 164
Murray, Ray, 164
Nelson, Rocky, 165
Niarhos, Gus, 165
Nichols, Chet, 166
Nicholson, Bill, 65
Nixon, Willard, 166
Noren, Irv, 167
Northey, Ron, 167
Nuxhall, Joe, 65
Olson, Karl, 168
Ostrowski, Joe, 168
Overmire, Stubby, 169
Pafko, Andy, 66
Page, Joe, 66
Palica, Erv, 169
Parnell, Mel, 67
Pellagrini, Eddie, 170
Perkowski, Harry, 170
Pesky, Johnny, 67
Philley, Dave, 171
Phillips, Jack, 171
Pierce, Billy, 68
Pillette, Duane, 172
Pitler, Jake, 172
Podbielan, Bud, 173
Poholsky, Tom, 173
Pollet, Howie, 68
Porterfield, Bob, 174
Posedel, Bill, 174
Post, Wally, 69
Pramesa, Johnny, 175
Presko, Joe, 175

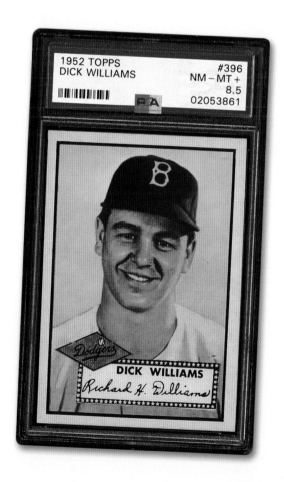

About the Authors and Contributors

Tom Zappala is a businessman in the greater Boston area who is passionate about maintaining the traditions and historical significance of our National Pastime. He is co-author of the award-winning books *The T206 Collection: The Players & Their Stories*, *The Cracker Jack Collection: Baseball's Prized Players*, *The 100 Greatest Baseball Autographs*, *Legendary Lumber: The Top 100 Player Bats in Baseball History*, and *An All-Star's Cardboard Memories*. In addition to co-hosting a popular Boston area radio talk show, Zappala co-hosts *The Great American Collectibles Show* with Red Sox Hall of Famer Rico Petrocelli, which airs nationally every week. As co-owner of ATS Communications, a multimedia and consulting company, he handles publicity and personal appearances for several authors and a variety of artists in the entertainment field. He enjoys collecting vintage baseball and boxing memorabilia, using the simple philosophy of collecting for the love of the sport. Proud of his Italian heritage, Zappala authored *Bless Me Sister*, a humorous book about his experience attending an Italian parochial school.

Ellen Zappala is president of ATS Communications, a multimedia marketing and consulting company. Co-author of the award-winning books *The T206 Collection: The Players & Their Stories*, *The Cracker Jack Collection: Baseball's Prized Players*, *The 100 Greatest Baseball Autographs*, *Legendary Lumber: The Top 100 Player Bats in Baseball History*, and *An All-Star's Cardboard Memories*, Zappala also worked with former welterweight boxing champ and Boxing Hall of Famer Tony DeMarco on his autobiography *Nardo: Memoirs of a Boxing Champion*. Zappala was publisher of a group of weekly newspapers in Massachusetts and New Hampshire for many years and served as president of the New England Press Association. She works closely with various publishing companies on behalf other authors and handles publicity in both print and electronic media. She especially enjoys bringing the stories of the Deadball Era and Golden Age players to life.

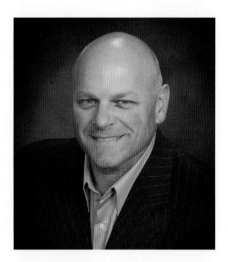

Joe Orlando is the president and CEO of Collectors Universe, Inc., the parent company of Professional Sports Authenticator (PSA), the largest trading card and sports memorabilia authentication service in the hobby. Prior to taking on his new role, Orlando acted as the PSA president for 16 years. Editor of the nationally distributed *Sports Market Report* (SMR), a Juris Doctor, and an advanced collector, Orlando has authored several collecting guides and dozens of articles for Collectors Universe, Inc. Amongst other book projects, he authored *Collecting Sports Legends* (2008), and he was the lead author of the award-winning *Legendary Lumber: The Top 100 Player Bats in Baseball History* (2017). Orlando contributed to the award-winning *The T206 Collection: The Players & Their Stories* (2010), *The Cracker Jack Collection: Baseball's Prized Players* (2013), *The 100 Greatest Baseball Autographs* (2016), and *An All-Star's Cardboard Memories* (2018). As a hobby expert, Orlando has appeared as a featured guest on numerous radio and television programs, including ESPN's *Outside the Lines*, HBO's *Real Sports*, and the Fox Business Network.

John Molori is a columnist/writer for *Boston Baseball Magazine*, *Northeast Golf Monthly*, and EBSCO Publishing. He contributed to the award-winning books *The Cracker Jack Collection: Baseball's Prized Players*, *The 100 Greatest Baseball Autographs*, and *Legendary Lumber: The Top 100 Player Bats in Baseball History*. Molori has also written for ESPNW.com, *Patriots Football Weekly*, *Boston Metro*, *Providence Journal*, *Lowell Sun*, and the *Eagle-Tribune*. A rotating co-host on *The Great American Collectibles Show*, his radio and TV credits include: ESPN, SiriusXM, FOX, Comcast, NESN, and NECN. Molori has lectured on writing and media at Emerson College, Boston University, Lasell University, and Curry College. His awards include: New England Emmy Award, CableACE, Beacon Award, and the New Hampshire Association of Broadcasters Award. For his contributions as a sports journalist and commentator, Molori is an inductee into the Methuen, MA, Athletic Hall of Fame alongside 1987 Cy Young Award winner Steve Bedrosian.

Christina Good is a senior photographer for Collectors Universe, Inc. A Seattle native and 2005 graduate of Brooks Institute of Photography in Santa Barbara, Good initially honed her skills on portraiture and wedding photography. Since joining the company in 2013, she has become a key part of the photography team and especially enjoys the opportunity to use her photography skills to artistically document rare coins and collectibles. Her beautiful, artistically styled images have also appeared in the award-winning book, *An All-Star's Cardboard Memories*.